A Short History of Sweden

1   Sweden: provinces, lakes and principal towns

STEWART OAKLEY

❉

A Short History of
SWEDEN

FREDERICK A. PRAEGER, *Publishers*

NEW YORK · WASHINGTON

BOOKS THAT MATTER

Published in the United States of America in 1966
by Frederick A. Praeger, Inc., Publishers
111 Fourth Avenue, New York 3, N.Y., U.S.A.

DL
648
O2

11/18/cc Easton 6.05

Originally published in Great Britain
by Faber and Faber Limited under
the title of The Story of Sweden

51700

Printed in Great Britain

Contents

7

Contents

8

Illustrations

PLATES

9

Illustrations

MAPS

GENEALOGICAL TABLES

Preface

I have attempted in this book to provide the reader who is interested in Sweden but has little or no knowledge of her history with an introduction to the main lines of her development. I hope in particular that it will prove of some use to those who intend to visit the country, for whatever purpose, and even that it may encourage some to go who have not previously been tempted to do so; Sweden is not, after all, so difficult to reach from Britain, and, as I have tried to indicate, there are still many memorials of the past to be seen there.

While providing a framework of political events, I have devoted a good deal of space to economic, social and cultural factors. This seemed especially desirable in view of the fact that it is just these aspects of Swedish life which have attracted most attention in recent years. Since so much of what makes Sweden what she is today lies deeply rooted in her past, in which there has been no sharp break such as many other countries have suffered, I have chosen to go back to the very beginning, and have paid due attention to medieval as well as to modern times. The exigences of space have often forced me to oversimplify (but not, I hope, excessively to distort) many issues and to omit some altogether. For this I must ask the expert's indulgence.

At the end of the book will be found a rather full bibliography of works in several languages, classified under subjects. The general reader may perhaps wish to pursue one topic or another; and the student, especially, may have felt the lack of such a general guide.

For saving me from a number of errors and for helping to make clearer many passages, I wish to record here my heartfelt thanks to Professor Denys Hay of the University of Edinburgh, Professor Michael Roberts of the Queen's University, Belfast, and Dr. Ragnhild Hatton of the London School of Economics, all of whom have read chapters of the book. For errors and obscurities which remain I take full responsibility.

Edinburgh   STEWART OAKLEY
May 1965

NOTE ON THE SPELLING OF PROPER NAMES

I do not claim to have been consistent in this. Where a proper name may be more familiar in its English than its Swedish form, I have adopted the former, e.g. Gustavus Adolphus for Gustav Adolf; Gothenburg for Göteborg; and Scania for Skåne. But I have preferred the briefer and more euphonious Dalarna to Dalecarlia; Västergötland to West Gothland, etc. I realize that this often raises difficulties of pronunciation, but hope that here the note below will be of some assistance.

NOTE ON SWEDISH PRONUNCIATION
(Most values are only approximate)

å   like *aw* in l*aw* (e.g. R*å*d)
ä   like *e* in p*e*t (e.g. V*ä*ttern) or *ai* in r*ai*n (e.g. l*ä*n)
e   when long, like *a* in c*a*ne (e.g. S*e*rgel)
g   before e, i, y, ä, ö, like *y* in *y*et (e.g. Väster*g*ötland; De *G*eer). After r at end of word, like *y* (e.g. Strindber*g*). Otherwise like *g* in *g*et (e.g. *G*otland)
gn   like *ng* (e.g. Te*gn*ér)
j   like *y* in *y*et (e.g. *J*ämtland) (But see also under *s*)
k   before e, i, y, ä, ö, like *ch* in *ch*urch (e.g. Norr*k*öping). Otherwise as in English. (But see also under *s*)
o   when long, like *oo* in r*oo*m (e.g. B*o*rås)
ö   like *er* without the *r* sound in timb*er* (e.g. Lagerl*ö*f)
sk   before a, o, u, å as in English (e.g. real*sk*ola)
sk   before e, i, y, ä, ö; and *sj, skj, sti* and *stj* in all positions, like *sh* in *sh*ore (e.g. *Sk*änninge; *Sti*ernhielm)
u   like *ou* in y*ou* (e.g. R*u*dbeck)
w   like *v* in *v*ast (e.g. *W*rangel)
y   like *i* with rounded lips (e.g. N*y*stad)
Other letters as in English.

CHAPTER I

Sweden Before History

The earliest traces left by man in Sweden have been dated to between 10,000 and 8,000 B.C. By this time the great ice-sheet which had covered north-eastern Europe for many thousands of years had withdrawn far enough to lay bare the extreme south of the country, and small groups of reindeer-hunters crossed the land-bridge which then joined Sweden to the Danish islands. They left, however, few surviving traces of their presence behind them—little more than some implements made of bone. The ice continued its retreat northwards, and, as it did so, the melted waters raised the level of the Baltic, which burst through to the North Sea, drowning central Sweden. Later still, the land rose again, and the Baltic turned into a great freshwater lake. The climate improved and became drier with warm summers, although the winters were still cold. Aspen trees and later fir replaced the tundra: bear and elk drove the reindeer to the north. It was under such conditions that men began to arrive in Sweden in fairly large numbers from the south, to fish off the west coast and in the rivers which flow into the North Sea and to hunt farther and farther into the interior. By 6,000 B.C. the whole of Sweden was free of ice. The climate grew wetter and the winters milder; deciduous forests of oak and elm, inhabited by deer and wild boar, appeared. A fresh sinking of the land broke the link with Denmark about 5,000 B.C. (at the same time that Britain became an island), and for a long time after this a large area of eastern Sweden was submerged under a great arm of the sea.

Nearly all the habitation-sites which have been dated to this period are situated in the extreme south and along the river-valleys of the west and south-west, for long the most thickly populated parts of the country. Even here they were probably used only intermittently, but archaeological finds are well scattered throughout the whole of the country then above sea-level as far north as the modern province of Jämtland. Here the southern culture which has been described met the offshoots of another coming from the north and east, which manifested itself in elaborate rock-carvings with an apparently magical purpose. The tools used by these earliest Swedes for fishing and hunting alike were made of bone, wood and—in the south and west, where it was plentiful—flint. The only animal which had been domesticated was the dog. Primitive religious beliefs are suggested by the presence of weapons in the earliest graves which have been discovered; it was apparently thought that the dead man would have need of them in an after-life.

The appearance, some time during the first half of the third millennium B.C., of pottery, soon followed by the practice of raising cattle, goats, pigs and sheep and the growing of barley and wheat in certain parts of the country, announced the arrival of the New Stone Age in Sweden. With it came a more settled way of life for a fair number of her inhabitants. The change, which suggests an immigration from the south, was fostered by a further alteration in the climate, which became drier with much warmer summers than are experienced today; even grapes could be grown in central Sweden. Further evidence of a more highly-organized existence is provided by the great stone monuments raised over graves in the coastal regions of the south and west, but this 'megalithic' culture, which probably originated in western Europe, never penetrated far into the interior of the country. For by this time men had reached central Sweden in large numbers and were settled on the shores of the great bay referred to above, on the south coast of Norrland and on the island of Gotland in the middle of the Baltic. Even the heart of Norrland was thickly populated for a time, but the inhabitants of this region, who had probably come from the east and north, had for long little contact with the rest of the country and never developed beyond an Old Stone Age culture.

The extent of the change which occurred at this period must not be exaggerated. Agriculture was firmly established only in the south and west. In some places, such as modern Söderman-land, it was the dominant means of livelihood for only a brief

time, and, even where the land was cultivated, cattle-rearing
was probably the major occupation and fishing and hunting
still practised to supplement the diet. Flint remained the most
important material for the making of tools and weapons,
although workmanship was of a far higher standard than in the
Old Stone Age. Denmark and Scania in the far south began to
export flint from their rich deposits to the more northerly parts,
where it was exchanged for fish and furs. Much of this trade
was for some time in the hands of fishermen who came from the
lands east of the Baltic to settle along the whole coastline of
southern Sweden. From the same direction there came about
2,000 B.C. an even more important immigration—of the Boat-
Axe Folk, so-called from the shape of their beautifully designed
stone axes. These were nomads who established themselves
inland and spread rapidly—probably with the assistance of
horses—throughout the countryside not already occupied by
the fisher-folk and the megalith builders. They swamped the
small agricultural communities in east and central Sweden.

They also played a large part in a trade which not only
linked the various parts of the country together and fostered the
development of a common culture, but also united Sweden with
the rest of Europe, especially with the British Isles and the more
advanced peoples of the middle Danube.

Along these trade routes, which eventually reached as far as
northern Italy and southern Spain, flowed the first metal objects
to be seen in Scandinavia. Copper axes were imported as early
as 2,500 B.C., but Sweden's Bronze Age proper (i.e. when
articles of bronze occurred on a large scale) did not begin until
nearly a thousand years later. Flint and wood continued to be
used for everyday tools, except those like sickles where the use
of metal had decided practical advantages. Bronze was, after
all, an alloy of two comparatively rare ingredients—copper and
tin—which had to be imported and could be afforded by only
a small minority of the population, which constituted an aristocracy. This, some historians believe, was provided by the
Boat-Axe Folk, who imposed their culture on the whole of
southern Sweden and who drew their wealth from the improved agriculture which came with the use of the horse- or ox-
drawn plough and was favoured by the mild climate. The
sharp class distinctions of the age, which are found in all Bronze

Age communities, are well illustrated by the contrast in graves. All along the west coast, and in other places also, the noble dead were buried in coffins of oak or stone, accompanied by a wealth of metal articles for use in the life hereafter and covered with great mounds of earth or stones visible for miles around. The peasant, on the other hand, often had no goods of any kind in his grave and certainly no great monument to mark the spot.

Swedish smiths, who seem to have learnt their art from Britain, were at first content to copy the designs of the swords, clasps and other bronze objects imported from the south. But fairly quickly they developed their own distinctive styles, which they executed with great delicacy. Bronze statuettes and ceremonial axes dating from the period are probably connected with worship of the sun; on the elaborate rock-drawings of the same age, found particularly in the province of Bohuslän, this often appears in the guise of a wheel or a disk carried by men or in a carriage drawn by horses. The centre of the bronze industry lay in the south-east of Sweden, where there was an abundance of soap-stone particularly suited to the making of moulds, and the products of this region were sent all over the country. The whole age was one not only of high artistic attainment but also of great material prosperity. This was especially marked during the latter part of the period in the area around Lake Mälaren, now largely risen from the sea to take on its present shape; this, the historic heartland of Sweden, springs into a prominence which it was destined to retain. It seems to have been the centre of an extensive trade in furs obtained from Norway and Finland as well as from Norrland, which continued to import flint from the mines of Scania.

Among the objects depicted on the rock-drawings mentioned above are ships with high prows and sterns and propelled by oars (see plate 2). The importance attached to seafaring is also demonstrated by the boat-shape of the grave enclosures found on the east coast and on Gotland, which, even at this early date, was an important centre of Baltic trade. From finds in Denmark it is possible to reconstruct the costume of the men and women of this age. The men wore a simple tunic covered by a cloak. The younger women—at least during the warm summer months which then prevailed—wore a sleeved blouse fastened at the waist with a belt and a large bronze clasp, a fringed skirt and bronze pins, necklaces and armlets. Only one house of the period has been unearthed in Sweden. It is a simple rectangular structure with a stone floor and walls of wattle and daub similar to New Stone Age dwellings.

About 400 B.C. iron began to be used in Sweden for the first time, although until the beginning of the Christian era only in the form of imported finished articles. For some time the climate had been growing wetter and colder. This necessitated the growing of hardier crops such as rye; favoured cattle (which now, however, had to be wintered indoors) at the expense of agriculture; and compelled men to build more substantial houses with thicker walls. The challenge and the greater permanence of settlement which all this involved may well have encouraged social development. But there is a striking paucity of remains from this period, which has so far not been satisfactorily explained. It may simply flow from a misdating of the evidence, but the most widely accepted theory is that the spread of the Celtic peoples across central Europe at this time destroyed the old Bronze Age trade routes; the new ones flowed from east to west instead of north to south as formerly. The more difficult climatic conditions may also have brought about a sharp decline in the population.

In the first century B.C. the climate improved again to become much as it is today, and the replacement of the Celts in central Europe by Germanic tribes closely related to the Swedes themselves re-established contact with the world to the south of them—a world increasingly dominated by the power of Rome. Prosperity returned to Scandinavia. Iron began to be worked in Sweden itself from the rich deposits laid down during the previous wet period, and a stream of goods—bronze cooking-pots, glassware, gold ornaments and silver coins—began to reach the country from the south. At first they came mainly from Italy via middlemen in Bohemia and along the River Elbe, but after A.D. 100 Gaul became the main centre of export and the River Rhine the main artery of trade. During the fourth century strong influences also flowed into Sweden from the dominions of the Goths, a people who may themselves have emigrated from southern Sweden at an earlier period to settle near the Black Sea (the King of Sweden numbers among his titles that of King of the Goths). It seems likely that such influences included the primitive letters adapted from the Roman and Greek alphabets and known as *runes*, which first made their appearance in Sweden in the third century A.D. They were, however, long prized more for their supposedly magical properties than as a means of communication (the very name rune signifies 'secret'), and it was not until Viking times that inscriptions in them became at all common.

The great migrations of peoples across Europe between the fourth and the sixth centuries A.D. which led to the destruction of Roman power in the West brought even greater prosperity to Sweden. The art of working in metal, especially gold, which was now present in the country in large quantities as a result of raids or of legitimate trading, reached a new peak; the carved picture-stones of Gotland (mostly dating from the eighth century and depicting some of the stories familiar from the old sagas) have been hailed as among the artistic wonders of the age. But for Sweden, as for the rest of the Continent, this period was also one of considerable unrest. Evidence of this is to be found in the numerous hill-forts on the islands and in the coastal regions of the country; the vast booty mutilated and cast into bogs as offerings to the gods; the huge hoards of gold coins from as far afield as Byzantium buried against the return of more peaceful conditions; and the number of habitation-sites on the islands of Gotland and Öland which were abandoned and often burnt.

Out of these disturbed conditions, there emerged around 500, or perhaps earlier, the first Swedish state. This was the kingdom of the Svear, centred on Uppland on the north side of what is now Lake Mälaren but which was then still an arm of the Baltic. Under the name of *Suiones* the Svear were described by the Roman writer Tacitus at the end of the first century as 'strong not only in arms and men but also in their fleets. The shape of their ships is uncommon in having a prow at both ends always ready to be put ashore. They do not use sails or fasten their oars in banks along the sides. . . . Power is highly esteemed among them, and that is why they obey one ruler, with no restraint on his authority or mere casual claim to obedience.' Tacitus's information came to him through many hands and must thus be treated with some caution, but ships such as he describes have been discovered in Denmark and dated to the fourth century. In the middle of the sixth century, the Gothic historian Jordanes wrote of the *Suehans* as possessing fine horses, delighting in rich apparel and trading in furs. Mälaren and its archipelago provided the Svear with excellent easily-defended harbours, from which they could sail forth to raid and trade in the furs and other produce of Norrland, now, it seems, again sparsely populated; and the rich pastures provided by the land recently risen from the sea gave them excellent grazing for their cattle. At Old Uppsala, two miles to the north of the modern town in Uppland, lay their great religious centre and the meeting-place of their assemblies or *things*. To this day three great mounds there mark the graves of some of their early kings. Svear chieftains were interred in their ships and lavishly equipped with the weapons, horses, hunting dogs and food which they would need for their journey to the next world; the coming of iron had obviously not brought with it a more democratic society. This practice, which was rarely followed in other parts of Sweden, where cremation was the rule, was also followed in the case of the seventh-century East Anglian king whose memorial mound (for some mysterious reason without its body) was set up at Sutton Hoo in Suffolk and discovered just before the Second World War. It was lavishly furnished, and many of the objects uncovered in the course of excavation bear a striking resemblance to finds from a rather earlier period in the Mälaren region. A close link therefore seems to have existed between this particular part of Sweden and Britain long before the Viking raids; it has even been mooted that the royal house of East Anglia was of Swedish origin.

In time the power of the Svear spread. According to some historians, by the end of the eighth century—that is on the eve of the Viking period—they were ruling directly or indirectly over all the inhabited areas of Sweden except the extreme south. There is certainly evidence that Gotland was paying tribute to them in the ninth century, and it and other islands may well have been conquered much earlier than this. It was from Gotland and Uppland that settlements were made on the south and south-east coasts of the Baltic—in Latvia and near the mouth of the River Vistula—in the seventh century. That economic motives lay behind this early expansion is certain, and it foreshadowed much more dramatic developments to come.

CHAPTER II

The Vikings and the Conversion

Towards the end of the eighth century, the Scandinavian peoples suddenly emerged from their comparative obscurity to play for a time a dominant rôle in European history. During the three centuries which make up the Viking Age, their bolder spirits established settlements in Iceland and Greenland; struck terror into the inhabitants of Europe's Atlantic coast; penetrated into the western basin of the Mediterranean; and established a kingdom in England and a principality in northern France. In many of these westward expeditions—at least in the later stages of the movement—the Swedes played a part, as is recorded in many of the runic inscriptions on the over 2,500 memorial stones set up in their homeland. A small number of Swedish families are numbered among the earliest settlers in Iceland in the middle of the tenth century, and Swedish warriors served in Canute's bodyguard in England and helped to collect the *danegeld*, much of which found its way to Sweden. But in these more familiar fields of Viking activity Norwegians and Danes were overwhelmingly preponderant; the main Swedish effort was directed south-eastwards across the Baltic and was an extension of the settlement mentioned at the end of the last chapter. Previously the Swedes had traded with the Arab world, with all its riches, only through the Franks in western Europe; now they sought direct contact with the Near East through regions which offered little organized resistance to their advance but furs and slaves in plenty for exchange. Thus the Swedish expansion was of a rather different character from that of the Norwegians and Danes (these can now be spoken of as separate peoples for the first time; distinct languages, as can be learnt from the runes, were beginning to emerge from

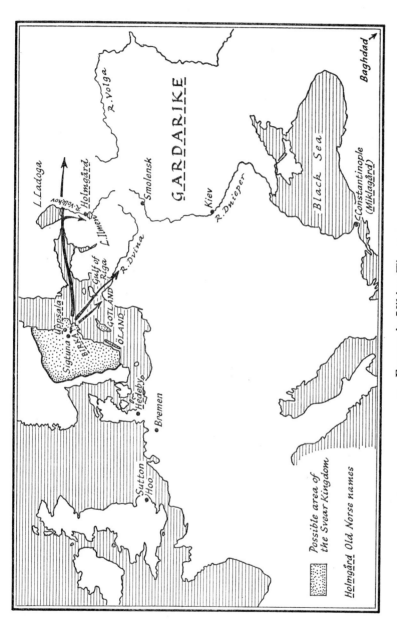

2   Europe in Viking Times

Common Norse, and Old Swedish was being born). The accent was on trade rather than on the seizure of booty. But the difference must not be exaggerated, for economic motives certainly played a large part in the western raids, while the Swedes in the east also sought to subject neighbouring peoples.

From bases in the region of Lake Ladoga, they first penetrated down the River Volkhov to Lake Ilmen, and there established a number of settlements including one which they called Holmgård on the site of the later city of Novgorod. From here they could exploit much of what is now northern European Russia, then inhabited by primitive Finnish tribes. Some ventured farther—to the River Volga, which was reached by dragging their boats overland on rollers, and so on down the river to the more highly organized peoples on its lower reaches. With these they could exchange their wares for gold and other precious goods from farther south. Arab writers reported them in this region in the tenth century, and even earlier they are recorded as selling and buying in the Arab capital of Baghdad itself. Other Swedes and Gotlanders travelled from the Gulf of Riga, up the Dvina to its headwaters and thence overland to their settlement on the River Dnieper at Smolensk. From here they had to negotiate dangerous rapids before reaching the Black Sea and Constantinople, the capital of the Eastern Roman Empire, where Swedish warriors were enlisted in the emperor's Varangian (= Viking) Guard. On the Dnieper Swedish settlers founded the town of Kiev, which eventually grew into an independent principality under rulers of Swedish descent, who exercised authority as far as Holmgård. The numbers involved in these operations were probably small, and those who stayed in Russia were fairly rapidly absorbed into a predominantly Slav population; all ties with the homeland had been broken by the end of the Viking age.

The trade-links which were established by the spread of the Scandinavian peoples made the Baltic a great commercial centre. To it during the ninth century flowed precious metals (especially silver), silk from as far afield as China and spices from the Arab world. From it in exchange went furs, fish, weapons, slaves and goods obtained from western Europe. The most important single mart of the area was the town of Hedeby, situated on the neck of land at the base of the Jutish peninsula through which today runs the Kiel Canal. For a brief period at the end of the ninth and beginning of the tenth century this was held by the Swedes, but an almost equally important trading centre lay in Sweden itself—the extensive town of Birka on an island in Lake Mälaren. Although not yet fully investigated, the existence of over 3,000 graves in its cemetery gives some estimate of its size and importance. Its international merchant community introduced urban organization to Sweden for the first time. Birka, however, suffered attacks from Finnish pirates and in the second half of the tenth century was largely abandoned. The nearby, but more defensible, Sigtuna took its place to a certain extent, but by this time the great days of Scandinavian expansion had passed. The trade-routes were again changing, leaving Sweden on their periphery; only the peasant-traders of Gotland continued to flourish.

The reasons for the great explosion which took place in the North at this time will doubtless always be hotly debated by historians. One plausible explanation lies in land-hunger caused by a natural growth of population, although this would be more effective in Norway than elsewhere. But some part was almost certainly also played by the process of political unification, which reduced the field for individual initiative at home. As has been suggested, we do not know how far this had gone before Viking times. A traveller's account, included in one of King Alfred's writings at the end of the ninth century, claims that the province of Blekinge in the south of Sweden and the islands of Öland and Gotland were in the hands of the Svear, but the hold of their kings on the provinces outside Uppland was probably for long very insecure.

These kings supported themselves largely from their personal estates, but they may also have claimed—as they certainly did later—a proportion of the fines imposed on malefactors in the area under their control. They headed the national levy in time of war and organized the annual campaigns across the Baltic, to which the coastal regions of the kingdom were expected to contribute men and boats. But their coercive power, such as it was, rested mainly on the personal bodyguard of professional warriors which they and all nobles maintained and bound to themselves by an oath of allegiance. Contact with more highly-developed states of western Europe hastened the development of political organization. Olof Sköttkonung, the first King of Sweden of whom much at all is known—the first ruler indeed who can safely be given that title—employed, at the beginning of the eleventh century, an English mintmaster to strike coins with inscriptions in the Latin alphabet—the first example of its use in Sweden. Below the king stood the chiefs or nobles. Originally these might have been, like the king, elected to lead the men of their district into battle, but they rapidly became an hereditary class with power in land and followers. Next came the broad mass of freemen; and at the bottom of the social scale the unfree *thralls*—many of them prisoners-of-war—who served all the other ranks.

The local communities in Viking times were left very much to run their own affairs; poor communications and the isolation of the early settlements made this inevitable. Their members would discuss matters of common interest at *things*, which met regularly in the open air at some prominent landmark. Once a year representatives would be chosen to attend a provincial gathering, where a *lawman*—one learned in the unwritten customs of the province—was elected to act in effect as the headman of the district. The *thing* of the province of Uppland became particularly important as the power of the Svear spread, for each new king had to submit himself to it for approval and to promise to respect the laws of the province. In theory each province elected its own king, and the choice of Uppland had to be ratified by all the others after he had been solemnly proclaimed on the traditional site at Mora. Rather later than the period being discussed here, although the custom probably dated back to it, we find Swedish kings journeying through five of their provinces to make declarations in each similar to that which they had first made before the Uppland *thing*. This *eriksgata* (= oath-confirmation-journey) was undertaken as late as the eighteenth century.

Each province continued to enjoy its own laws long after the Viking Age had passed. Justice seems to have been administered in much the same way as in Anglo-Saxon England. A man could clear himself of an accusation before the local *thing* by gathering together a sufficient number of his fellows who were willing to swear to his innocence; there was no question of examining evidence. Nor, it seems, were imprisonment, torture

24

or even the death penalty inflicted as punishments. The guilty party either had to pay the injured man's family a sum of money graded according to the enormity of the offence and the social standing of those involved or, for serious crimes such as murder, suffer outlawry from the province. Such forms gradually replaced the ancient blood-feud, but this continued to be practised even after Viking times.

It must be remembered that most freemen were not pirates or adventurous traders but farmers, making a precarious living from the scanty produce of a recalcitrant soil. We know little about agriculture in early Sweden. Rye was the main crop in most parts, and, in the comparatively thickly-populated lowland belt which runs across the middle of the country from west to east, village land was probably divided into strips periodically reapportioned among the inhabitants, as in much of England during the Middle Ages. But only a small proportion of the land was suitable for tillage, and cattle-rearing was of equal—if not of greater—importance in many areas. In the mountainous regions of the west, of which the central districts were settled from Norway at an early stage and lost to Sweden until the seventeenth century, a pastoral life undoubtedly predominated. The noble might still, as in pre-Viking times, take pride in fine clothes and richly ornamented swords, but even for him the standard of material comfort was low. All buildings—even the largest—were made of wood and still lacked both windows and chimneys; the fire was placed on an open hearth in the middle of the main structure, and the smoke was allowed to find its way out through a hole in the roof or through the door. There was a bare minimum of furniture.

Reference has already been made to Old Uppsala as the religious centre of the Svear kingdom. By the end of Viking times it had become the site of a great temple, which served not only the people of the Mälar region, but also much of the rest of Scandinavia yet to be converted to Christianity. Here, every nine years, at a particularly solemn ceremony, men and women were offered as sacrifices to the dread triumvirate of the Nordic pantheon—Freya, the god of plenty and fertility; Odin, the god of wisdom and war, who ruled over Valhalla, whither were borne the bodies of warriors who were fortunate enough to die in battle; and Thor, the god of justice, with his great hammer.

These were only the leaders among a multitude of gods, many of whose names have survived in place-names and in whose honour cattle were slaughtered and weapons, pots and ornaments cast into sacred lakes; each locality had its own favourite. But to the ordinary Swede, *trolls* and other mysterious inhabitants of the mountain and forest were probably more familiar and felt to be more approachable than the rather distant gods and goddesses. There seems to have been no organized priesthood except at Uppsala, and buildings for worship were rare; the necessary ceremonies were conducted at some natural site by the chief landowner of the district.

The first evidence of Christian missionary activity in Sweden concerns the visit to Birka of the monk Ansgar, the first distinct personality known to Swedish history, thanks to the life of him written by his companion Rimbert, a fellow monk. Ansgar was sent in 829 by the Frankish king Louis the Pious, the son of Charlemagne, in answer to a call from a certain Swedish king or chieftain named Björn, who wished the conversion of his subjects and satisfaction for the spiritual needs of the Christian traders and slaves in the town. Ansgar preached and built a church in Birka, but after his departure his successor was forced to flee the country as the result of a popular uprising on behalf of the old gods. About twenty years later Ansgar, now archbishop of the German town of Bremen, which was the main centre of missionary enterprise in the North, returned to Birka, and Rimbert was still preaching there when he died in 865. But no firm roots were struck, and after this no more is heard of Christianity for the rest of the ninth century.

Swedes returning from trading or raiding ventures in the West did, however, bring back with them Christian influences, and a large number of Christian graves dating from the tenth century have been discovered in central Sweden. The Church was making great strides in both Norway and Denmark by this time, and even the newly-established Church in Russia exerted a certain influence in a Sweden still linked to the principalities of Novgorod and Kiev by ties of blood and commerce. After the conquest of England by Canute of Denmark in the early eleventh century and his conversion to Christianity, English missionaries began to arrive in Sweden, parts of which he claimed to rule, in appreciable numbers. But even before this, in

1008, Olof Sköttkonung is said to have been baptized by an Englishman named Sigfrid, who spread the faith through the province of Södermanland and founded the first Swedish bishopric at Skara; two Englishmen are named among its first bishops. Two other saints named David and Botvid (the latter, we are told, a Swede converted in England and martyred in Sweden) are supposed to have evangelized the south of the country, but, as with so many of the early missionaries, little that is at all trustworthy is known of them, and their very existence has been doubted by some authorities. English influence remained strong for a long time—especially in western Sweden, the earliest part of the country to have been permanently converted—and left its mark on the ecclesiastical vocabulary of the Swedish language as well as on the design of her earliest stone churches, which date from the end of the eleventh century. But it had to face stronger and finally overwhelming competition from the south; the Archbishop of Bremen claimed jurisdiction over the whole of Scandinavia until 1103, when a provincial see was established at Lund in Scania, then under the Danish Crown.

The Church had an exceptionally hard struggle in Sweden, especially among the Svears of Uppland, who remained pagan long after their neighbours had been converted. In 1060 the bishop of the new diocese of Sigtuna was driven from the town, and soon after 1080 an even more serious pagan reaction came to a head. King Inge, like Olof Sköttkonung before him, was compelled to flee to the safety of Västergötland after refusing to perform the rites pertaining to his office at the Uppsala temple. It was apparently during this reaction that the English Bishop Eskil was murdered. His body was taken for burial to the town of Tuna, which soon appears as Eskilstuna in his honour. Inge soon regained power, and it was probably he who finally destroyed the temple and had a church built on its site; its successor stands there to this day. Christianity seemed finally to have triumphed throughout the kingdom, yet at the beginning of the twelfth century an Anglo-Danish monk could still write that 'The Swedes and Goths seem outwardly to honour the Christian faith as long as everything is going as they would wish. But, should the winds of adversity blow over them; should the earth fail to yield its harvest or the sky its rain; should the storm rage and the fire ravage; then will they persecute the religion they appeared to respect.' As late as 1177 parts of the remote province of Dalarna were accounted pagan, and in the form of charms, *trolls*, folk-tales and traditional festivities paganism has lived on in Sweden—as in other parts of Europe—into modern times.

CHAPTER III

The Early Middle Ages

It is not always realized how fortunate the English historian is in the relative confidence with which he is able to describe the course of events in the early medieval period of his country's history. A great wealth of contemporary evidence in the form of laws, charters, chronicles and administrative records has survived, not only from the period after the Norman Conquest, but even from Anglo-Saxon times. For Sweden during the same epoch such written evidence simply does not exist. There is no Swedish equivalent of either the *Anglo-Saxon Chronicle* or *Domesday Book*; no Swedish law-code was recorded until the thirteenth century, and this was the first document written in the Swedish language; no register of writs issuing from the royal chancery or accounts of sums received by the royal exchequer, such as we have in England from the twelfth century, has survived in Sweden for any part of the Middle Ages. We are thus for long dependent for our knowledge of her past on descriptions written long after the events they purport to relate; on references in foreign histories; and on isolated documents which lend themselves to a large number of interpretations. For events even as late as the fourteenth century we are chiefly reliant on a single source—a verse chronicle composed in the 1320's and based largely on oral tradition. The historian of Sweden must perforce often describe major events occurring quite late in time only as having 'possibly' or 'probably' taken place.

That this is so emphasizes the backward character of Swedish society—at least up to the thirteenth century—when compared even with her Scandinavian neighbours, of whom Denmark retained the predominant position which she had enjoyed in prehistoric times. When the Normans conquered England even

Sweden's kings had been Christian for less than a century, and the great heathen temple at Old Uppsala was not only still standing but was still being used for worship. The country was a collection of semi-independent provinces administering their own laws and recognizing little more than the nominal overlordship of the king. No town existed where the modern capital stands. Indeed there were few towns at all in the modern meaning of the term then or for many years to come.

The ancient line of Svear kings to which Olof Sköttkonung belonged died out about 1060. To succeed its last representative the Uppland *thing* elected a pious noble from western Sweden called Stenkil. His reign was, however, brief and was followed by a struggle for the succession, which resulted in the acknowledgement of his sons as co-regents. It was during their reign that occurred the pagan reaction mentioned in the last chapter and the destruction of the temple at Uppsala. After the death of the last of these brothers about 1100 the Crown was again divided between their sons, but within little more than twenty years these had all died without issue. It is interesting to note how the Crown, while remaining elective, continued in the possession of one family, whose hereditary right, at least to be considered for it, seems to have been recognized. This remained a feature of early Swedish political life; descent from a king always gave one a very strong claim to the throne.

A further period of strife, which seems to a certain extent to have taken the form of rivalry between the various provinces, ended after about a decade with the emergence as victor of a noble named Sverker. He strengthened his position by marrying the widow of the last Stenkil king and by establishing good relations with the Church, which had become by now a formidable power in the land. He fully supported the reforms carried out in the late eleventh century by the great pope Gregory VII and especially favoured the new Cistercian Order of monks, to whom he granted land on which to build their monasteries. He was murdered in 1155, according to one account by one of his own servants while on his way to hear midnight mass on Christmas Eve, and was succeeded by a noble from Västergötland called Erik. All that we know about this man, of whom there is no contemporary record, is contained in a much later life written after he had become Sweden's patron-saint and highly coloured by this fact. It tells of a crusade against the pagan Finns, on which he was accompanied by an English-born Bishop Henry, who became the patron-saint of Finland after he had been martyred there. And it tells of Erik's death on 18th May 1160 at the hands of a Danish prince, who claimed his throne and came upon him in the market-town which grew into the modern Uppsala. His body was buried in the church at Old Uppsala and for reasons by no means clear—unless the later accounts of his exceptional piety are to be taken at their face value—soon became the centre of a cult; before the end of the century the date of his death was being celebrated as a Church festival. The adoption of this obscure man as the country's patron-saint must be seen partly as a manifestation of national pride and independence like the campaign being fought at the same time for the establishment of a separate archbishopric for Sweden; she had to match Norway's St. Olav. But it was also encouraged by his descendants in their struggle to win the throne and by the Archbishops of Uppsala, who certainly strengthened their position by having such a holy relic in their cathedral.

The descendants of Sverker and Erik ruled Sweden alternately for nearly a hundred years after the latter's death. This was not, it seems, the result of any formal arrangement, but of a series of bitter struggles between the adherents of each family at the end of each reign. To some extent these feuds may represent the opposition of different attitudes to the Church. The Sverkers apparently stood for a pro-papal, the descendants of St. Erik for a more national policy; it was in any case to the Sverkers that the Church generally gave its support. But it was Erik's son Knut who won the crown about 1173. His reign, which lasted until 1196, was an eventful one and may be said to mark the re-emergence of Sweden on the European scene.

The king himself is a rather shadowy figure, but at his side stood Birger Brosa. He was the first of the great *jarls* or justiciars, who were to wield enormous power for much of the thirteenth century as the king's chief ministers. They led the army in time of war, acquired vast property in land and often married into the royal family; the last and greatest of them finally managed to place his own son on the throne. It is to Birger Brosa that most of the achievements of Knut Eriksson's reign have been ascribed. He took a great interest in developing Sweden's economic ties with the rest of the Continent; concluded a commercial treaty (the first in Swedish history) with the powerful ruler of Saxony in north-west Germany, whose port of Lübeck was destined to play a decisive part in Swedish history as leader of the Hanseatic League of north German merchant-towns; built a harbour at the mouth of the River Göta on the only strip of coastline facing west which was then in Swedish hands; and even welcomed a trade mission from Henry II of England, although little seems to have come of it. Sweden minted her own coins (using German models) for the first time since the beginning of the eleventh century. The defences of the realm were strengthened against pirates after they had murdered the Archbishop and burnt Sigtuna; a series of forts was built around the coast, including one on an island at the eastern end of Lake Mälaren which was to form the nucleus of the town of Stockholm.

Birger retained power after his master's death, which was exceptionally a natural one, and consolidated his position by marrying his daughter to the new king—Sverker, the son of Knut Eriksson's predecessor. The favours which the younger Sverker showered on the Church—the exemption, for example, of its lands from taxation and of its servants from the jurisdiction of lay lawcourts—were in the tradition of his family, but they made him unpopular with many of the nobles, who called on Knut Eriksson's son to replace him. Sverker made himself even more disliked by calling in Danish troops to help him crush the revolt, and when he was overthrown in 1208 and killed in battle in 1210, the events were regarded as somewhat in the nature of national victories. Erik, the son of Knut Eriksson, reconciled himself to the Church, which had understandably supported his rival, and was crowned at the first coronation in Sweden of which there is any record. He was succeeded by Sverker's son in 1216, and when he died childless six years later the line of Sverker came to an end. His predecessor had, however, a posthumous son also named Erik, and it was he who was next elected to fill the throne.

Throughout all these changes the office of *jarl* was held by one of the descendants of Birger Brosa. Associated with them was a group of nobles known to history as the *Folkungs* after

Birger's son Folke. This group steadily opposed the growing
centralization of royal power which was taking place at this
time and which meant that they had to compete more and
more with royal officials in local affairs; they stood for the
ancient traditions of provincial self-government. And in 1229

3   Sweden in the Middle Ages

they deposed Erik Eriksson. He fled to Denmark, and, although he was allowed to return to his realm a few years later, the real power continued to rest in the hands of a noble faction who supported the *Jarl*, a nephew of Birger Brosa also named Birger. Birger Jarl, as he is known in Swedish history, married the king's sister and, since the king had no children, was soon suspected of harbouring designs on the throne. The great power which he already wielded as *jarl* made this highly un-desirable in the eyes of the *Folkungs*, and in 1247 they turned against him. He crushed the revolt with considerable severity, clearing the way for him to forward a claim to the crown—not for himself but for his son Valdemar, Erik's nephew. Every-thing in these years seemed to be working in his favour. He won the support of the papacy through a papal legate who had been sent to Sweden to try to reconcile the opposing factions; in 1249 he carried out a highly-successful crusade in Finland which confirmed Sweden's hold on the south-west of the country; and in the following year King Erik died, and Valde-mar Birgersson was elected to succeed him.

Just to confuse matters for the historian, the name *folkung* was later applied to Birger Jarl's family, so that Valdemar is now spoken of as the first king of the Folkung dynasty,[1] although the appellation was (and is) also used for his enemies. Hardly had he been crowned when these once more rose in revolt. They were again ruthlessly crushed, and the hold of the new house was strengthened by making one of the king's brothers a bishop and giving another, Magnus, the title of Duke of the Svear; this is the first time that such a rank is heard of in Sweden and is a reflection of the growing influence of Conti-nental feudal ideas in the land. It was intended that Magnus should after his father's death occupy a position near the throne equivalent to that of a *jarl*, but Birger lived on for another six-teen years and for the whole of this time acted as the real ruler of the country. It was a period of considerable prosperity for Sweden, during which she can be said to have drawn level with her neighbours in many respects. Provincial law-codes were written down for the first time. Foreign merchants were en-couraged to settle under the walls of Stockholm's castle, and the town which grew up there as a result was developed as a com-

[1] See the table on p. 55.

mercial centre to replace Sigtuna, which had, it seems, been largely abandoned after the pirate raid. Two trade-missions were also sent to England; but Sweden's trade was falling more and more into the hands of German merchants, and just as little came from this attempt to establish closer links with western Europe as from those which Birger's uncle had made in the previous century.

Birger died at last in 1266. And with the removal of his strong hand, strife broke out once more. It took the form of a family-feud between the king and his brothers. One of these, Erik, had been excluded from the benefits conferred on the others and persuaded Duke Magnus to join him in a revolt. Valdemar, who seems to have made himself thoroughly unpopular with his subjects, was defeated and deposed in 1275. Magnus was elected king, and Erik became Duke of the Svear. But Valdemar did not give up the struggle; he enlisted Danish support and forced Magnus to grant him extensive lands. The *Folkungs* then staged yet another uprising, but came to terms with the king behind the back of his brother, who had to surrender the lands he had been given. After a rebellion in 1280 the *Folkung* party finally disappeared from history.

For the remaining ten years of his reign King Magnus enjoyed comparative peace. His son Birger was accepted as his successor in 1284—an event which seemed to presage the disappearance of the elective monarchy—and the end of the *Folkungs* enabled him to assert royal power to a degree hitherto unknown in Sweden. He forbade the council of nobles and ecclesiastics, with whose aid previous kings had ruled, to meet without his approval and issued decrees on his own authority alone. The crime of *lèse-majesté* (i.e. injury to the Crown, which could be interpreted very widely) was introduced—a formidable weapon, since any man convicted of it could suffer loss of life and lands. Magnus forbade his nobles to claim from the peasants maintenance for themselves and their followers as they travelled about the countryside from estate to estate; it was probably this ordinance which earned for him the nickname of *Laduslås* or Barnlock. He also encouraged the introduction into his kingdom of new cultural influences from the more advanced states of western Europe, including the whole apparatus of chivalry with tournaments and the dubbing of new knights.

While he failed to subdue the nobility for very long—and indeed increased its power to some extent by giving the magnates a more clearly defined position in government and society and a recognized relationship to the Crown in the royal council—his reign undoubtedly marks an important stage in the consolidation of the Swedish State. On his death in 1290 he was buried in the new church being built on the island of Riddarholm (Knight's Isle) to the west of Stockholm to serve the Franciscan abbey in the town and destined to be the last resting-place of many of Sweden's rulers.

*   *   *

In the course of the twelfth and thirteenth centuries Sweden had thus made rapid strides towards the attainment of political unity and strong government. But she was, at the death of Magnus Ladulås, also in other ways very unlike the land which had sent out contingents to join the Viking hosts.

The change which had most affected the life of every Swede was the establishment of the Christian Church. Its priests taught a morality radically different from that of their pagan predecessors, to whom such virtues as humility were unknown. The canon law often clashed with the unwritten law of the folk, in allowing, for example, a man to bequeath his property to the Church without consulting the wishes of his family and heirs. The grants of land made by successive kings and nobles constituted a revolution in the distribution of the principal form of wealth, which involved not only the owner but also all who worked on it. As in England, it was the clergy who introduced the Latin alphabet and the written record, a device which was gradually adopted also by secular society. Kings came to rely on churchmen, as the most highly—for long indeed the only—educated class in their realm, to conduct diplomatic negotiations and to fill their Chancery, the department of government which dealt with all the paper- (or in this age parchment-) work essential for the development of administration; a bishop filled the office of Chancellor throughout most of the Middle Ages in Sweden. Not only this, but kings relied on abbots and bishops, often themselves members of great noble families, to administer large areas of their kingdom in the same way as lay nobles and to give advice when called upon to do so as members of the royal council.

In 1120 there were six sees in Sweden, all concentrated in the region of Lake Mälaren, where the most intensive missionary effort had been made—at Skara, Sigtuna, Linköping, Eskilstuna, Strängnäs and Västerås. It was, however, probably some time before precise diocesan boundaries, which corresponded roughly with those of the existing provinces, were fixed, and fifty years later the picture had changed. Eskilstuna had ceased to be a bishopric; a new one had appeared in the south at Växjö; and the see of Sigtuna had been transferred to Old Uppsala and raised to the dignity of an archbishopric. Moved finally to the modern Uppsala about 1276, this latter was by far the richest and largest of the dioceses throughout the period; it included the whole of thinly-populated Norrland. Its first incumbent was an English Cistercian monk named Stefan (Stephen).

The method by which bishops were chosen long remained undefined. The earliest were probably the king's nominees, and the Crown, as in England, always had a considerable say in the appointment of all the more important ecclesiastical officials. But there was also a popular element, and as late as the early thirteenth century the Archbishop himself is spoken of as having been chosen by 'the clergy and people of the diocese'. Soon after this, however, the bodies of priests gathered round a bishop—his 'family'—began to be organized into regular cathedral chapters under a dean and given the duty not only of helping to administer the diocese and run the cathedral services, but also of electing each new incumbent. In the parishes the local landowner, whose ancestors had built the church and granted the land for its upkeep, for long nominated the priest to serve it, but in time his rights were confined to that of recommending a candidate to the local bishop, who would give his consent to appoint only if he were satisfied with the man's fitness.

Education and all forms of cultural life were, as throughout the rest of Europe during the Middle Ages, closely bound up with the Church. The main teaching centres were the schools attached to the cathedrals and run by members of the chapters. All those who wished to be ordained priest were expected to study in these schools for at least two years. If they

wished, they could stay on for a total of eight years and pass
from a study of Latin grammar and philosophy to that of
music, astronomy, arithmetic and geometry, all taught from
set texts by classical authors. For the really ambitious or
scholarly there were the great centres of learning outside
Scandinavia, and by the thirteenth century Swedish clerics
were to be found in the schools of both Paris and Bologna; at
the end of the same century a special house was acquired in the
former town for the use of clergy from the diocese of Uppsala,
and in time two other dioceses came to be served in the same
way. The Dominican friars, who prized learning as a weapon
against heresy, gave a considerable impetus to Swedish culture
and education. Their friaries, which were usually built in towns,
became important study centres with well-equipped libraries,
and the Latin annals and calendars in which their inhabitants
recorded events are of considerable importance to the historian.
Only slowly did the clergy lose its monopoly of literacy, but it
is obvious from the writing down of the provincial law-codes in
the early thirteenth century, about which more will be said later
in this chapter,[1] that some at least of the lawmen, for whose
guidance they were provided, could read. A vernacular
literature did not, however, emerge until after 1300.

It was the Church which provided the first stone buildings
seen in Sweden. Indeed it appears that it was not until the
thirteenth century that any secular buildings were constructed
of anything but wood; and even then an exception was made
only in the case of some royal castles (such as that at Stockholm), some private forts and a few of the richer merchants'
houses in Stockholm, Kalmar and Visby on Gotland. Until the
twelfth century, the style adopted for churches was the simple
Romanesque, but the Cistercians then introduced the bolder
Gothic from northern France. The church of the great Cistercian
monastery at Varnhem, south of Lake Vänern, is a fine example of this style from the thirteenth century; among others are
a number of the ruined churches in Visby. But the outstanding
monument to Early Gothic in Sweden is the cathedral at Uppsala, begun about 1273 to provide a fitting resting-place for the
bones of St. Erik. It took over a century and a half to complete,
but the main plan was the responsibility of a Frenchman,

[1] See p. 41.

Etienne de Bonneuil, who arrived in Sweden in 1287 and adopted a style familiar to him in his homeland. Brick was employed by the friars for their town houses, but it was some time before it was used elsewhere.

Even the minor arts were largely ecclesiastical. Paintings covered the walls and ceilings of even the humblest parish churches, to instruct the illiterate layman in the Scriptures and make more vivid the torments of the damned, the joys of the blessed and the majesty of the Almighty (see plate 3). A wealth of carved fonts on Gotland bears witness to the skill of the twelfth- and thirteenth-century sculptor, as well as to certain Russian and Byzantine influences on his work. That the metal worker had lost little of the cunning which he had possessed in Viking times may be seen on a church door at Rogslösa near the eastern shore of Lake Vättern.

After the changes in Swedish society brought about by the Conversion, probably the most far-reaching were those which flowed from changing methods of warfare among Sweden's neighbours. Sweden never knew a fully-fledged feudal society such as developed in Germany, France or Norman England. Land was not held from the Crown in a graded hierarchy by hereditary succession in exchange for the service of a definite number of mounted warriors; important offices and the territories intended to support their dignity never passed automatically from father to son but remained, as they had originally been elsewhere, tenable for one life only; estates were generally small and scattered. But the problems posed by the armoured knight, which the kings of Sweden did not have to face until the thirteenth century, led to important changes in the administration of their realm and in relations between the various classes of their subjects. The old national levy, to which every freeman was expected to contribute in person, gradually became obsolete, but the raising of a body of knights was a very expensive business, and only the nobility could be expected to afford the requisite horses and armour. Old systems of taxation had to be reformed or replaced by new ones, while the obligations of the upper classes to the king had to be more closely defined. The levy of ships and men formerly imposed on the coastal districts of central Sweden was converted into a regular tax, and the food claimed by the Court during its journeys about the realm became a steady burden paid to the stewards of the royal estates. The nobles, on the other hand, were exempted from all financial impositions on condition that they should aid the king with their dependents whenever called upon to do so; Magnus Laduslås decreed that all bishops and nobles and all who served another with a horse should be freed from the burden of entertaining the Court. These and similar measures helped to transform the Swedish nobility from a rather amorphous group of landowners into a distinct military class with common interests to defend against the Crown, the Church and any outsiders who appeared to be usurping its rightful place near the monarch. During the late thirteenth century it began to meet at irregular intervals in *herredagar* (= assemblies of lords).

The nobles formed a comparatively large class representing many different grades of wealth and responsibility. At the top stood the magnates. From these were chosen the members of the royal council or *Råd*, a body which emerged in the thirteenth century from the more informal gatherings of advisers previously called by the king, and a body which, as will be seen, gradually became the principal mouth-piece of noble aspirations against the Crown. It was the magnates who held the leading offices in Church and State and who acted as custodians of the castles which began to spring up on royal estates throughout Sweden around 1250; considerable districts or *län* were provided for their support, and over these the custodian enjoyed complete control. It was the magnates, closely linked to the Court as they were, who were most deeply influenced by the new concept of chivalry which reached Sweden from western Europe at this time; the title of knight (*riddare*) was for long a rare privilege and did not denote simply a rank below that of noble. Many magnates held lands in various parts of the country, which gave them a strong interest in the maintenance of national unity, an important factor when the Crown was weak.

It was also from the ranks of the higher nobility that were chosen the lawmen, who, through the provincial *things*, administered such land as had not been bequeathed to the Church and was not royal. The laws pronounced by them and the methods of judgment changed little for a long time after the end of the Viking Age. But, as the power of the king grew, significant developments took place. Certain serious crimes came to be deemed breaches of the 'king's peace' and were tried by the king or his representative, though still in the *thing*. This concept applied to all the provinces alike, and conviction meant outlawry, not only from the province in which the crime had been committed but also from the realm. Thus the legal system began to acquire a certain unity, but it was to be many years before there was one law-code for the whole country. From the early thirteenth century the provincial law-codes began to be written down. The oldest of these to survive—and the oldest document in the Swedish language—is the Code of Östergötland, dating from 1220 and attributed to the brother of Birger Jarl. Others followed, and in 1296 the king himself took a hand and appointed a commission to examine the laws of Uppland; the code which resulted was issued significantly by royal decree. All courts, it should be emphasized, were either royal or popular. The Swedish nobility never acquired independent judicial rights; private courts were unknown.

The changes outlined above naturally affected the peasants. These became more and more clearly divided between a majority who performed labour services and/or paid rent to a lay or ecclesiastical lord and were exempt from taxation, and a minority who worked on royal estates or who owned their own land and were liable to pay taxes to the king. The slave slowly began to disappear from the scene after the Conversion under the impetus of clerical disapproval, but the freedman remained dependent on his former master and his descendants for several generations, and the law dealt harshly with the man who had little or no land; he was forced to work for another. But life in the countryside was fundamentally much as it had been in Viking times; the same crops were grown, the same primitive implements were used and the same low standard of living endured. The population of the country was, however, growing and with it the area of cultivated land. A host of place-names indicating new settlements date from this period; the forest of Norrland was retreating slowly but steadily northwards; and more and more heathland in the south was used for grazing cattle as the opportunities for the export of dairy produce improved. The distribution of the village land seems to have become more regular in the twelfth and thirteenth centuries, and the two-field system of crop rotation, by which half the village arable was left fallow every year in order to allow it to recover its fertility, became standard in central Sweden; only in the richer, wheat-growing areas of the south was the more familiar three-field system to be found in operation.

The end of the Viking Age did not mean that the Viking trade-routes ceased to be used. The peasant-traders of Gotland maintained links with places as far afield as Novgorod in the east and Britain in the west, and merchants from the Swedish mainland were still active after 1000. Skara, Eskilstuna and Västerås (all, it may be noted, seats of bishops) were important centres of inland trade, while Lödöse, near where Gothenburg now stands, provided an outlet to the North Sea, and Sigtuna was, until the twelfth century, one of the hubs of international commerce in the Baltic. In the twelfth century, however, the rise of ports on the Baltic coast of Germany headed by Lübeck proved at once a stimulus to Sweden's economic development and a threat to her economic independence. German merchants first settled in Visby, which soon became an almost exclusively German town, and took over much of the trade with the east which had previously been exploited by the Gotlanders themselves. Then they began not only to trade with but also to live permanently in towns on the Swedish mainland, especially Kalmar and, from the middle of the thirteenth century, Stockholm. They also penetrated inland to the smaller centres, where their presence seems to have been particularly resented.

Wherever they went they brought new skills, capital (of which Sweden was in dire need) and a form of town government with burgomaster and council which was new to the Swedes. The Swedish name for town—*stad*—is itself of German origin, a reminder of the importance of German influence not only on the country's urban development but also on her language. New towns were built on the German model around a central market-place, and craft-guilds were organized on German lines. Many of the early town councils were dominated by Germans, and their settlement was encouraged by successive Swedish kings, who saw that the increase in trade which they brought would augment the royal income from tolls. But the rulers were nevertheless determined to retain ultimate control in their own hands. As a result, the Germans in Sweden never attained the privileged position in society which they won in

Denmark and Norway in the course of the Middle Ages; they gradually became absorbed into the native merchant community. Such privileges as they did obtain, such as a monopoly of all trade in the vicinity of the town where they resided, were granted by royal charters, of which that to Jönköping in the reign of King Magnus Ladulås is the earliest to have survived. Stockholm did not become a royal capital until after the end of the Middle Ages, but very early in its life it was the leading commercial centre of the country. In this capacity it replaced Sigtuna, which was in decline even before the pirate raid of 1187; and the conquest of the south-west Finland further favoured that part of Sweden which lay closest to it. Most of the other towns were very small indeed by modern standards; Bergen, which was the largest town in Scandinavia in the thirteenth century, had no more than 6,000 inhabitants.

Nor must the extent of foreign trade be exaggerated. The sole article which can be classed as an essential import into Sweden was salt, needed to preserve meat through the long winter months when there was not enough fodder to keep many of the cattle alive. Otherwise imports consisted of luxury or semi-luxury goods for the rich, like fine cloth. In return the Swedes could provide not only furs and fish as in prehistoric times, but also dairy produce and, towards the end of the period, increasing quantities of iron ore.

CHAPTER IV

The Fourteenth Century

T he rise and decline of monarchical authority in medieval
Sweden parallels to a certain extent that in England at
the same time, although there was no basis such as that
laid by William the Conqueror in an occupied country. Just
as in the England of Edward I at the end of the thirteenth
century the king wielded greater power than ever before and
his death was followed by a long and disturbed period, during
which the nobles sought to control the administration, so the
reign of Magnus Laduslås is a high-water mark of royal
dominance in Sweden, not to be attained again until the sixteenth century.

When Magnus died in 1290 his son Birger was only eleven
years old, and the government of the realm was placed in the
hands of the council of magnates headed by Torgils Knutsson;
he made his office of Marshal the most important in the land.
The period of internal peace which had commenced with the
final overthrow of the *Folkung* party continued into the new
reign. Birger was crowned in 1302, and, as had been the practice under Valdemar, his brothers, Erik and Valdemar, were
granted extensive territories over which to rule under him. The
latter was given Finland, and it was here that the most striking
work of the Marshal, who retained the reality of power after the
king's coming-of-age, was done. He conquered western Karelia
in a war with the principality of Novgorod, Sweden's main rival
for control of the Gulf of Finland and the Russian market beyond;
and he built a great fortress at Viborg to protect his acquisi-
tions. The peace at home, however, was broken when he
attacked the privileges of the Church. Erik and Valdemar, who
had grown increasingly restless and jealous of the Marshal's

44

power, sided with the opposition which this policy aroused. They
agreed to an outward reconciliation in 1305, but at once set about
trying to persuade the king that his overmighty subject constituted a serious menace to the throne. Their success resulted in
Torgils's arrest and execution.

Then, however, the brothers rounded on Birger himself, who
turned to Denmark and Norway for assistance. This was
readily obtained; the other Scandinavian monarchs seldom
missed an opportunity to fish in Sweden's troubled waters.
With their help, a settlement was reached in 1310 by which the
country was divided between the three contestants. Erik, who
had claims on the hereditary Norwegian crown through his
marriage with the wearer's daughter, gained what amounted to
a petty kingdom in the west of Sweden; Valdemar was given
Uppland; and the king kept the rest. Sweden seemed to be
going the way of countries like Germany, where the nominal
ruler had become little more than one great hereditary landowner among several others with like power. From this fate,
however, she was saved. Birger was understandably little satisfied with the arrangement and in 1317 had his brothers arrested
and confined; they were subsequently starved to death in
prison, but it is not clear how far the king was personally responsible for this. Erik in particular had been very popular with his
fellow nobles, and Birger's action drove them to revolt. They
forced him to flee to Gotland and thence to Denmark, where he
died shortly afterwards. The victors proceeded to elect the
three-year-old Magnus, son of Duke Erik and already King of
Norway, as King of Sweden also. The event is significant for
three reasons. Firstly, the Scandinavian peninsula, with the exception of the Danish provinces in the extreme south and south-
west, was now united under one ruler. Secondly, the principle
of elective monarchy was reasserted after having been threatened by the practice of kings' naming their sons to succeed them
during their life-time. And thirdly, representatives of the tax-
paying peasants attended the election ceremony for the first
time.

The most notable event during the regency which preceded
the personal reign of Magnus Eriksson was the conclusion of a
treaty with Novgorod in 1323. This established a definite
frontier in eastern and northern Finland which left the Swedes

in undisputed control of the south-western half of the country but also marked for some time the limit of their expansion in the area.

King Magnus was declared of age in 1332. The very same year saw the opening of the so-called Scanian Question, which dominated Swedish politics for the rest of the long reign. Denmark was at this time rent by squabbles between her king and the Count of Holstein to the south. One of the groups in Denmark who were opposed to the Crown offered Sweden the two provinces of Scania and Blekinge, which the Count was holding in pledge from the Danish king against loans which he had made to him. The offer was an extremely attractive one, for it would give Sweden both complete control of the eastern shore of the Sound and, in the case of Scania, an area richer than any Swedish province. Magnus, however, preferred to gain the territory by negotiation and agreed finally to accept it in return for a promise to pay the Count the sum owed to him by the King of Denmark. This was enormous and very much more than the Swedish king could afford; his finances were already in a sorry state, and the peasantry was grossly over-burdened with taxes. Stability eventually returned to Denmark with the accession of King Valdemar Atterdag in 1340, and he immediately refused to recognize Sweden's right to the two provinces. He called in the wily Albert, Duke of Mecklenburg on the southern shore of the Baltic, to assist him in making good his claims. But Albert was King Magnus's brother-in-law and as such had been granted extensive privileges in Sweden in exchange for loans. He seized this opportunity to extend his influence in the North still further by offering to act as mediator in the dispute. As a result of his intervention, Valdemar was persuaded to acknowledge the loss of Scania, Halland and Blekinge, but only on condition that he should be paid a further large sum of money.

The burden which all this placed on the Swedish Crown made Magnus's position intolerable, and his troubles were speedily exploited by Valdemar and Albert. He tried to save himself by pledging large areas of the royal domain to his nobles against loans, but this not only failed to win him their support but worsened his financial position still further, for such land was exempt from taxation. So he tried to reverse the process, and began to demand the return of territory already granted on the grounds that its holders had not performed the military service for which they had originally been given their privileges. At the same time he attacked the similar privileges enjoyed by the Church. The hostility caused by this policy forced him to come to terms, but the peace did not last long. Magnus's eldest son Erik, peeved at his powerlessness after his younger brother had succeeded to the throne of Norway, joined his father's enemies and in 1356 headed a revolt.

Once more Albert of Mecklenburg, who had encouraged the opposition, stepped in as mediator and forced the king to grant Erik Finland and a large part of southern Sweden; Albert himself received certain important districts in Scania in payment for his services. Magnus now approached King Valdemar with a plan to turn the tables on his son and arranged for the marriage of his younger son Håkon, King of Norway, to Valdemar's daughter. But Erik drove out the invading Danes and became reconciled to his father. In 1359 he died without heirs.

Magnus's position, however, remained perilous. He decided to appeal to his subjects' loyalty in a national assembly made up of representatives from the four main 'estates' of the realm—the nobles, the clergy, the burghers or townsmen and the tax-paying peasants. Some historians have regarded this as the first Swedish *riksdag* or parliament, but while the appearance of the burghers for the first time in such a context is interesting, there is unfortunately no evidence that a body of this kind ever met. Even if it did, it was not imitated for at least thirty years, and it was long after that before such assemblies became other than extraordinary. Magnus at the same time broke his contract with the King of Denmark and found himself faced with both a Danish invasion and the renewed hostility of Albert of Mecklenburg. In 1361 the Danes overran Gotland and massacred its peasant army in a great battle outside the walls of Visby, whose German inhabitants refused to grant the Swedes refuge. Visby's trading privileges were confirmed after it had payed a huge ransom, but the Danish occupation of what was still the greatest trading centre in the Baltic considerably alarmed the towns of the Hanseatic League, who tendered their services to Sweden. Magnus, however, found the price they demanded for their support too high and turned down the offer. This was too much for his nobles, who rose against him yet again and elected his son Håkon in his stead. But, as had happened before, father and son were reconciled and opened negotiations with Denmark. As a result of these, Håkon was finally married to Valdemar's daughter Margaret. The way was thus prepared for a union of all three Scandinavian kingdoms, but, in view of the elective nature of the thrones of Denmark and Sweden, this was by no means a foregone conclusion.

Once more the Swedish nobles rebelled and in 1363 offered the crown to Albert, the son of Albert of Mecklenburg. They threw King Magnus into prison, but his son fought on and gained Danish assistance. The Hanseatic League, discontented with the treatment meted out to its merchants in Norway and Denmark, joined Albert and enabled him to reoccupy Scania. But they began to grow fearful of the rising power of Mecklenburg and withdrew from the war in 1369.

It was now King Albert who was in serious trouble, from internal as well as external enemies. His employment of Germans, upon whom were lavished offices and *län*, made him very unpopular with many of his new subjects, especially the magnates, who saw what they regarded as their rightful place in society and government being usurped by foreigners. The king managed to make peace with Valdemar in return for Gotland, but in 1371 King Håkon raised a revolt and marched on Stockholm. Albert hurriedly agreed to appoint only native Swedes to be governors of royal castles, to surrender the lands his father had been granted in Sweden and to do nothing without the consent of his *Råd*. Magnus Eriksson was released, but he was drowned in a shipwreck three years later.

Albert had saved his crown but at the cost of handing over all real power to the magnates of the Council and in particular to Bo Jonsson, the Steward, an office now more important than that of Marshal. Nicknamed Grip from the griffin (Swedish *grip*) on his coat of arms (the usual source from this time on of the surnames adopted by Swedish noble families or by commoners on being ennobled), this man had already acted as marshal for King Magnus Eriksson and on the accession of King Albert was granted powers equivalent to those once wielded by the *jarls*. He proceeded to use these to build up—often by highly questionable means—an enormous fortune in

The Fourteenth Century

land and castles. He acquired a dozen great fortresses and over a thousand separate estates and in the end was virtual ruler of Finland and central and south-east Sweden. On the south shore of Lake Mälaren he built himself Gripsholm, one of the most famous castles in Sweden, although the one now standing on the site dates from the sixteenth century.

When he died in 1386, Grip's vast property was placed in the hands of a committee of leading nobles and ecclesiastics named in his will, part of their task being to pay off the considerable debt which the Steward had incurred while creating his empire. King Albert naturally wished, as Grip had foreseen, to obtain as much of the estate as possible for the Crown, but the methods he employed in his attempts to do this aroused the hostility of his nobles, headed by Grip's executors. They turned to King Håkon's wife Margaret, who was at this time acting as regent for her son Olof, King of Norway since his father's death and of Denmark too since the death of King Valdemar in 1375. The prospect of a united Scandinavia appealed especially to the many Swedish magnates who owned lands in the other kingdoms or whose estates lay near the frontier and were frequently ravaged in the course of disputes, but the idea was also attractive to those who wished to erect a bulwark against further German interference in the affairs of the North.

Olof died in 1387, but, at a meeting of some of the leading Swedish nobles in the following year, his mother was proclaimed 'first lady of Sweden and her lawful mistress', a position similar to that which she already enjoyed in Norway and Denmark. She was given the right to dispose of the crown as she chose and control of all Grip's castles and much of the remainder of his estate. In return she confirmed all the privileges claimed by the nobility as a class. The rest of the Swedish nobles accepted these terms and drove Albert from the realm. He returned with an army of German mercenaries in 1389 but was defeated and taken prisoner. Stockholm held out on his behalf for nine more years with help from Mecklenburg, but the rest of the country came under Margaret's sway. The way was clear for a union under a king of her choice, and in 1396 her great-nephew Erik of Pomerania, already King of Norway, was proclaimed ruler of Denmark and Sweden.

* * *

D 49

The political history of Sweden in the century before the union of the three Scandinavian kingdoms is thus essentially the history of the largely successful attempts of her nobles to defend their privileges against the efforts of successive kings, beset by growing financial difficulties, to impose on the country with the help of councillors and castellans, often foreigners, of their own choosing and of mercenary knights, all-powerful hereditary monarchy. This did not, however, result, as in some other European countries, in the break-up of the realm into semi-independent principalities. The centralized administration introduced in the course of the twelfth and thirteenth centuries survived under the control of the *Råd*, which by the middle of the fourteenth century was made up of all the bishops and chief officials like the Steward and Marshal, together with most of the lawmen; all appointments of interest to the magnates, such as that of custodian of a royal castle, and all grants of Crown land were considered to lie within its competence. Indeed the work of centralization went on. The provincial *things* became to an increasing extent purely judicial bodies, and even as such they grew more and more dependent on the king and his council, where the lawman usually had a seat; while the latter might still in theory be elected by the assembly of freemen, he was in practice appointed by his peers.

It is also in the field of law that is to be found perhaps the most striking evidence for this process of unification. About 1350, during a period when Magnus Eriksson was temporarily reconciled to his nobles, there was drawn up for the first time a law-code for the whole realm, a code which remained in force until the eighteenth century. But it was more than a law-code, for it opened with a section laying down that Sweden was an elective and not an hereditary monarchy and specifying both the way in which the election should be carried out and the powers and compositions of the Council. It is thus also a kind of constitution and occupies a place in Swedish history similar to that of Magna Carta in the history of England; it defined the ancient rights—for so they were regarded—of the nobility against the king, who would overstep the line drawn at his peril.

The fierce struggle by the Swedish nobles to retain their powers and privileges must be viewed against the background of an economic depression which affected them no less than the

Crown. The agricultural prosperity which was found in most parts of Europe in the thirteenth century did not long survive its close. The precise cause or causes of this recession remain obscure, but a decline in population appears to have played a major part. In Sweden this was to a certain extent the result of emigration from the more thickly populated central areas to Norrland and Finland, combined with the growing burden of taxation imposed by an impoverished Crown; but the process was greatly aggravated by the Black Death, which reached Sweden from Norway in 1350.[1] The exact extent of its ravages will never be known, but it has been calculated that only a sixth of the population of Uppland survived, and whole parishes were certainly deserted in many parts of the country. Marginal land which had been put under the plough in the thirteenth century was allowed to return to forest and waste, and a shortage of labour caused a catastrophic fall in the value of land which hit all who owned it. The effect of these developments on the peasantry became most dramatically apparent in the fifteenth century and will be examined in the next chapter.[2]

During the same period, other departments of Sweden's economic life were falling more and more under the control of North Germans, who, as we have seen, had begun to arrive in large numbers in the previous century and whose rôle in political life has already been described. The fleets of swift and roomy ships from the Hansa towns, especially Lübeck and Danzig, had by now largely driven the less economically-run Swedish craft from the main Baltic trade routes. Among the goods which they carried, a leading place was occupied by high-grade Swedish iron and copper ore, the mining of which on a large scale depended on German capital and expertise, although the Crown and native nobility showed an early appreciation of its potentialities. Mining, as distinct from the extraction of ore from dried-out bogs, which had been carried on even in the prehistoric period, can be traced back to the twelfth century; but it was not apparently until the end of the thirteenth that the great deposits of iron in the Bergslagen district to the west and north-west of Lake Mälaren, for which Västerås was

---

[1] Its effects in Norway are vividly described at the end of Sigrid Undset's masterly novel *Kristin Lavransdatter*.

[2] See pp. 64–5.

the main outlet, or the Great Copper Mountain (Kopparberg) at Falun in Dalarna were seriously exploited. The mine-owners, many of them of German origin, were for long numerous, and their individual enterprises were on a small scale. They might even work in the mine themselves, but as their labour force was increased in response to demand, a clearer distinction emerged between masters and men. The former organized themselves into powerful co-operative guilds, to which the Crown granted extensive privileges, including exemption from taxation and from provincial administration; the charter granted to the Kopparberg miners in 1347 is one of the earliest still surviving to be composed in Swedish, and on its basis the company which today controls the workings claims to be the oldest in the world. While criminals might be committed to the mines as a punishment, and prisoners-of-war were sometimes used, most of those who worked either underground or in the smelting-sheds, where the ore was refined, were drawn from the local peasantry, who continued to own plots of land which they cultivated in their spare time. The mining areas thus developed easily into distinct self-governing communities isolated from the rest of the country; in the fifteenth century they were to constitute a formidable force in political life.

Under the impetus of German trade and traders, Swedish towns continued to grow and organize themselves. Among them Stockholm was by now undoubtedly the most important; its customs became a model for those of most of its fellows and formed the basis for a general urban code for the whole country, drawn up in the middle of the century. Its provisions included one that at least half the members of the town council and its clerk should be Swedes. This reflects the importance of the German element among the burghers, for even if it was only in Stockholm and Kalmar that this was predominant, it must be remembered that elsewhere many who could claim to be Swedish were of German origin. A further result of German influence was the emergence of craft guilds, of which the first (of Stockholm tailors) appeared in 1336, but these were confined to the largest towns, which alone had a population of sufficient size to make them necessary, and, unlike their equivalents in many other countries, they seem to have played little part in town government.

But it was not only in the political and economic field that Germany loomed large over late-medieval Sweden. In intellectual and artistic life it was no longer France who provided the main inspiration. Little new ecclesiastical building was undertaken after 1300, but the additions and alterations made to churches already in existence are distinctly German in character. This can be seen in the cathedral of Linköping, which is mainly of the fourteenth century but took even longer to complete than Uppsala. The increasing use of brick is partly a reflection of the poverty of the time, and in general this is a bleak period of Swedish art, to which nothing of note can be attributed.

Swedish scholars, though continuing to frequent Paris, gravitated in the fourteenth century more and more to new universities in northern and central Europe; Prague was particularly popular with them. And they were no longer only churchmen who wrote Latin but also included laymen who write in Swedish. The vernacular, which was absorbing an increasing number of German borrowings, began to be employed for the first time in private documents, and French romances in verse were translated into it for the delectation of the Court. Nothing of great literary value was produced in Swedish, but the *Chronicle of Erik*, a history in verse of Sweden's kings from 1220 to the time when it was written about a century later, has some merit, and is certainly better than the efforts in the same genre which succeeded it; it is an important—if highly-coloured—source for the historian of the thirteenth and early fourteenth century. The most outstanding corpus of literature produced by a Swede in this period—or indeed until modern times—was, at least in the form in which it has come down to us, written in Latin. This was the seven books of the *Revelations of St. Bridget*. More must, however, be said about this remarkable woman, the only Swede to gain a European reputation in the Middle Ages.

Bridget (more correctly Birgitta Birgersdotter) was born in 1303 to the wife of the lawman of Uppland, a member of one of the most powerful and wealthiest families in the land, and one in addition with an outstanding record for piety. She was married at the age of thirteen to a young nobleman to whom she bore eight children. Even at this period in her life she appears to have acquired a widespread reputation for good works and had as her confessor the leading theologian in Sweden. She accompanied her husband on a pilgrimage to Spain, but he died shortly after their return in 1344 and was buried in the Cistercian monastery of Alvastra on the shore of Lake Vättern. This event led to a great crisis in Bridget's spiritual life, during which she experienced a vision in which Christ declared to her 'that you shall be my bride and my mouth-piece and that you shall hear and see spiritual things, and my Holy Spirit shall remain with you unto death'. She settled at Alvastra and there received further revelations on various matters, which were faithfully recorded by the sub-prior Peter Olovsson, who became her most devoted follower. She then persuaded King Magnus Eriksson, whose queen she had served as lady-in-waiting, to grant her a royal estate at Vadstena, not far from Alvastra. Here she proposed to build a monastery for both monks and nuns under an abbess, similar to the 'double monasteries' found in Anglo-Saxon England and the later Gilbertine houses, but as part of an entirely new religious order.

Other means having failed, and the king having withdrawn his support, in 1349 she set off for Rome in an attempt to persuade the pope both to bless her enterprise and to return to the Holy City from his self-imposed exile in Avignon. She never saw her native land again, but took a keen interest in Scandinavian affairs and encouraged the nobles in their opposition to Magnus, whose conduct she attacked bitterly in further revelations; her son Karl took a prominent part in a revolt against him in 1362.

In Rome she settled in a house built by the pope's brother and, in a city rent by disorder, led a life of regular devotion, although she never appears to have taken the vows of a nun. Pope Clement VI remained adamant before her entreaties— and threats—but his successor, after a brief visit to Rome, finally agreed to allow her to build a house at Vadstena for monks and nuns who were to belong to the Augustinian Order but follow a rule drawn up by Bridget herself. Two years later, although nearly seventy years of age, she made a pilgrimage to the Holy Land accompanied by her son Birger and daughter Catherine, both of whom had inherited their mother's piety. Soon after her return to Rome she died. Her body was taken back to Vadstena, where a small community had already established itself, and the monastery rapidly became the most popular place of pilgrimage in the whole of Scandinavia. Bridget's daughter stayed on in Rome to work for her mother's canonization, a task in which she received every encouragement from the Swedish Crown and nobility alike. Their efforts received their reward in 1391, and monasteries following the Rule of St. Saviour (or in popular parlance 'of the Brigittine Order'), constructed according to the detailed specifications laid down by the foundress herself, spread throughout Europe and beyond. A house was established in England, on a royal estate at Isleworth in Middlesex, by Henry Fitzhugh, who had visited Scandinavia on the occasion of the marriage of Philippa, the daughter of Henry IV, to Erik of Pomerania; at the time of the Dissolution in the sixteenth century Syon, as it was called, was among the wealthiest monasteries in the country.[1]

THE FOLKUNG DYNASTY

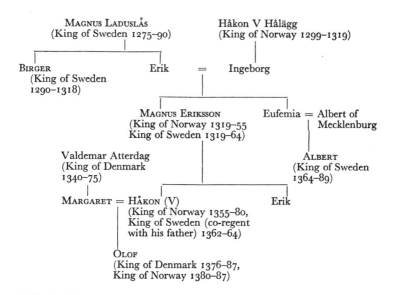

[1] The Brigittines returned to England in 1861 and now have a house at South Brent in Devon. The last of their 'double monasteries' (in Bavaria) lost its monks in the early nineteenth century.

Even before her death, the task of editing the Saint's revelations (over 600 of them) had been undertaken by members of her entourage. They cover a wide range of topics including harsh criticisms of individuals, both lay and ecclesiastical, and a long dialogue between Christ and a doubting monk, in which the necessity of evil is explained. But all are marked by a wealth of imagery and a depth of feeling which gave them a European reputation in the fifteenth century. In addition, Bridget left behind her a number of prayers which found their way into all English pre-Reformation religious primers.

CHAPTER V

The Union of Kalmar

W hile the overthrow of King Albert and the acceptance of Erik of Pomerania in his place united the three Scandinavian realms under one crown, it was several years before the full implications of such an arrangement could be discussed. A body of Albert's supporters held out in Stockholm, while others harassed the Swedish coast and brought relief to the besieged from Gotland and Mecklenburg. Finally, in 1395, the Hanseatic League mediated a peace by which Albert was to be released and Stockholm handed over to Margaret after three years.

On the occasion of Erik's coronation at Kalmar in 1397, negotiations between the magnates of the three countries were set on foot to regulate their mutual relations and the powers of the new king; it was hoped in this way to give the Union a firmer foundation. Only the draft of an agreement arising out of these discussions has survived, and historians have long argued as to whether any final treaty was ever made. But a compact very similar to that set out in the draft, allowing for a common foreign policy but the maintenance of existing laws and separate national councils, was often referred to in later years as if it were considered valid. The so-called 'Union of Kalmar' had, in any case, become a reality eight years before the negotiations took place.

Erik was only fourteen at the time of his election, and the real power remained in Margaret's hands until her death in 1412. She ruled with great ability, but her firm assertion of the Crown's rights did not make her popular with the Swedish nobles. She insisted on the return of all lands acquired by them and the Church during Albert's reign, lands which had in this

57

way become exempt from taxation. It is true that nobles were allowed to participate in the commission which carried out the survey, and that much of the land involved had gone to foreigners, but many of the magnates feared that this *reduktion* might prove to be only the first step in the resumption of all land once held by the Crown. In spite of the increase in her income which resulted from these measures, the Regent found herself obliged to levy heavy additional taxes to enable her both to pay for a war with the Order of Teutonic Knights, to whom Albert had sold Gotland, and then to buy the island back from them. The peasants and burghers grumbled at these exactions, while the nobles muttered against the appointment of Danes to be custodians of royal castles; this, they claimed, was a breach of the promise Margaret had made to them when they had offered her the kingdom.

While she lived, everything remained fairly quiet, but from the beginning of Erik's personal rule his troubles began to multiply. The new king was possessed by an inordinate ambition, and wished to make his three kingdoms the centre of a great Baltic empire similar to that which Sweden alone was to win in the seventeenth century. Not content with the enmity of German nobles in the south of Denmark, who were struggling for their independence in alliance with the Hanseatic League, he made enemies also of the Teutonic Knights; his marriage to Henry IV's daughter and the favours he bestowed on English merchants in his dominions were aimed at enlisting the help of the distant realm against his foes. Constant warfare made heavy demands on the Exchequer and forced him not only to increase taxation but also to debase the coinage, which made the economic situation still worse. At the beginning of the reign, he tried to appease the Swedish nobles by abandoning the resumption of lands granted by his predecessor and even returned some which Margaret had confiscated. But any good will this might have engendered was soon dissipated by his appointment of Danes and Germans to the command of his fortresses; such men were responsible to him alone to a much greater degree than his great-aunt's appointees had been to her. He spent little time in Sweden and grew wholly out of touch with feeling in the country.

When discontent finally came to a head, however, it did so

amongst the magnates, but among the miners of Bergslagen. They had been particularly hard hit by the blockade imposed on the Swedish coast by the Hansa towns, a blockade which prevented the export of iron and copper on which their livelihood depended. In 1432 they rose in revolt under the leadership of a mine-owner named Engelbrekt Engelbrektsson, a member of the lesser nobility and, like so many mine-owners, of German origin. He could rely for support not only on the miners, but also on other members of his own class, which was being seriously affected by the agricultural depression, and on the free (i.e. tax-paying) peasants, oppressed by royal taxation. The magnates on the Council promised to intercede with Erik for the rebels, but they obtained little satisfaction from their master, and in 1434, when he seemed on the point of victory over his various foreign enemies, a new revolt under Engelbrekt swept all before it. This time it was joined by the burghers, who were also deprived of much of their income by the blockade, and by several bishops, resentful of the king's attempts to foist his own candidates into ecclesiastical vacancies with papal support. The magnates themselves, though with considerable misgivings, finally sided with the rebels, to whom castle after castle fell. Erik agreed to negotiate.

In January 1435 Engelbrekt was elected Guardian of the Realm at a meeting he called at Arboga in Södermanland. But it was the *Råd* which really controlled the situation and which conducted the negotiations with the king. The magnates were alarmed by the new forces which Engelbrekt had unleashed and connived at his murder early in 1436, when war had again broken out. His grave soon became a place of pilgrimage for the lower classes, whose cause he had seemed to champion and who regarded him as a saint. He seems, from all accounts, to have been an attractive figure, though easily outmanoeuvred on the political plane by the powerful nobles. For the romantic historian of the nineteenth century, he was a national hero fighting for independence against foreign oppression, but there is no real evidence that he wished, any more than did the magnates, to break the Union; his aim was, rather, to force the king to end the war and all the misery which went with it.

The magnates continued to strengthen their position after his death. They ruthlessly crushed further peasant risings;

executed Engelbrekt's lieutenants; and forbade all non-nobles to wear swords. They elected one of their own number, the Marshal, Karl Knutsson, to act as regent, and in 1439 finally deposed Erik. This did not mean a dissolution of the Union, for the Swedish revolt had sparked off risings in Norway and Denmark, where Erik's nephew, Christopher of Bavaria, was chosen to succeed him, and in 1441 the Swedes followed suit. Erik's power was soon confined to Gotland.

Christopher had to promise to respect all the rights and privileges of the Swedish nobles, who ruled the country in his name through a council drawn from their ranks. In the most important contemporary chronicle he is pictured as a weak man, but it was written largely to glorify his successor, and its judgments must thus be treated with caution. His reputation certainly suffered from his failure to win back Gotland from Erik, who turned the island into a pirate base from which to harry Swedish and Danish ships, and from a run of bad harvests, for which he was in no way to blame but which earned him the nickname of Bark King on account of the bread made from bark which the peasants were forced to eat. He was given no opportunity to redeem his good name, for he died suddenly in 1448.

This led to the first real breach in the Union, although it was a temporary one and probably unintentional. While Karl Knutsson, whom Christopher had retained as his marshal, was elected King of Sweden, the Danes and Norwegians chose Christian of Oldenburg to be their monarch. Erik handed over Gotland to the latter and retired to Pomerania. That there was still strong support for the principle of union among the magnates of all three realms was shown in 1451, when Karl reached an agreement with the Danish king, by which whoever should live the longer was to inherit the other's kingdom. Several points, however, remained in dispute, and war broke out. Although the Danes were joined by the Hanseatic League and the Teutonic Knights, their attacks on Sweden were successfully repelled, but the war forced Karl to impose heavy taxes on his subjects, and the Hansa renewed its blockade. The king found himself faced by a growing opposition, led by Archbishop Jöns Bengtsson of the powerful Uppland family of Oxenstierna, who had a long-standing personal quarrel with him. In 1457 he was forced to flee the realm, and Christian was elected in his stead.

It soon became apparent, however, that the new king had little sympathy with the constitutional aspirations of the Swedish magnates, and in 1464 he even imprisoned the Archbishop for defying his orders. This was the signal for yet another revolt, which resulted in Christian's defeat and Karl Knutsson's recall. He in his turn fell foul of the Oxenstiernas, who compelled him to abdicate after only a year on the throne and to retire to Finland. There followed a period of near-anarchy, which degenerated into a civil war between, on the one side, the Oxenstiernas and their friends, who wished to retain the Union on their own terms, and, on the other, what may be called without too much exaggeration a nationalist group. This was led by the sons of the Danish immigrant Axel Tott, who had acquired land in south Sweden which gave them control of the very valuable export trade in cattle and dairy produce from that area, and the family of Sture, to whom the Totts were related. In 1467 the latter party managed to obtain the return of Karl to the throne.

Three years later he died, and power was seized by his nephew Sten Sture. With the support of the burghers of Stockholm and the peasants of the traditionally-turbulent province of Dalarna, he made himself Guardian of the Realm, the title which Karl Knutsson had once held. But the Unionists under the Oxenstiernas remained formidable, and Christian could rely on their support when he sailed to Stockholm in 1471 with a large Dano-German army. He came to negotiate with the Swedish magnates with a view to resuming the government of the country. But Sture held aloof, and on October 10th his army attacked Christian's. This was drawn up on Brunkeberg, a ridge running north from the island to which Stockholm was still confined but in the heart of the modern city. The Danes and their Swedish allies (for the Oxenstiernas had raised the Uppland peasants on Christian's behalf) were decisively defeated; the king was compelled to sail back to Denmark and make peace.

The Battle of Brunkeberg is as famous in Sweden's history as is the Battle of Agincourt in England's, and, like the latter, it greatly encouraged the growth of national—in this case of specifically anti-Danish—feeling, especially among the lower classes; the great wooden statue of St. George slaying the Dragon which Sten Sture ordered to commemorate it can still be seen in Stockholm Cathedral. But it must not be forgotten that it was in some degree a battle of Swedes against Swedes, and, while the Oxenstiernas were temporarily discomfited, feeling in favour of the Union was still strong enough among the magnates to compel the victor to continue negotiations for its re-establishment. These resulted five years after Brunkeberg in a Swedish promise to recognize the Danish king, on certain conditions. Whether Christian every contemplated accepting these we do not know, but he died in 1481 without ever having returned to Sweden.

His son Hans succeeded him in Denmark and Norway and was promised the Swedish crown, though on more stringent terms than those offered to his father. He accepted them, but Sture fought long and hard to prevent the implementation of the agreement, which was demanded by the *Råd*. For a time he was successful, but his position was weakened by an unsuccessful war against the Prince of Muscovy, who was becoming a serious menace to Sweden's position in Finland. In 1497 he succeeded in making peace, but on his return to Stockholm he was deposed. A peasant army was formed in his defence, but this was defeated by Hans, who became king. Sten Sture, like Karl Knutsson before him, was granted Finland as a fief and given a seat on the Council. Instead of being won over by this generosity, however, he used his power to reunite his former followers and plan for a new *coup* at the first favourable opportunity. This came in 1501, when Hans suffered a catastrophic military defeat on the River Elbe. Sture had himself appointed regent in Sweden, which was soon completely under his control. At his moment of triumph he died.

He had done much to prepare the way for the Vasa kings in the sixteenth century by trying to establish a strong, centralized state, based on the consent of a much wider section of society than the nobility alone. To provide this state with a firm financial basis, he fostered foreign trade, but within a nationalist framework, and, while he avoided an open clash with the Hansa, he took advantage of the League's declining power to reduce the privileges enjoyed by German merchants in the

Swedish market. These and other aspects of his work make the period of his rule an important watershed in Sweden's history.

He was succeeded in the regency by Svante Nilsson from a family also named Sture, but quite unrelated, it seems, to Sten's. Svante tried to govern the country in co-operation with the magnates, but as time went on his position became more and more difficult. Hans remained irreconcilable, and Sweden had to withstand constant Danish attacks from both land and sea, as well as a blockade of her coasts. Svante Sture refused to compromise, but the general misery caused by the war and the seemingly endless nature of the struggle strengthened the hand of the Unionist opposition. The nobles became extremely jealous of the Regent's power and fearful of the peasant unrest which he might, they suspected, use to increase it still more. In 1512 he was killed, apparently accidentally, by a fall in a mine he was visiting, and his place was taken by his son.

Although still in his teens, Sten Sture the Younger managed to win over the suspicious magnates of the *Råd*. Like his namesake, however, he based his power principally on the unprivileged classes, especially the Dalarna peasants. But he did so in a far more radical way, and his open ambition, which seemed to be drawing him towards the crown itself, imposed a severe strain on his relations with the nobility, a large section of which was driven to join the Unionists, now led by the unscrupulous new archbishop, Gustav Trolle. An open breach between Trolle and Sture took place in 1517 over the immunities which the prelate claimed for his estates, and the Regent had him deposed and imprisoned.

King Hans died in 1513 and was succeeded by his son Christian II. Like the Stures, the new ruler of Denmark set about building up an efficient, centralized state based on the middle and lower classes, and he was not the man to forgo voluntarily his rights in Sweden. Sture's violent handling of the Archbishop provided him with an excellent opportunity to assert them. He persuaded the pope to have the Sture party excommunicated and to appoint him leader of a crusade against them. In 1520 he attacked Sweden by land and defeated and mortally wounded Sten Sture in a battle on the frozen lake of Åsunden in Vastergötland. Trolle, now free, joined the Danes, and he was followed by many of Sture's former supporters among the nobles. The peasants remained loyal to the latter's cause rather longer, but they knew of Christian's reputation as a friend of the lower classes, and were finally gained by promises. Only Stockholm held out under the command of the Regent's widow, Christina Gyllenstierna, and she surrendered the city after Christian had promised a general amnesty. In November he made a triumphal entry into the capital, and a divided Council proclaimed him hereditary king. Then, in the midst of the coronation celebrations, the Archbishop suddenly demanded the trial of Christina, together with twelve nobles and the leading burghers of Stockholm, on a charge of heresy for their part in his deposition and imprisonment. Just how far the king himself was a party to the plot has never been established, but there can be little doubt that he welcomed this opportunity to be rid of those most likely to stand in his way. He readily assented to Trolle's request, and 82 people, including two bishops, were condemned to death and executed in what came to be known as 'The Stockholm Bloodbath'. Christina was thrown into prison, and her husband's body burnt.

Christian then began a tour of his new kingdom. But before this was completed, rumours of insurrection began to reach him. Persecution of Sture's followers had spread to the provinces and had evoked a formidable reaction. The example was set by the Dalarna peasants, who rose under a nephew of Christina Gyllenstierna named Gustav Eriksson Vasa. The fate of the Union was sealed.

*   *   *

One of the most remarkable features of the political life of Sweden in the fifteenth century is the part played in the shaping of events by the freehold peasants, who probably owned about half the land in the country. They helped Engelbrekt to his short-lived victory; the Stures leaned heavily on them as a counter-poise to the magnates; and Gustav Vasa found their help essential in his revolt against Christian II. In the latter part of the century their importance was recognized by calling their representatives regularly to national assemblies. While this

1. Typical Swedish lakeland scenery (Hälsingland). *Swedish Tourist Traffic Association*

2a. Rock-drawing in Tanum parish, Bohuslän. *Photo ATA*

2b. The Old Town of Stockholm with a view of
the thirteenth-century Cathedral.
Swedish Tourist Traffic Association

development reflects to a certain extent changing methods of warfare and especially the replacement of the armoured knight (never very suitable for use in the wooded terrain which covered so much of Sweden) by the foot-soldier as the decisive factor on the battle-field, it is also closely linked to changing economic conditions. Throughout Europe during the later Middle Ages there occurred a series of peasant revolts of which the most familiar to the majority of readers will be that which took place in southern England in 1381. Historians can still not agree on the cause or causes of these movements, but a decline in living standards does not seem to have been one. Rather do they seem to have flowed from the rising prosperity enjoyed by a large body of the rural lower class, which made already existing or newly-imposed restrictions and burdens more irksome than they would have been earlier. The effects on the peasants of the decline in agriculture which began in the fourteenth century varied according to their individual wealth and status within their class. Some nobles who were entitled to labour services were able to overcome their difficulties by increasing them, but often, especially on the small estates in the south of Sweden, land-lords had to offer their tenants better conditions and accept lower rents from them in order to get their land cultivated at all. And the well-to-do freeholder could exploit the fall in land values by purchasing the holdings of an impoverished noble.

But, while conditions were improving for a good number, life for the majority remained hard. A run of bad harvests like that during the reign of Christopher of Bavaria might, as has been seen, drive the peasant to live on bread made of birch-bark, and for most Swedes starvation was always in any case only just around the corner. There was rarely enough grain for export, and the frequent blockades imposed by the Hansa as well as Danish raids on Baltic commerce cut off supplies of the salt from France and north-west Germany on which the peasant relied, both for the preservation of meat and fish, very little of which was eaten fresh, and for the butter which absorbed most of the milk supply. The internal strife of the Union period also caused much misery to those who found themselves in the path of contending armies or who lived near the national frontier.

Housing in the countryside was of the simplest. A one-roomed wooden hut, with an open hearth and no windows

E

(apart from a skylight covered with calf-skin to keep the rain out), served most families for both sleeping and eating in. A number of outhouses, how many depending on the remoteness of the settlement, were used as larders and to house the farm's animals. In the living-room, beds and benches were fixed to the walls; the only movable pieces of furniture were trestle-tables and storage chests for the few personal possessions. All common utensils were made of wood, and the diet was confined to root vegetables and thin, flat loaves, not eaten until long after they had been baked, supplemented very occasionally with dried meat and fish. The complexes of buildings to be seen in modern open-air museums like Skansen in Stockholm, and still used in some parts of the country, are based on medieval prototypes, but such prototypes belonged to the upper ranks of the peasantry (see plate 5). These alone could afford to cover their interior walls with hangings on festive occasions; to wall-in a fireplace in one corner of the room; to eat off dishes made of pottery or metal; and to build separate, though unheated, sleeping-rooms for the use of younger members of the family or guests. For the whole class clothing was almost exclusively of wool, cut in the simplest style; only on feast days and at weddings might its sombre browns and greys be brightened with a splash of colour.

It was probably the lesser nobles who suffered most from the depression. This may account for the support they gave to Engelbrekt and the Stures and their leadership of the peasant armies. They often had to sell at least a part of their land to their wealthier neighbours, and in this way a number of magnates, especially in the south of the country, were able to build up considerable estates, although the large and compact domain found in other parts of Europe remained a rarity in Sweden until the seventeenth century; usually the lord's holdings were widely scattered among those of other freeholders. But the decline in the price of agricultural produce and of land, combined with the shortage of labour and a legal ban on the acquisition of land belonging to a tax-paying peasant, made it more and more difficult even for many magnates to make ends meet. And to make matters worse, the standard of living within the reach of the wealthy was rising steadily; new luxuries like silks and spices were being imported, and the cost of maintaining the state thought suitable for one of high rank was mounting. The successful could build themselves stone castles, to serve not, as previously, as temporary refuges in times of trouble, but as semi-permanent residences. These were still, however, built with defence rather than comfort as the prime consideration. Windows were small (except in some great halls), and glass was a luxury; furniture was almost as sparse as in the peasant's home and distinguished only by superior workmanship and the use of upholstery. A much larger proportion of the noble's income went on food, drink and fine clothes; for it was considered a social duty to entertain lavishly, and accounts of the period speak of meals with innumerable courses, amongst which eel was esteemed a particular delicacy. Drink consisted of imported wine or German beer, which was much stronger than that brewed in Sweden at this time. Foreign cloth also made up a large part of Sweden's imports in the fifteenth century, and some of the dresses which were worn by wealthy women in the later Middle Ages may be seen among the 'traditional' peasant costumes worn today in parts of Sweden on special occasions.

Some of this luxury could also be enjoyed by the rich merchants of Stockholm and Kalmar. Here they could live in stone houses, which usually served also as offices and storehouses for the goods in which the merchants dealt; some might even have chimneys. While the traders of Lübeck and Danzig were having to face growing competition in the Baltic from the Dutch and—until they were driven out again in the middle of the fifteenth century—the English, the German element in the population, in Stockholm and Kalmar at least, retained its importance for most of the period; in the latter town over a third of the burghers around 1450 were of German birth, and they paid over half the taxes. After the Battle of Brunkeberg, however, those in Stockholm suffered a serious set-back. They were forced to become naturalized Swedes, and some historians have interpreted the execution of so many of the leading citizens of the capital in the Bloodbath of 1520 as an act of revenge by the German community for the loss of their privileges.

German influence in the field of culture, which we saw to be growing in the fourteenth century, had by Union times become overwhelming. Most of the outstanding works of art of the period, like the painted triptychs and reredoses found in a large number of Swedish medieval churches, are of north German or Dutch origin; only remote areas like Dalarna seem to have been able to keep alive a native tradition. The greatest monument of the age is undoubtedly the wooden statue of St. George and the Dragon in Stockholm Cathedral, which has already been referred to. This was the work of Bernt Notke, a Lübeck woodcarver who also undertook a number of commissions for smaller churches in Sweden. Another artist of distinction was Albert Pictor, also probably a German. He decorated the interior walls and roofs of many churches in the central provinces and produced some fine embroidery in pearl on ecclesiastical vestments. But not all the Swedish art of the fifteenth century was produced by foreigners or for the Church; a fair proportion of the work of the eighty-five goldsmiths known to have been employed in Stockholm in Union times must have been intended for the laity. What is most striking about all the art then being produced when compared with that of the earlier Middle Ages is its realism; many of the portraits are recognizable personalities.

While art was flourishing, even if largely in the hands of foreign craftsmen, the weakening of Sweden's ties with southern and western Europe, exacerbated by the schism in the Church between 1378 and 1417, which led to different parts of Europe owing allegiance to different popes, brought a general decline of culture from the heights it had reached in the thirteenth and early fourteenth centuries. St. Bridget's monastery at Vadstena, formally consecrated in 1430, had the largest library in Sweden (about 1,400 books); was the most lively intellectual centre in the country; the origin of most of the religious literature produced in the fifteenth century; and the training-ground for most of Sweden's leading ecclesiastics. The Church retained her dominance in education; even the schools for the laity which had been set up in some of the leading towns were run by clerics. But the number of upper and middle class Swedes who were literate was growing rapidly; it was they who were the targets for the spate of political propaganda which came out of the struggles of the period. Knowledge of Danish plans to found a university in Copenhagen prompted the government of Sten Sture the Elder to agree to the establishment of one at Uppsala in 1477, the first in Scandinavia. One of the first teachers there was Erik Olai, generally considered to be the father of Swedish history. His great Latin *Chronicle of the Kingdom of the Goths* is still valuable for its remarkable objectivity and its use of sources long since lost. Like the University, it is an expression of the national pride which was beginning to become prominent. But this is found even more specifically in the myth of Gothicism, which Erik helped to propagate and which traced all European civilization back to the Goths, from whom the Swedes claimed descent. Swedish scholars continued, however, to be attracted to German universities, especially to the new foundation at Rostock in Mecklenburg, where Erik Olai himself studied, and King Hans found it necessary to forbid his subjects to attend these before they had spent at least three years at the university in Copenhagen or Uppsala.

The first printing-press in Sweden was set up by a Lübecker, who came to Stockholm from Denmark in 1483 (seven years after Caxton had begun working in London); but it was another twelve years before anything in the Swedish tongue appeared in print—and then it was a translation of a French work. The struggles of the fifteenth century did produce a large number of political tracts in Swedish, like the popular rhymed chronicles describing the deeds of Karl Knutsson and the Stures, and the ballad which commemorated the Battle of Brunkeberg. But the only ones of any literary merit, and the only ones which can be ascribed to an individual author are *The Song of Freedom* and *The Song of Loyalty*, written by Bishop Thomas of Strängnäs at the time of Engelbrekt's revolt. The refrain of the former, which begins

> *Freedom is the finest thing*
> *Which may be sought the whole world round*

has been treasured by all subsequent generations. Of the vernacular Court poetry of an earlier period, and of imaginative literature to compare with St. Bridget's *Revelations*, no trace has survived. What we have is marked by the same realism, often violent and brutal, as is found in the plastic arts; satire was a popular medium.

CHAPTER VI

Gustav Vasa and His Sons

G ustav Vasa, who was twenty-five in 1520, had already
taken part in the struggle against Christian II as a
member of Sten Sture's army, and had been carried off
to Denmark as a hostage. He had, however, escaped to Lübeck
and thence returned to Sweden. When news reached him
of the Stockholm Bloodbath, he was in hiding on the family
estates in Södermanland. He at once determined to travel to
Dalarna to rouse the peasants of the province, who had supported the Stures in the past. On his arrival, however, he found
that the lower classes were little interested in the fate of the
nobility. After nearly falling into the hands of Danish troops on
more than one occasion, Gustav fled in despair towards the
Norwegian frontier. But before he could reach it, he was recalled
by two messengers sent by the very peasants who had previously
rejected him; confirmation of the rumours of outrages committed by Christian's supporters had persuaded them to accept
him as their leader in revolt. After emerging victorious from
its initial encounters, Gustav's army grew rapidly. He seized
Västerås, which gave him control of Bergslagen, and nobles
and clergy also began to join him. In 1521 he was proclaimed
Regent of the Realm at a meeting at Vadstena. By this time
most of the country and Finland was under his control, but a
number of important forts held out against him, and Stockholm was protected by the Danish fleet. Gustav needed both
warships and experienced troops, and both these the merchants
of Lübeck were able to supply. While he had been among them
they had refused him aid; now his success and the hostile attitude adopted by Christian II towards the Hansa towns determined them to join him. But their price was a high one. They

demanded extensive trading privileges, the exclusion of Swedes from any commerce through the Sound and a large sum of money. Gustav had to agree to these terms and, with the consequent aid, managed to reduce the remaining Danish strongholds and capture the capital itself in 1523.

He entered Stockholm as King of Sweden, for shortly before its fall he had been elected such by the Estates assembled at Strängnäs. The Danes had also deposed Christian with the help of the Lübeckers, but their new king, Frederick I, refused to recognize the break-up of the Union, and the war continued. Lübeck offered to mediate. Gustav naturally expected that he would gain thereby a settlement favourable to himself, but by the peace concluded in 1524, he was compelled, in exchange for an acknowledgement of his right to the Swedish throne, to surrender the southern provinces of Scania, Halland and Blekinge together with the island of Gotland; Norway remained united to Denmark. The two Scandinavian powers tended thereafter to draw closer together, for the Swedish king's embitterment against the German merchants was matched by Frederick's resentment of their power; and both countries were faced by a continuing threat from Christian II, who was still at large and determined to regain his crowns.

The demands of war and defence and the large debt outstanding to Lübeck placed a very heavy strain on Gustav's financial resources and fed his envy of the great wealth of the Swedish Church, which held about a fifth of all the land in the realm. It seemed to him that he was entitled to expect a larger contribution from the ecclesiastics towards the cost of government, and, in his desire for greater control over them, he found willing allies in the growing band of Swedish Lutherans. These were led by Olaus Petri, who had become one of the German monk's disciples in Wittenberg before returning to Sweden in 1518, and Gustav's own secretary, Laurentius Andrae, Archdeacon of Strängnäs. The king in 1524 appointed Olaus preacher in Stockholm Cathedral. But for the moment he was more interested in Luther's teachings on relations between Church and State, according to which the prince should have the final word, than in his purely theological doctrines, on which Gustav refused to commit himself. The bishops, led by Hans Brask, Bishop of Linköping, met his growing demands for financial assistance with stubborn opposition, until finally, in 1527, faced by internal disorders brought about by the heavy taxation which he had been forced to impose but which had done little to improve the state of the Treasury, Gustav called a *riksdag* at Västerås. There, using the homely imagery of which he was such a master, he pictured the pitiful plight of the kingdom, and appealed to the nobles to help him to wring more from the Church. Brask protested vigorously against any proposals to interfere with ecclesiastical privileges, and the nobles were divided. Gustav then played his trump card. He threatened to abdicate. According to one account, he did so in the following words: 'I do not wonder that the peasants are wild and disobedient when I see that they have such instigators. If they get no rain, they throw the blame on me; if they get no sun, they blame me likewise. I can expect no better reward for my pains than your desire to see my skull cleft in two, though no one dares to wield the axe. Pay me then what I have sacrificed of my property for the sake of the realm, and I shall go my way and never return to my ungrateful fatherland.' Such an appeal had the effect he had hoped for; the nobles granted all he asked. He received their sanction to take over as much of the lands of the Church as he should think necessary for the common weal and to deprive the bishops of their castles. He in fact made far more extensive use of this power than most of the nobles probably intended. The bishops and lower clergy were permitted to retain only such land as was considered necessary for their immediate needs; the rest was incorporated in the royal domain, which grew at a single stroke from less than a twelfth to over a quarter of Sweden.

Although nothing specific had been said at Västerås about relations with Rome, Sweden had *de facto* renounced her allegiance to the pope. But the king, like Henry VIII of England after the Act of Supremacy, long refused to commit himself to Lutheran dogma; the Reform Movement was strong only in Stockholm, where alone services were being conducted in Swedish. In 1529, however, certain moderate changes, such as the abolition of many saints' days, were agreed to at a church assembly in Örebro; two years later Olaus Petri's brother Laurentius was appointed archbishop; and vacant sees began to be filled with Lutherans.

Gustav Vasa and His Sons

The *Riksdag* at Västerås met against a background of considerable social unrest, which the king accused the bishops of encouraging. The peasants of Dalarna and the miners of Bergslagen had rapidly become disillusioned with the master they had helped to power, and rose in 1525. The revolt was easily put down, but another soon broke out under a leader who claimed to be the son of Sten Sture, although at the time this young man was living at Court. Gustav temporized until after the Västerås meeting and then turned on the rebels, who were once more crushed; the pretender fled to Rostock, where he was executed at the king's request. In 1531 an order was sent to all parishes to provide one church bell or its equivalent in money, with which it was intended to pay off part of the debt still outstanding to Lübeck. Fresh disturbances resulted, and many parishes too poor to pay in cash refused to part with their bells, which they regarded as sacred objects. The situation was particularly grave since Christian II chose this time to return to Norway in a bid for his lost inheritance. Gustav restored order for the moment by a show of force and the promise of an amnesty, but, after he had helped the Danes to defeat and capture Christian, he returned to Dalarna, which was again the centre of unrest, had the ringleaders of the so-called Bell Revolt executed and destroyed the autonomy hitherto enjoyed by the mining communities of Bergslagen.

Soon after this he was at last given an opportunity to free himself from many of his obligations to Lübeck. War broke out between the town and Denmark, and Sweden joined in on the side of the Danes. When peace returned in 1536, the latter agreed to act as mediators between the other two antagonists, and, as a result, the remainder of the Swedish debt was cancelled and the privileges enjoyed by the Lübeckers in Sweden suspended.

Meanwhile, the reformation of the Swedish Church went forward. During the late 1530's, when Denmark also broke with Rome, the mass in Swedish became universal, and in 1541 there finally appeared an edition of the whole Bible in the vernacular. While the bishops continued to exercise their priestly functions, the administration of their dioceses was placed in the hands of committees consisting of two priests and a layman. Gustav appointed his eldest son's tutor George Norman as Superintendent over all with the task of subordinating the Church to the royal will. As might be expected, all this was not accomplished without arousing serious opposition, and religious motives seem to have played a large part in the last and most serious rebellion with which Gustav had to deal. This was the rising of the peasants of the poor province of Småland in 1542 under one of their own number named Nils Dacke. They were finally suppressed, though with considerable difficulty, and Dacke was slain by his own followers.

Immediately after this success, the king called another *riksdag* at Västerås and obtained the Estates' support for the conversion of Sweden into an hereditary monarchy. This was the culmination of the first and most important stage of his policy of centralization in the Sture tradition. It was also a reflection of the powerful position which the Crown had acquired during the first two decades of the reign. Just as the weakness of the Swedish kings of the later Middle Ages flowed largely from the meagreness of their financial resources, so Gustav Vasa's strength lay in the wealth which he was able to command at this time. He had not only the lands and castles which had been confiscated from Union supporters after his victory and the vast property of the bishops and monasteries, but also silver from veins recently discovered at Sala in Västmanland; control of this enabled him to relieve his subjects of much taxation. After the defeat of the Bell Revolt, the Crown enjoyed considerable profits in addition from the iron mines of Bergslagen. Much of this income went on defence; substantial castles, capable of withstanding the assaults of the more formidable artillery then coming into use, were built up and down the country, and a navy of forty-eight vessels was constructed. In 1527 the military service owed by the nobles to the king was closely defined for the first time. But such a semi-feudal host was no longer suited to the changing methods of warfare; what was needed was a professional standing army, and for some time this could only be provided by German mercenaries whose pay absorbed a large part of the royal revenue.

German influence on Gustav's policy was particularly strong during the late 1530's and early 1540's, so much so that the period immediately after the Dacke Rebellion is often referred to as 'The German period' of the reign. It is typified by the employment not only of German troops, but also of Germans in the highest civil offices. In 1538, one of them named Conrad von Pyhy was appointed Chancellor and helped the king to reorganize the administration in a more rational manner. The Council was turned from a mere collection of the king's advisers into a genuine organ of government; a separate Foreign Office was set up; and the Treasury was reformed. But after 1543 Swedes regained control. Swedish troops replaced the German, although German officers still trained and led them; Pyhy was thrown into prison; and many of the new departments ceased to function.

The centralization under royal control which is characteristic of Gustav Vasa's government is also the hall-mark of his economic policy, which was closely linked to his financial needs. A strict control was exercised over both imports and exports, and while passive trade conducted by foreigners was preferred to active trade by Swedes, efforts were made to reduce the influence still wielded by the Hansa by encouraging other nationals—especially the Dutch—to visit Swedish ports. The king himself became a considerable merchant, with his own warehouses, in which were stored the yields of his taxes (which he usually insisted on having paid in kind), and his own ships. To ensure proper supervision, he attempted, rather unsuccessfully, to limit all internal trade to the towns.

Gustav Vasa does not emerge as a particularly attractive figure, in spite of the vigorous efforts he made to justify all his actions by means of a well-organized propaganda machine in the Sture tradition. He was intensely suspicious, perhaps with justification, of those around him, and would brook no opposition to his policy. In 1540 he had Laurentius Andrae, Olaus Petri and Olaus's brother condemned to death for criticizing some of his more high-handed actions, although they were later pardoned; von Pyhy was condemned largely because the king wanted a scapegoat for the Dacke Rebellion; his condemnation of the leaders of the Bell Revolt three years after the event does him little credit. But when he died in 1560, Sweden had been free of internal disorders for nearly twenty years; her economy was flourishing; the Treasury had a large surplus; and a formidable military power had been created.

Gustav Vasa was married three times. By his first wife he

had one son, who ascended the throne on his death, as Erik XIV.[1] His second presented him with three sons, John, Magnus and Charles, each of whom was granted, at the end of their father's reign, a large duchy with which to support himself. Charles, who was still under age in 1560, received the provinces of Värmland, Närke and Södermanland to the west of Stockholm; Magnus, who was mentally unbalanced, obtained most of the south of the country; and John was given Finland and the Åland Islands. Thus the new king found a large part of his kingdom already removed partially from his control, with Duke Charles in a particularly threatening position. But he had inherited all his father's imperiousness and was determined to have absolute dominion over all his subjects. Any checks which the nobles attempted to place upon the exercise of the royal prerogative only increased his irritation, and he became even more morbidly suspicious than Gustav had been. He resolved from the outset to make his half-brothers submit to his will and to deprive them of their privileged status. John at least made it quite clear, on the other hand, that he meant to retain his independence. The quarrel between the two men, in which the nobility were compelled to take sides, dominated the whole of the eight-year reign. The king won the first round by bribing a number of nobles with the new titles of count and baron and lands to go with them. He also persuaded the Estates to agree to the imposition of royal control over the duchies. But John remained defiant.

The situation was complicated by the confusion which reigned in the eastern Baltic at this time. The decline of the Teutonic Knights left a vacuum there which their neighbours were only too anxious to fill. The Tsar of Muscovy, Ivan VI (The Terrible), was eager to provide himself with an ice-free coastline, which would enable him to trade directly with western Europe. But the Swedes had long entertained ambitions of dominating the south as well as the north shore of the Gulf of Finland and of controlling the port of Reval, an outlet for the valuable trade in

[1] Sweden's kings were not numbered in this way until the sixteenth century, and I have followed the practice of modern Swedish historians, who identify medieval rulers by the names of their fathers. There is, in any case, little historical evidence for the existence of the first six Eriks; the seventh was Olof Sköttkonung's father.

Russian produce; and Poland and Denmark had their eyes fixed on the same area. The stage was thus set for a four-cornered fight for power in the Baltic which was to last for the next century and a half. The crisis opened in 1558 when the tsar broke through to the Baltic and captured the port of Narva. The Knights of Livonia and the town of Reval appealed for help to their neighbours, including the King of Sweden. Gustav hesitated to intervene, but Erik on his accession promised his protection to Reval and the adjacent Estonian provinces in exchange for recognition of Swedish sovereignty. He sent troops to the town and imposed a blockade on Narva.

Duke John in Finland, however, began to conduct his own independent foreign policy, and, to gain Polish help, married the King of Poland's daughter. Erik replied by arresting a number of his adherents and servants and accusing them of treason before a new supreme court, made up minor nobles and civil servants, which he had formed at the beginning of his reign to deal with such eventualities. He then called a *riksdag*, before which he intended to arraign the duke himself. When John refused to appear, he was arrested and imprisoned in Gripsholm castle.

To offset this domestic success, Erik found himself faced by new complications abroad. While Denmark and Sweden had been at peace since the beginning of Gustav Vasa's reign and had even concluded an alliance in 1541, the wounds caused by the break-up of the Union of Kalmar had never fully healed. The Danish kings still hoped for an opportunity to reassert their claim to the Swedish throne, and both Gustav and his son were fully aware of the danger which threatened them from the south. It was largely to protect himself against it that Erik offered his hand in marriage to the young Elizabeth of England, and, when this project fell through, to a number of north German princesses. When, however, Sweden's entanglements in the east persuaded the Danish king to launch an attack on her in alliance with Poland and Lübeck, Sweden was still without an ally. Her fleet more than held its own against the Danes, and managed to keep the Baltic sea-lanes open, but on land she suffered a number of serious defeats.

Meanwhile, the opposition to Erik at home was growing. The nobles were becoming increasingly resentful of the king's policy of employing low-born secretaries in his administration and especially of the favours he bestowed on a certain Göran Persson; as in earlier centuries, they reacted strongly against any attempt to dislodge them from what they regarded as their rightful place at the monarch's side. And as criticism grew, so did the king's suspiciousness. He was already showing definite signs of insanity, and finally became convinced of the existence of a vast plot headed by the Sture family to depose him; in 1567 he had the latter's leading members arrested and murdered in their prison-cell while he looked on. Soon after this he became quite incapable of carrying on the business of government, and his duties were taken over the the *Råd*. While Göran Persson was arrested and Duke John released, there was, however, no move made to depose the king. He indeed recovered, and resumed control of the administration. But when he restored the hated Persson to office, John and his brother Charles raised the standard of rebellion; and no one lifted a finger in defence of the Crown. Erik was thrown into prison, where he languished until his death in 1577; Persson was broken on the wheel; and at a *riksdag* in 1569, Duke John was proclaimed king.

One of John III's first acts was to open negotiations with Denmark. By this time both sides were exhausted by a struggle in which neither could win a decisive victory, and at the Peace of Stettin, which ended what is usually referred to as the Northern Seven Years' War, both kings renounced all claims on the other's territory. The accession of the brother-in-law of the King of Poland to the Swedish throne had already caused that country to make peace, but the struggle with Russia in Estonia continued, until in 1581 the Swedes succeeded in capturing Narva. This enabled them to arrange an armistice which left them in control of their conquests.

Erik XIV had been deposed largely because he had refused to grant his nobles what they regarded as their rightful place in government. It was therefore expected of John that he would rule in accordance with their wishes. He did indeed confirm their ancient privileges at the beginning of his reign, and even added new ones, such as the exemption from military service of all nobles' tenants who lived within a league of their lord's main seat. But he had no intention of allowing himself to become a mere *primus inter pares*—no Vasa would ever stoop to be this and the nobles soon found that they had gained far less from the change of ruler than they had at first imagined. The king's financial needs, exacerbated by the continuing war with Muscovy and the indemnity which he had agreed to pay Denmark at Stettin, led him to impose new tax burdens from which the nobles could not claim exemption. After initial protests, however, they acquiesced. A steady rise in prices during the reign made the offices and estates which the king could bestow attractive, and isolated trouble-makers could usually be silenced by threatening to confiscate their fiefs.

In such conditions of comparative political stability, John was at last able to tackle the problem of making a final ecclesiastical settlement. At the end of his father's reign, the struggle for power between the conservative bishops, led by Laurentius Petri, and the more ardent reformers, who wished to make sweeping changes in doctrine, liturgy and Church government, was far from settled; Gustav Vasa, like his contemporary Henry VIII, found it in his interests to maintain a rough balance between the two factions at his Court. Erik XIV, while he retained the bishops as the pillars of Church organization, was attracted by the ideas of the reformers, but the accession of his half-brother brought a distinct swerve to the right. John not only accepted a conservative settlement drawn up by the Archbishop, which Erik had rejected, but in 1576 had a new liturgy published which was little else than a translation of the Roman mass; it became known as *The Red Book*. It seems unlikely, however, that, although he was married to a Catholic, he envisaged a return to the papal allegiance in the near future, and his policy was dictated as much by political as by religious motives. He wanted the support of the Catholic powers of Europe, and when he failed to attract them and found himself faced with a fierce pamphlet war at home, he decided to go no further. *The Red Book* remained, and its critics were silenced, but a theological college which a Jesuit had been allowed to open in Stockholm was closed.

One of the reasons for John's desire to end religious strife at home was undoubtedly the attitude which his brother Charles was adopting in his great duchy in central Sweden—an attitude similar to that which John had taken up when Erik came to the throne. Charles patronized the reform party within the Swedish

Church; refused to apply the new religious settlement to the lands under his control; and led the opposition to *The Red Book*. But it was the way in which he exploited his privileged position to build up his political power that caused his brother most alarm. Finally, in 1587, the king, strongly supported by the magnates of the Council, forced Charles to agree to a considerable limitation of his independence. But soon afterwards an event took place which helped to draw the two men closer together. In 1587 also, John's son and heir Sigismund was elected King of Poland, but he fell out with his subjects, and his father tried to persuade him to abdicate and return to Sweden. On this matter the *Råd* opposed the king, and in revenge he dismissed a number of its members and cancelled the treaty with the duke.

Sigismund did not abdicate, and on John III's death in 1592, became King of Sweden also. Charles was determined that any attempt by the new ruler, who had been raised a Catholic, to force Sweden back into the Roman fold should be resisted with all vigour and was backed in this resolve by a large proportion of the nation. Before Sigismund arrived for his coronation, the Duke called a meeting at Uppsala which rejected *The Red Book* and affirmed Sweden's allegiance to the Augsburg Confession, the central creed of the Lutheran faith. In face of this, the monarch agreed not to interfere with the religious settlement, but, on the other hand, refused to grant Charles the powers to which, as the foremost member of the Council which ruled the country in the king's absence, he felt himself entitled.

As soon as Sigismund had returned to Poland, the duke persuaded the *Råd* to extend his privileges, and threatened his nephew that he would call a meeting of the Estates on his own initiative to ratify them if Sigismund himself did not do so. Since the latter refused, Charles carried out his threat, but the magnates would not risk an open breach with the king, and the duke felt it prudent to draw back for the time being. In 1597, however, he made another bid for power. Still only the peasants supported him with any enthusiasm, but he decided to gamble on rebellion, and seized the ports of Kalmar and Älvsborg. They were speedily recaptured, but in September 1598 the royal army was decisively defeated and the king compelled to retire once more to Poland. The whole of Sweden and Finland

3b. *Gustav Vasa* by Jakob Binck (1542).
Svenska Porträttarkivet

3a. Interior of Södra Råda Church, Värmland. *Photo ATA*

4a. 'King Erik XIV's Room' in Kalmar Castle.
Photo ATA

4b. Läckö Castle, Västergötland (late seventeeth century).
Photo ATA

was soon under Charles's control, and in 1599 Sigismund was declared deposed. But the duke did not immediately take the crown which was offered him; he declared that he would act as regent for Sigismund's half-brother John or his own son Gustav Adolf until they should come of age, when the Estates could choose between them. At the end of 1603, however, he allowed himself to be proclaimed king as Charles IX. This usurpation was made even more heinous by the execution of a number of Sigismund's magnate supporters in the so-called Linköping Bloodbath.

While still only duke, Charles had persuaded the Estates to forbid Catholic worship in Sweden and had dissolved Vadstena, the last monastery which had been allowed to function. As king, he began to move in a Calvinist direction, but he met with such opposition that he decided to leave well alone; his subjects had had change enough. And from that time to this the overwhelming majority of Swedes have been—at least nominally—members of the State Lutheran Church, episcopal in organization but with the king as 'supreme administrator'. Sweden was mercifully spared the fierce religious controversies which divided so many European countries in the course of the seventeenth century.

The truce which had been signed with Russia in 1581 was broken at the end of John III's reign, but a definite peace was finally concluded in 1595 at Teushina, near Narva. This confirmed Sweden's hold on Estonia and Narva, and the Tsar promised to conduct his overseas trade through Reval and Viborg in Finland. But he could still use Archangel in the far north or the ports of Latvia and Lithuania, which were under Polish control; over neither of these exits did the Swedes have any influence. And Poland after 1599 was Sweden's national enemy, determined to restore the personal union which the accession of Sigismund had created, and to assert its claims to Estonia. It was not, however, until the death of Tsar Boris Godunov in 1605 precipitated a war for his inheritance that Poland and Sweden came seriously to blows. Boris's successor appealed to Charles IX for help against a pretender who was supported by the Poles, but in 1610, before the King of Sweden could respond, Polish troops occupied Moscow. The encirclement of Sweden was completed the following year, when Denmark attacked her and captured Kalmar. At this critical point Charles IX died, leaving his kingdom to his seventeen-year-old son Gustav Adolf, better known to English readers as Gustavus Adolphus or The Lion of the North.

CHAPTER VII

Sweden in the Age of the Renaissance and Reformation

I n spite of the perilous position in which Sweden found herself at the death of Charles IX in 1611, she stood in fact on the threshold of the most brilliant period of her history, when she became the greatest power in northern Europe. Such a status could not have been won or sustained for as long as it was without the development of a healthy economy at home in the sixteenth century.

The attainment of independence coincided roughly with the end of the late-medieval depression in European agriculture. While methods of farming changed little, if at all, and a poor harvest could still bring near-starvation to large sections of society, a rise in prices made it again worthwhile to bring new land under cultivation. The population increased—if slowly by later standards—to about three-quarters of a million, and, from the somewhat scanty evidence which has survived, it seems that the bulk of this population was enjoying in the sixteenth century a higher standard of living than it was to enjoy again until comparatively recent times. Finance never ceased to be a serious problem for the Vasa kings; Gustav Vasa's sons had to resort to debasement of the coinage, and were forced to sell to the nobility some of the lands which their father had seized from the Church. But they never found themselves in such desperate straits as those to which the rulers of the fourteenth and fifteen centuries had been reduced, and their subjects were better able to sustain the taxes which they imposed. Doubtless the end of the serious internal strife which had marked Union times helped to bring about this happier state of affairs, but it is not clear what weight we should give to this factor.

It was not to the surface of the land alone that Sweden's kings looked for their income. Production at the silver mines of Sala sank sharply after the death of Gustav Vasa, and their working became unprofitable, but a new source of wealth soon took their place—and more. The mining of copper at Falun was still relatively unimportant to the Swedish economy in the early sixteenth century, and flooding caused serious difficulties as the shafts were driven deeper into the mountain, but the introduction of a copper coinage in Spain in the 1580's brought a great increase in the demand for the metal, at the same time as production in Sweden, which enjoyed almost a European monopoly of it, was again rising. The Crown had always taken a keen interest in all mining operations within the kingdom, and John III and his brother succeeded in imposing a control over this increasingly important asset, which turned it for a short time at the beginning of the seventeenth century into almost a royal industry.

The iron mines of Bergslagen were also increasing—somewhat more steadily—in importance during the same decades, and in the latter half of the sixteenth century the value of Sweden's iron exports doubled. This was partly because of the improved quality obtained as the result of the introduction of larger blast furnaces which turned out refined metal in the form of bars. These fetched a far higher price on the European market than the small pieces known as *osmunds* which had been previously exported; *osmunds* did not cease to be produced, but by 1600 they accounted for only half the output. As for most of its history up to this date, the Swedish iron industry relied heavily on techniques introduced by German experts, whose settlement in Bergslagen Gustav Vasa and his sons continued to encourage. The traditional organization of small mine-owners changed little, but, as with copper, the Crown acquired a larger and larger foothold in it, through the ownership, for example, of many of the great hammers set up by German engineers to shape the new bars.

The considerable expansion of iron- and copper-mining in Sweden in the latter half of the sixteenth century caused a striking change to take place in the pattern of her overseas

trade. Iron had always stood high on her list of exports, but by
the reign of Charles IX it had acquired an importance far beyond that which it had enjoyed even at the death of Gustav
Vasa, and accounted for about three-quarters of the total;
copper, although much less significant as yet, was also rising in
relation to the livestock and dairy produce from the south of the
country which made up most of the remainder. Otherwise, however, although trade grew appreciably, its character changed
little. With the exception of salt, the kingdom remained largely
self-supporting, and most other imports were, as in the fifteenth
century, in the luxury class—fine cloth, German beer, wine,
silk and spices. In spite of the abolition by Gustav Vasa of the
Hansa's privileges, and the general decline of their European
trade, German merchants retained much of their old dominance in the Baltic, although from the middle of the century
Dutch and Scots traders began to appear in Swedish ports in
larger and larger numbers, at first via Danzig and Lübeck, but
later from their homelands direct. Foreigners were officially forbidden to participate in inland trade, but a number of Scots undoubtedly engaged in it, and at least one of them, named John
Waterstone, was prosecuted on several occasions in the 1570's
and 1580's for doing so. He had probably come to Sweden as a
member of one of the numerous mercenary bands raised in
Scotland at the request of Gustav Vasa's sons to help them in
their foreign wars, but other Scots were genuine merchants who
established themselves as burghers in the leading ports.

Of these, Stockholm, with a population at the end of the
century of about 8,000, was by far the most important, although
it was still confined within the walls which surrounded the island
on which it stood. But in 1607 Charles IX founded a town,
which was, after various vicissitudes, to rival the capital as a
commercial centre and to grow in step with the expansion of
Sweden's trade beyond the Baltic. At the mouth of the River
Göta, which was the country's only outlet to the west, between
the Danish provinces of Halland and Bohuslän, Gothenburg
was established to replace the older settlement at Lödöse farther
upstream. The important part already being played by the inhabitants of the northern Netherlands in north European commerce in the early seventeenth century, as well as the special
favours bestowed on them by the Calvinistically-inclined king,

is evidenced by the fact that the new town's first burghers were overwhelmingly Dutch in origin; municipal business was conducted in their native tongue.

Whatever might have been the good effects of Sweden's breach with the Catholic Church under Gustav Vasa, it constituted a definite set-back for her education and culture, both of which, in spite of the spread of lay education in the later Middle Ages, were still closely tied up with the fate of the Church. The seizure of much of the latter's wealth meant that little was left for educational purposes; the closing of the monasteries deprived the country of important centres of learning; and a great patron of the arts disappeared. Gustav Vasa, in spite of the attractiveness of his prose style, was not a cultured man. He seems to have appreciated the need for trained servants in government, but did little to provide them with the necessary intellectual equipment. Uppsala University was closed during the civil wars at the beginning of the century, and it remained closed for the whole of the reign; Swedish scholars had to depend on foreign Protestant universities like Wittenberg and Rostock. On the other hand, the king took great pains to ensure that his sons were well educated, although it is significant that he found it necessary to rely largely on foreign scholars for this purpose. They did their job well; Erik XIV was a Renaissance prince in his learning as well as in his public policy.

He re-opened the University in 1566. After fourteen years it was again closed owing to the opposition of its professors to John III's *Red Book*, but during the latter's reign something was at last done to repair the breach in secondary education caused by the Reformation: included in the Church settlement of 1571 was a detailed provision for the establishment of three- and four-class schools on German lines, and within thirty years every cathedral town at least possessed one of these. Instruction in them was, however, largely confined to Latin grammar with perhaps a little Greek and Hebrew, and Charles IX expressed deep dissatisfaction with his kingdom's educational system. At the very end of his reign work was begun on a new ordinance, but this was not implemented until after his death. His predecessor Sigismund had, in 1595, witnessed the reopening of the University, to which extensive privileges were granted, and shortly after his deposition it was again granting degrees. But

Charles IX objected to the independent attitude of its teachers, and in 1607 withdrew the rights granted by his nephew. For a few years the very existence of the institution seemed again in jeopardy, and, although it managed to survive, it did so in a very unsatisfactory state.

In spite of this rather gloomy picture, Swedish culture, even in the reign of Gustav Vasa, was far from dead. Olaus Petri, besides being responsible for various religious works and the oldest surviving drama in the vernacular, played a large part in the translation of the Bible into Swedish and wrote a prose history of his native land from its beginnings to 1520. The *Swedish Chronicle* is an admirably objective work, written in an attractive style, and far in advance of anything of its kind produced hitherto, but it unfortunately suffered from the king's enmity toward its author, and it was not published until the early nineteenth century. The last two Catholic archbishops—the brothers Johannes and Olaus Magnus—were more fortunate in this respect. While in exile in Rome in the 1550's, they both published histories in Latin. Olaus's survey of Scandinavian culture was translated into several languages, had a wide circulation and is still of value, but his brother's chronicle, although very popular for a long time after his death, is marred by a fanciful account of the early period, which revived the Gothic myth favoured by Ericus Olai, but eschewed by Olaus Magnus.

In Swedish literature the latter half of the sixteenth century is a barren period, but this is not true of other arts. Even Gustav Vasa took an interest in music, and appears to have been responsible for the formation of a permanent Court orchestra. Erik XIV went further, and himself both performed and composed; an eight-part motet by him has survived, and shows him to have had a considerable talent. His half-brother and successor, the most cultivated of all the early Vasa kings, was more interested in architecture, and was no mean draftsman. It was in his reign that the Renaissance or Early Baroque style appeared in Sweden on a large scale, having been brought in by foreign artists and craftsmen whom John enticed from as far afield as Italy, to remodel the royal castles in accordance with the latest fashions and add to them entirely new structures. Even in Gustav Vasa's castles (like the new Gripsholm with its characteristic rectangular walls and massive round towers), although they were built primarily for defence, there is evidence of a growing attention to the demands of comfort. While still rather grim when viewed from the outside, the interiors of the castles reconstructed by the first Vasa's sons were often lavishly decorated with elaborately carved and painted panelling and stuccowork, as can still be seen in the State Chamber in Kalmar Castle, to which Erik XIV devoted much attention (see plate 4).

The Crown was thus coming in some measure to replace the Church as the greatest single patron of the arts and artists, although as yet these were mainly foreigners. Gustav Vasa in 1542 commissioned the earliest Swedish royal portrait—from a German who was in Stockholm on a brief visit (see plate 3). A Dutchman named Willem Boy, who was one of John III's leading architects, carved for him the monument to Gustav Vasa and his wives in Uppsala Cathedral, as well as several other pieces. Another Dutchman made for the coronation of Erik XIV the magnificent gold crown which still forms part of the Swedish Crown Jewels. But one of the best-known works of art of this period may have been produced by a native Swede. This is the earliest painting of Stockholm to survive. Commissioned by Olaus Petri in 1535 to commemorate the 'mock sun' which was observed over the city in that year and which is included in the picture, it can now be seen in Stockholm Cathedral.

Beyond the confines of the Court, there was as yet little sign of any 'new movement'. The Gothic style continued to be used for the few new ecclesiastical buildings; and most of the nobles rested content with their simple country houses, made of wood and little different in design from the farmhouses of the richer peasants—sometimes indeed less prominent than these. But a time was to come when it would be not only the king who could afford to spend great sums on richly-furnished homes embellished by foreign and native artists, a time when Swedish culture would emerge from the dark days through which it had passed. And at the end of the sixteenth century that time was not far off.

CHAPTER VIII

Sweden Becomes a European Power

In spite of his youth, Gustavus had already had considerable experience in government by the time he came to the throne, and those around him considered that he was ready to take over full control of the administration. The regency for which Charles IX had arranged was therefore dispensed with; it was also felt that the crisis which faced Sweden—war with Russia, Poland and Denmark—demanded firmer leadership than a regency council could be expected to provide. But in return for agreeing to proclaim his majority, the nobles, led by the young Axel Oxenstierna, who was made Chancellor in 1612, demanded certain concessions; an opportunity at last presented itself to rid the realm of the low-born secretaries, upon whom all Gustav Vasa's sons had relied to a greater or lesser extent, and to restore the privileged position under the Crown which the nobles had claimed for themselves ever since they had become a distinct class. The new king had to promise to reserve for them all senior posts in both central and local government; to seek the consent of the *Råd* before imposing new taxes or hiring fresh troops; and to have all new laws and foreign alliances approved by the *Riksdag*, which was dominated by the magnates. Further guarantees were included in the oath which Gustavus had to take at his coronation in 1617; he bound himself to respect all alienations of royal land made by his predecessors as well as the increasingly important grants of tax-revenue from peasant freeholds.

Meanwhile the war—or rather wars—went on. The most serious menace was Denmark, who could strike so easily at the very heart of the kingdom; and in 1612 King Christian IV launched an attack on Stockholm. This, however, failed, and the Danish armies advancing from the south, although they did manage to destroy the new settlement at Gothenburg, were constantly frustrated by the Swedes' adoption of a 'scorched-earth' policy. Both sides eventually accepted English mediation, and made peace at Knäred in 1613. The most important provision of this was that the Danes should keep the fortress of Älvsborg at the mouth of the River Göta—thus blocking Sweden's main outlet to the west—for five years, and would then return it only on payment of the enormous sum of one million *dalers*. The effects on the Swedish economy of this demand is discussed elsewhere,[1] but the temporary loss of the castle and the area surrounding it also made the Swedes realize how dependent they were on Danish good will for the maintenance of their growing trade with western Europe, and how desirable it was to command at least a longer stretch of the west coast, if not the whole southern part of the peninsula.

The struggle with Russia lasted rather longer. The Poles had been unable to maintain themselves in Moscow for very long, and had had to retreat before a national uprising which had placed Michael Romanov on the throne. Michael agreed to open peace negotiations with the Swedes, again under English mediation, and the Treaty of Stolbova was concluded in 1617. By this Gustavus completed Russia's isolation from the Baltic by the acquisition of Ingria and the eastern half of Karelia, and was enabled to devote all his attention to the war with Poland, where Sigismund continued to assert his claims to the Swedish throne.

The king's frequent absences abroad on campaign, if nothing else, necessitated the introduction of a more sophisticated form of government to replace the rule by secretaries practised in the sixteenth century. The work of reform was undertaken, with considerable enthusiasm, by the Chancellor. The scheme which he favoured was one based on the five great officers of State— the Chancellor himself, the Marshal, the Admiral, the Treasurer and the Steward. Each of these was now to head a 'college', or small committee jointly responsible for policy in a particular sphere of administration under the overall authority of the *Råd*. The Chancery was to take charge of foreign affairs as well as of relations between the Government and the provinces; the

[1] See p. 124.

Treasury was to concern itself with all financial matters; affairs relating to the army fell to the College of War under the Marshal; the Admiralty was to control the navy; and the administration of justice was to be the job of a college under the Steward. It naturally took some time for all this to be worked out in detail, and the process was not completed during Gustavus's reign. As early as 1614 the Steward was made chairman of a new supreme court—the *Svea Hovrätt* in Stockholm. But this was soon found to be inadequate, and similar courts of appeal were established at Åbo (to serve Finland) and at Dorpat in Livonia (for the newly-conquered Baltic provinces). The Treasury was reorganized in 1618, and the Chancery achieved its final form in 1626. The Marshal's department did not become a college until after Gustavus's death in 1632, but much was done before this to bring the Swedish army up to date, with an eye especially on the military achievements of the Dutch. A form of conscription had been in existence ever since the days of Gustav Vasa, but its workings left much to be desired, especially when the scope of military operations was enormously widened. Under the system now introduced, each of the nine districts into which Sweden and Finland were divided for this purpose was expected to provide a regiment of foot, and one in every ten able-bodied men was liable to be called to the colours. At the same time, improvements were made in weapons; pikes, muskets and cannon were all reduced in size and weight. Speed and mobility were also stressed in the new tactics which were adopted. The cavalry—rather a cinderella since the downfall of the armoured knight—was taught to charge home with drawn sword and became once more a formidable factor on the field of battle; the size of formations was much reduced with the same end in view; and various arms were interspersed so that they could support each other more effectively.

The origin of the Swedish *Riksdag* of four Estates has been the subject of as heated a controversy as surrounds that of the English parliament. Some historians have traced it as far back as 1359, when King Magnus Eriksson called a meeting of nobles, clergy, burghers and tax-paying peasants; but, as has been pointed out, there is no evidence that this ever took place. The 'traditional' date—the equivalent of 1265 for the English parliament—is 1435, when Engelbrekt was elected regent by a gathering at Arboga, but this is also open to dispute, since no mention is made on this occasion of the presence of tax-paying peasants. They did take part in similar assemblies about this time, but—as with the Commons in England—only slowly, during the latter half of the fifteenth century, did they come to be recognized as an essential element in them. And not until the early years of the seventeenth century, when Charles IX was seeking national support in his struggle with his nephew and called a *riksdag* nearly every year, was the Diet accepted as a regular part of the machinery of government. Even at the accession of his son it was still a disorganized body, whose exact composition and powers were uncertain. In 1626, however, the nobility at least was formed into a definite Estate as in western and central European countries and divided into three classes—the counts and barons; the families of royal councillors; and the mass of lesser nobles. Since each of these classes carried equal weight when it came to a vote, the magnates, as long as they remained united, could always be sure of dominating the Estate and through it the whole *Riksdag*. Further, while the nobles and Crown remained in harmony, as they did throughout Gustavus's reign, the 'unprivileged' (*ofrälse*, literally 'unredeemed') Estates of clergy, burghers and peasants could be easily managed.

In 1618, the year after Stolbova, the acceptance of the crown of Bohemia by the Elector Palatine, the Calvinist Frederick V, in defiance of the Catholic emperor, precipitated the Thirty Years' War in Germany. In essence this was both a religious conflict, in which the emperor and his cousin in Spain tried to bring the whole of Germany back to the Catholic faith, and a political struggle, in which he tried to assert his hegemony over the princes of the Empire. A united Catholic Germany, especially if allied to a Catholic Poland whose king was claiming the Swedish crown, would obviously constitute a grave threat to both the religious settlement in Scandinavia and Sweden's position in the Baltic, control of which seemed to be coming within her grasp. There were, however, two obstacles to Sweden's intervention in Germany against the Habsburgs. She had still to settle with Poland; and she was deeply suspicious of Denmark, who, she feared, might use her strong strategic position to stab her neighbour in the back once that neighbour had committed herself to a German campaign. Thus, when Gustavus was invited in 1624 (by which date he had conquered Livonia) to join an alliance with England and Denmark against the emperor, he made demands, aimed at protecting his realm's security, which Denmark refused to accept because they threatened her own. The Danish king, Christian IV, finally entered the fray alone and was decisively defeated. No barrier now stood in the way if the brilliant Imperialist general Wallenstein's drive to the Baltic, and by 1628 he had established himself along the whole of the north coast of Germany; only the port of Stralsund held out against him. Gustavus had already decided that he must act while there was still time; he sent troops to help in the defence of Stralsund, and the following year signed a six-year truce with a defeated Poland at Altmark, near Danzig, which gave him control of Livonia and the mouth of the River Vistula. In June 1630, he sailed from Stockholm with an army of 13,000 and landed at the mouth of the River Oder in Pomerania.[1]

He arrived in Germany without any allies. Even many of the Protestant princes were suspicious of his ultimate intentions; Denmark was cowed; and the Dutch resented the growing power of Sweden, which threatened their vital trading interests in the Baltic. But he was lucky. Wallenstein had just been dismissed by an emperor who feared his independent might, and there was nobody of equal ability to take his place; Gustavus was left largely unmolested while he extended his bridgehead and forced the Duke of Pomerania to join him. The German princes—even his own brother-in-law the Elector of Brandenburg—still hesitated for fear of Imperial reprisals for any defection should he fail, and only the great free city of Magdeburg on the River Elbe made an alliance with the Swedes. But help did come from further afield at the beginning of 1631. France, although a Catholic country governed in effect by a cardinal, saw in Protestant Sweden the means by which the rising tide of Habsburg power, which threatened her in the west as much as it did Sweden in the north, might be stemmed, and, by the Treaty of Bärwalde, granted Gustavus subsidies sufficient to support 36,000 troops. In the spring the king began to advance up the River Oder from his base, while the Imperialists laid siege to Magdeburg. But the Elector of Branden-

[1] For the campaign which followed, see map on p. 113.

burg refused to allow Swedish troops to march through his territories to its relief, and by the time Gustavus had decided to use force against the timid prince, it was too late; Magdeburg was a smouldering mass of rubble, and its inhabitants put to the sword. The king cannot escape all responsibility for this deed, which more decisive action on his part could have prevented, but he was able to take partial revenge later in the year, when he crushed the main Imperial army at Breitenfeld in Saxony, whose elector had just joined him only to flee from the field as soon as he smelt gunsmoke. It was a victory for the new tactics which Gustavus had already tried out with great success against the Poles.

Breitenfeld altered the whole character of the war. Allies now poured into the Swedish camp, and nothing seemed to stand in the way of a direct blow by Gustavus at Vienna itself. But the Swedish king wished first to make sure of western and southern Germany and then to attack the Alpine lands of Austria down the Danube. By the beginning of 1632, after a triumphal march through the Empire against little opposition, he was well established on the latter river, and prepared for the final stroke. But now his luck turned. In desperation the emperor recalled Wallenstein to lead his armies. The general managed to repulse the king's attack on a strongly fortified camp which he had built at Nuremberg on the line of the enemy's advance, and then marched into Saxony to menace the Swedes' dangerously-extended lines of communication and supply. Gustavus could not afford to ignore such a threat, and marched north to deal with it. The two armies met at Lützen, not far from Breitenfeld. The honours of the day went to the Swedes and their allies, but any advantage they might have gained was nullified by the death of Gustavus in the early stages of the battle. As he and a few companions passed, in a thick mist, from one part of the field to another across the enemy front, they were shot down.

Gustavus II is probably the most attractive king ever to have sat on the Swedish throne. He was certainly not without his faults. He had inherited the quick temper so frequently displayed by his father and grandfather, and he was equally adept in the use of propaganda, so that one must be careful not to take all that is said about him in official or semi-official publications at its face value; the Lion of the North, as he became for his admirers, certainly intervened in Germany just as much to protect Swedish national interests as to defend the Protestant faith, although, as has been seen, the two were closely linked. But his reign is particularly well documented, and it is possible to build up a much fuller picture of him than of most of his predecessors. It is evident that he inspired great

4   Sweden in the seventeenth century

devotion in his subjects and revived the Swedes' attachment to the Vasa family, whose reputation had been somewhat tarnished by the quarrels between Charles IX and his brothers. And he took the welfare of his countrymen genuinely to heart, not only in the army, where the comfort of the men always had first priority, but outside it as well.

He recognized his dependence on the nobles, and worked with them more successfully than any of his predecessors had managed to do, a fact which goes a long way to explain the smooth running of the government in his absence. For, in spite of all the work done by Axel Oxenstierna, it was the king himself who was ultimately responsible for the success of the new administrative organs, and in military, foreign and economic affairs his influence was paramount. His ultimate aims in foreign policy have been the subject of much dispute among historians, and their task has been made none the easier by the way in which he seems to have changed his ends as more powerful means came within his grasp. There can be little doubt that he wished from the beginning to provide his kingdom with a firm base or bases on the southern shore of the Baltic, such as would ensure command of all the main commercial arteries running into it—such as would allow Sweden, in fact, to dominate it both economically and politically. After Breitenfeld, however, he appears also to have entertained the idea of creating a great confederation of German Protestant princes under Swedish leadership to prevent a recurrence of the perilous situation in which they had found themselves at the end of the 1620's. With his death, all this came to naught.

In 1632 his daughter and heiress Christina was only six years old, and arrangements had to be made for a regency. This might have led to a dangerous struggle for power among the nobles, but fortunately the Chancellor was in full command of the situation. From Germany, where he had been visiting the king and where he remained for the next three years, he sent over a plan for the regency and future government of the realm, which—or so at least he claimed—had been approved by Gustavus just before his death. With such authority behind it, the project met with little opposition—at least at first. The Regency Council which was set up consisted of the five great officers of State, and, since Oxenstierna had his own brother appointed Steward and his cousin Treasurer, he was assured of complete control. The Form of Government—the nearest thing Sweden had so far had to a constitution—was ratified by the Estates in 1634 and was in most respects a completion of the work begun in the king's lifetime. The Admiral and the Marshal were finally given their own colleges, and the exact composition of a college was now determined; each was to contain at least two members of the *Råd*, except the Chancery and the Supreme Court, which were to have four. The Council itself was to be made up of twenty-four nobles. The membership of the non-noble Estates was also regulated for the first time, although their competence remained ill defined. The Estate of the clergy was to consist of the bishops and two priests from each cathedral chapter; each town was to send a burgher and burgomaster to the Estate of Burghers; and each hundred (*härad*) was to be represented by one tax-paying peasant. The effect of all this in practice was to strengthen the power of the officers of State—and thus of the Oxenstierna family—at the expense not only of the unprivileged Estates, but also of the nobles in the *Råd*, who, in spite of their position in the colleges, found themselves more and more frequently by-passed in the making of policy. Provision was made for the Regents to consult the Estates in the form of a select committee of nobles, bishops and burghers, and only in an emergency were they obliged to call a full meeting of the *Riksdag*.

There was naturally much discontent among all social groups at the way in which the Regents seemed to be trying to edge them out of government, but, while the non-noble orders did manage to present something like a united front under the able leadership of the fiery Johannes Rudbeckius, Bishop of Västerås and one of the foremost figures in the history of the Swedish Lutheran Church, they were divided from the nobles by their opposition to the latter's privileges. The Chancellor managed to quieten criticism for a time by playing on these divisions and making minor concessions, but a new danger to his power emerged in the person of the young queen, who was proclaimed of age in 1644. His enemies failed to profit from this to oust him from office, but Christina soon made it patent that she was no longer willing to submit to the tutelage she had suffered as a minor; from 1647 she ignored Oxenstierna more and more, and slowly undermined his position by favouring families not bound to him.

By this time the war in Germany was at last drawing to a close. The position of the Swedish army—if it could be called such when, after Gustavus's early campaigns, it contained only a small proportion of Swedes—had deteriorated rapidly after Lützen, and in 1634 it was decisively defeated at the Battle of Nördlingen. The Electors of Brandenburg and Saxony immediately made peace with the emperor, and by 1637 the Swedes were fighting desperately even to maintain their position in Pomerania. Their truce with Poland expired in 1635, and they were able to renew it for twenty-six years only by abandoning control of the Vistula estuary and the income from its tolls which formed such a large part of their war-chest. France, now herself officially at war with the emperor, had to come to their aid with more subsidies, which enabled the offensive to be resumed. A decisive victory in Germany continued to elude them, but the time seemed ripe to settle old scores with Denmark, who had played no part in the war since 1629. The provinces of Scania and Halland were occupied in 1643, and the following year General Torstensson attacked Jutland itself from the south. Christian IV had to sue for peace, and at Brömsebro in 1645 Sweden regained the island of Gotland and the province of Halland, and won for the first time the island of Ösel at the mouth of the Gulf of Riga, the province of Jämtland in central Norway and exemption from all tolls levied by the Danes on ships passing into the Baltic through the Sound. She failed to obtain Scania and Blekinge in addition owing to pressure from the Dutch, but Denmark ceased to be able to offer a serious challenge to her position.

This position was confirmed at the Peace of Westphalia, which ended the Thirty Years' War in 1648. By 1643 both sides had been ready to open peace negotiations, but since the war continued while these were going on, and the terms offered and accepted reflected the fluctuating military situation, the proceedings were drawn out for six years. Sweden was richly rewarded in the final settlement with territories which gave her control of the mouths of the three great German rivers which flow into the Baltic. From Western Pomerania she commanded the Oder, and from the bishoprics of Bremen and Verden she controlled both the Elbe and the Weser; the king's initial objectives at least had been attained. A glance at the map will show much more vividly than any words can describe the dominant position which Sweden had achieved in northern Europe in the middle of the seventeenth century; and she had not yet reached the limits of her expansion. But her power had already won for her a number of very jealous neighbours, and it remained to be seen whether, with her small population and her limited economic resources, she would be able to hold on to what she had gained.

CHAPTER IX

Crisis and Reconstruction: The Reigns of Christina, Charles X and Charles XI

The conclusion of the war naturally led the lower orders of Swedish society to hope for a lightening of the crushing financial burdens which had been imposed upon them to pay for it. But the newly acquired trans-Baltic territories proved unable to sustain the cost even of their own government and defence; the Crown needed more not less money than before, and discontent grew. This discontent was, however, directed not against the queen, but against the magnates. In fact the burghers, clergy and tax-paying peasants looked to Christina to join them; reduce the powers and privileges of the nobility and base royal authority more broadly, on the mass of her subjects. Their principal demand was for a drastic resumption of the Crown lands and taxes which had been alienated on an unprecedented scale in recent years. For the war had been paid for, not only out of heavier taxation, but also by means of lavish grants both to Swedes and to the many foreigners who had entered Swedish service and could be rewarded in no other way. As the Crown's income sank, a fear arose among the growing number of free peasants who paid their taxes to nobles' stewards instead of to royal bailiffs that they would gradually be absorbed into the mass of nobles' peasants, and even that serfdom might gain a foothold in Sweden, from where it had hitherto been excluded. The interests of the queen thus appeared to coincide with those of the non-noble orders, especially at a time when she was trying to rid herself of the tutelage imposed by the Oxenstierna family. But, resentful as she was of the latter's pretensions, she had

Crisis and Reconstruction: Christina, Charles X and Charles XI
nevertheless absorbed the Chancellor's teachings on the best
means of developing her kingdom's economic strength. To him
it seemed that exploitation of the land could be more efficiently
carried out by the nobility, while the State should look for its
main source of revenue, not to the traditional direct taxes but
to indirect taxes and customs dues; these could be expected to
increase with the growth of trade, which was to be the main
concern of the Government.

Thus, when the storm broke in the *Riksdag* of 1650, and the
lower Estates called on the queen to lead them in what amounted
to a war on the higher nobility, she encouraged them until they
agreed to her plans for the succession, but then rejected all their
demands for the institution of a *reduktion*. Not only this, but she
proceeded to grant away estates and taxes even more recklessly
than before. The *Riksdag* of 1652 saw a renewal of the attack,
and the Chancellor did agree on this occasion to make some
concessions to allay the fears of the tax-peasants, and persuaded
the nobility to make a voluntary grant for two years. There was
still, however, no sign of the Crown's giving way on the question
of a *reduktion*, although the new Treasurer, Herman Fleming,
was in favour of it, and was in the process of breaking down the
queen's resistance, when, in 1654, she announced her intention
to abdicate.

This was no sudden decision. As far back as 1646 she seems
to have made up her mind to abandon the throne at the first
favourable opportunity, and in 1651 informed the Council of
her resolve. What her motives were it is impossible to judge with
any degree of certainty, but perhaps the main one was a desire
to ensure an undisputed succession, and to avoid the dangers of
a new regency. The lower Estates had been urging her ever since
the beginning of her reign to marry her soldier-cousin Charles
Gustavus of Zweibrücken, the son of her father's sister, in the
hope that this would strengthen the Crown against the magnates. But Christina, like Elizabeth I of England, appears to
have entertained an aversion to marriage, and finally declared
before the Estates in 1649 that 'it is impossible for me to marry.
Such is the nature of the case. I cannot give my reasons, but
my heart is not in it. I have prayed diligently to God, but (in
vain).' At the same time, however, she worked to ensure the
recognition of Charles as her heir, and attained this objective

during the meeting of the Estates in the following year. The troubles which came to a head on this occasion doubtless strengthened her determination to abdicate; and her passion for intellectual and cultural pursuits, which were difficult to reconcile with her work as a ruler (although she enjoyed this as well), may also have played a part. For Christina was a true 'blue-stocking'. She was extremely well-read in the learning of her time; spoke French, Dutch and Latin fluently; and gathered round her a circle of intellectuals headed by the great French philosopher Descartes. But what finally made her abdication inevitable was her conversion to Catholicism. Her admiration for Latin culture drew her in this direction, but even more important must have been the attraction for a woman with her temperament of a faith which had not yet lost the fervour of the Counter-Reformation, and which contrasted favourably with the rather arid formalism which had overtaken Lutheranism. Immediately after abdicating in favour of her cousin, she left Sweden for ever, and at Innsbruck, on her way south to Rome, she was formally received into the Catholic fold. She lived in Rome, in a house once occupied by St. Bridget, until her death thirty-five years later.

The accession of Charles X brought a sharp break with his predecessor's policy both at home and abroad. The practice of granting away royal lands and taxes was at last reversed, although only temporarily, and the territorial expansion which had come to a halt at Westphalia was resumed. Christina was pacific by temperament. Her country needed peace in 1648; and Axel Oxenstierna wished it in order that he might concentrate on developing Sweden's overseas trade—a policy which actually antagonized the Dutch without bringing much benefit to the realm. Charles, however, had spent most of his youth fighting with the Swedish troops in Germany, and had ended up as their commander-in-chief; it would have been surprising if he had shirked any war which promised to enhance the power, prestige and safety of his kingdom. And such a war he seemed called upon to wage as soon as he came to the throne.

For three years Russia and Poland had been struggling for dominion over the turbulent Cossacks of the Ukraine, and the success enjoyed by the tsar was alarming, and yet at the same time encouraging, for the king. It alarmed him because, if

Poland should fall under Russian control, Sweden's strategic and commercial position in the eastern Baltic would be extremely parlous. But it also encouraged him, because Poland's embarrassment provided Sweden with an excellent opportunity to seize the Polish littoral, link her possessions in Germany to Livonia and gain complete mastery of Russia's growing export trade. It offered, in addition, a chance to compel the King of Poland, who was still a member of the house of Vasa, to surrender his claims to the Swedish throne and to turn the existing armistice with him into a definitive peace. The war on which Charles X embarked in 1655 was thus both a defensive and an offensive operation. It further promised to ease the internal social tensions from which the country continued to suffer.

At first all went well. The Poles were unable to put up much resistance to a two-pronged attack on them from Pomerania and Livonia while they were facing the Russian assaults in the east; Warsaw and Cracow soon fell, and the Polish king fled the country. But Charles soon found that Poland was far easier to conquer than to hold, and in 1656 the tide turned against him. The Poles rose against their heretical occupiers, and drove them back towards the Baltic; the Russians concluded a truce, and turned their attention to Livonia; and the Dutch, alarmed by the Swedish successes, sent a fleet to protect the great port of Danzig, through which flowed most of their vital trade in Polish wheat. In 1657 the Swedes found themselves fighting desperately in northern Poland; the Elector of Brandenburg, who had allied himself with them at the beginning of the war, changed sides; and in the middle of the year the Danes joined in the attack on what seemed to be an already-defeated foe. But they had seriously under-estimated their adversary. They managed to occupy Bremen, but then had to evacuate Jutland before the advance of the main Swedish army from the south. Charles could not, however, attack the Danish islands without a fleet, and this he did not command; the Dutch were latent enemies, and Cromwell, whom he approached, refused to become involved. The weather came to his relief, for the winter of 1657–58 was so severe that the narrow belts of water between the islands froze over deep enough to enable him to transport his entire army over the ice, and threaten Copenhagen. The Danes agreed

Crisis and Reconstruction: Christina, Charles X and Charles XI

to conclude peace under English and French mediation. By the Treaty of Roskilde, they surrendered all the territory which they still held in what is now southern Sweden—Scania, Blekinge and Bohuslän—together with central Norway and the island of Bornholm, which had never owed allegiance to the Swedish Crown.

But even these gains did not satisfy Charles X. He determined to destroy Danish power completely, and even had plans for turning Denmark into a Swedish province. A mere six months after Roskilde he attacked again. But he had over-reached himself. The Dutch sent ships to help Copenhagen defend itself, and a Polish and Brandenburg army occupied Jutland, and drove the Swedes both from Pomerania and the few footholds which they still possessed in Poland. Charles had already agreed to open negotiations when, at the beginning of 1660, he died aged only thirty-eight.

In internal affairs, his reign saw a breach between the Crown and the higher nobility which foreshadowed the establishment of absolute monarchy by his successor. Axel Oxenstierna died in 1654 and was succeded by his son, but when he too died two years later, the office of Chancellor was left vacant. The *Råd* found itself by-passed more and more frequently by secretaries attached to the private chancery which accompanied the king on his campaigns, a return in some respects to the system of government favoured by the earlier Vasas and abandoned by Gustavus Adolphus. In such circumstances, and faced by the financial demands of the war, Charles listened to the call of the lower Estates for a *reduktion* with more favour than Christina had done. He empowered the Treasurer to conduct an inquiry into the legality of all nobles' claims to their land, and, in the *Riksdag* which met on the eve of the war, the House of Nobles agreed, under strong pressure, to surrender all estates considered by the Crown to be indispensable for the defence of the realm, together with a quarter of all the taxes granted away since the death of Gustavus Adolphus. While a commission was determining exactly what territory was involved, the nobles agreed to pay annually for three years a sum judged to be the equivalent of the taxes which would be resumed when it had finished its work. In 1660, however, the report of the commission was still not ready; the resumption of 'indispensable estates' had only just begun; and the king's death allowed the nobles to launch a counter-attack.

For Sweden was to be ruled, for the third time in the century, by regents, always an opportunity for the magnates to strengthen their position at the expense of the Crown. And on this occasion it seemed that they could look forward to a long tenure of power, for Charles X's son was only four years old. The new government was headed by the Chancellor, Magnus Gabriel De la Gardie, but it was in the large *Råd* that the nobles found their best weapon, not only against the *ofrälse* but also against the Regents. They immediately asserted the rights of this body by securing the exclusion from it of the unpopular Treasurer, and by making additions to the Form of Government (now once more recognized as being in force after a long period in abeyance) which restricted the Regents' powers.

The first task which the latter had to face was the conclusion of a satisfactory peace with Denmark, Poland, Russia and Brandenburg. In view of Sweden's position at Charles X's death, she was extremely fortunate in having to surrender only Bornholm and the Norwegian provinces by the Treaty of Copenhagen; the other gains she had made from Denmark at Roskilde were retained. The Polish king agreed to renounce his claims on the Swedish throne and Livonia at a separate peace concluded at Oliva, near Danzig, while Russia and Brandenburg had to rest content with the *status quo*. The second problem, closely related to the first, was that of finance. In spite of the demands of the lower Estates, no attempt was made to implement the 'quarter-*reduktion*' decided on in 1655, and the refusal of the burghers and peasants to grant any new taxes, with which to reduce the large debt which burdened the Treasury, compelled the Government both to introduce drastic economies and to resume the alienation of Crown lands; there seemed to be no other solution. In 1668 a private bank which had failed was taken over by the State to become the first national bank in Europe, but control of it was vested in the Estates.

Such a situation dictated an extremely cautious foreign policy, one aimed at the protection of Sweden's extensive and vulnerable empire by means of alliances with powers outside the circle of those who would benefit from its collapse. The close ties established between Denmark and the United Provinces suggested an approach to the latter's main commercial rival, England, with whom an alliance was concluded in 1665. But the aggressive policy conducted in the Spanish Netherlands (modern Belgium) by France under Louis XIV drove the Dutch and English together, and in 1667 the *Råd*, although against the wishes of the pro-French Chancellor, determined to join them in what became known as the Triple Alliance, aimed at limiting the French king's gains. In 1670 the situation changed once more when Charles II and the latter concluded the notorious Treaty of Dover, which promised English support for a French attack on Holland. This time De la Gardie won his colleagues over to his point of view, and secured a French alliance. Sweden thereby obtained much-needed subsidies with which to equip a large armament in her German provinces, which, it was hoped, would discourage the Elector of Brandenburg from coming to the aid of France's enemies. It appeared to be a good bargain. Sweden's defences were considerably strengthened at no cost to the Treasury, and there seemed little immediate risk of war, for Brandenburg made peace after the first campaign in 1672. But in 1674 the elector re-entered the war against France, who now insisted that Sweden fulfil her treaty obligations and attack Brandenburg. Unwillingly the Regents complied.

To the surprise of most of western Europe, the Swedish army suffered a defeat at the hands of the elector's troops at Fehrbellin in 1675. What took place was little more than a skirmish, but its outcome was enough to encourage both the Danes and the Dutch to declare war on Sweden. The Dutch fleet secured command of the Baltic, and enabled the Danes to cross the Sound into their former provinces, where they could count on a considerable body of sympathizers. The Swedish army redeemed its honour at the Battle of Lund in 1676, and the Danes were slowly driven out of the country, but Sweden's German possessions had to be abandoned, and it was only thanks to French diplomatic pressure and divisions among her enemies that she had to make only minor territorial concessions (in Pomerania and Bremen-Verden) when the war ended in 1679.

The war had completely discredited the Regents and the nobility in general, and had greatly enhanced the prestige of the Crown. Charles XI had been declared of age in 1672, but he was in no way associated with the policies which had dragged his kingdom into such peril. He had, in addition, though an exceedingly shy young man, fought with great gallantry at Lund, and had personally led the army which expelled the enemy from native soil. After Fehrbellin, De la Gardie had ceased to play an active part in government which fell largely into the hands of the secretaries of the Field Chancery, as under Charles X, and of the king's favourite, Johan Gyllenstierna. But this was not enough to satisfy the lower Estates, who demanded a full-scale *reduktion* and an investigation into the record of the Regency, with just retribution for those found guilty. In the *Riksdag* of 1680 both demands received full royal support. A commission was set up to find evidence against the Regents, and in 1682 those members of the Council who had survived from the Regency period were dismissed, and the Regents themselves fined heavily. It is difficult to imagine their receiving such lenient treatment in any other European country at this period! At the same time the nobles were persuaded to agree to the resumption of all lands in Sweden's overseas possessions which had been alienated by the Crown, and of the more valuable estates given away in Sweden itself since the beginning of the sixteenth century.

For Charles and his supporters, however, this was only the beginning of a revolution in government. In 1660, after the war which had brought a national disgrace even greater than that which Sweden suffered fifteen years later, the King of Denmark had allied himself with the lower classes to crush the power of his nobles and to establish an absolutist monarchy. And by 1680 it seemed as if the future was to lie with absolute monarchy throughout Europe; even in England Charles II was on the point of overthrowing a government of his Whig critics and dissolving his last parliament. Sweden would merely be following the general trend if she now imitated her southern neighbour, and, as in Denmark, her monarchy became absolute as the result of an alliance between the Crown and the unprivileged classes against a nobility held responsible for recent disasters. In the *Riksdag* of 1680, the lower Estates absolved the king from any obligation to observe the Form of Government or to rule with the advice of the *Råd*; the latter body continued to serve as a court of law and as a forum for the discussion of foreign affairs, in which Charles was less interested than his father, but most other matters were handled by *ad hoc* committees or individuals favoured by the king. The colleges also henceforth lost much of their former authority, and several of the great offices of State were left vacant. The Estates continued to meet at irregular intervals (unlike Denmark, where they ceased to exist), but they became completely subservient to the royal will, and in 1682 gave Charles full control over legislation and the *reduktion*. Finally, in 1693, he and his heirs were declared 'responsible to none on Earth for their actions, but (having) all the power they may wish, with which to guide and rule this kingdom like Christian kings'.

The main uses to which Charles put the enormous power which he now wielded were to restore the financial position of the Crown, and to build up his realm's military might; the second, as he realized full well, was not possible without the first. In the years following, over 80 per cent of the estates which had been alienated by the Crown since 1500 were resumed, until at the end of the century a third of all land in Sweden was again part of the royal domain; the threat of serfdom was averted. The greatest gains were made in the overseas territories, which accounted for over half the increase in the king's income.

The land thus acquired was made the basis for the so-called *indelning* system. Under this, the revenue from certain estates was set aside for the payment of government employees, in particular army officers. But the system was also extended to the army as a whole, in so far as certain provinces were made responsible for providing regiments of horse and foot, and the troops chosen were granted houses and land on which they and their families could support themselves. It was not unlike the system tried by Gustavus Adolphus, but much more thorough and effective in its application. By 1700 the Swedish army consisted of over 25,000 foot and twelve regiments of cavalry. At the same time Admiral Hans Wachtmeister expanded the fleet, which had been allowed to dwindle almost to nothing, to thirty-eight ships of the line, and a fine new base, nearer than Stockholm to the likely fields of action, was built at Karlskrona in Blekinge.

Such sweeping changes necessitated a long period of peace

for their fulfilment, especially as the *reduktion* caused much discontent among the nobles, who might use a war to try to restore their former position. For a brief time in 1679–80, when Johan Gyllenstierna was the king's chief adviser, negotiations were conducted with Denmark aimed at the creation of some kind of union between the two countries, but it was to be a union in which Sweden would clearly be the dominant partner, and, with Gyllenstierna's death in the latter year, the attempt to win Denmark to such a scheme was abandoned; and the two realms resumed their traditional hostility. For the remaining seventeen years of the reign Sweden's foreign relations were directed by Bengt Oxenstierna, a distant relative of Gustavus Adolphus's great Chancellor. Under him Sweden drifted away from France, whose aggressive policy was threatening to upset the balance of power in Europe, towards King Louis's opponents, the Dutch and the emperor, with whom a series of alliances was concluded during the 1680's with the object of maintaining the existing settlement. But when a major war finally broke out in 1688, Sweden refused to become involved beyond supplying the troops which she was obliged to send to the Rhine under the terms of her treaties; and these were dispatched tardily and with a bad grace. In the following year, however, she nearly went to war with Denmark to compel the latter to restore the Duke of Holstein-Gottorp, who was Sweden's client, to the lands from which the Danes had expelled him. Denmark gave way without fighting, and the European war in fact brought the two Northern Crowns closer together in a limited sphere. Interference with their merchant shipping by Dutch, English and—to a much lesser extent—French privateers and warships forced them both to fit out convoys, and in 1691 to join together in a so-called League of Armed Neutrality, which threatened reprisals against the belligerents if their molestations continued. Under this threat, the Dutch, who were the worst offenders, agreed to pay compensation for the seizures for which they were responsible.

One of Charles XI's dearest wishes was to act as the peacemaker of Europe, and just before he died in 1697, he had the satisfaction of knowing that both sides had accepted the offer of mediation which he had been making for several years. Sweden may have gained some prestige from this, but she gained nothing else, and her representative at the negotiations conducted at Ryswick in Holland found himself reduced to giving his approval to agreements arrived at behind his back, and to restraining the participants from abandoning the congress altogether. Peace had nevertheless returned to Europe by the end of the year.

CHAPTER X

Charles XII and the Collapse of the Swedish Empire

Certain features of the situation after the death of Charles XI are reminiscent of that in 1611. Once again, the new king, Charles XII, was a boy below the age (he was not yet fifteen) when he would normally have been invested with all the powers of his office, but considered mature enough for the regency to be brought to an end after only a few months of life. Here, however, the similarities end. At the beginning of Gustavus Adolphus's reign, the nobles had used the occasion to to wring promises from the young ruler which enabled them to resume the place in government which they had lost under the early Vasas. In 1697 no conditions were made, and no changes took place in the constitution; there was no relaxation of the absolutism so recently introduced. Indeed it is by no means clear exactly what lay behind the declaration of Charles's majority by the Estates. The unprivileged orders may have feared the effects of another regency, even if it must last for a much shorter time than that for the new monarch's father; the nobles certainly hoped for a relaxation in the *reduktion* programme; and the Chancellor probably expected to enjoy greater control of affairs under a young and inexperienced sovereign than at the head of a regency council containing his rivals. If the latter was the case, Oxenstierna must have been bitterly disillusioned, for his influence was soon completely overshadowed by younger men round the king, and Charles himself proved most unwilling to take advice from anyone at all.

One of the main reasons why Gustavus II had been declared

of age so early was that conditions at home and abroad seemed to demand unity of leadership. In 1697 Sweden was at peace. But the situation abroad was threatening, more threatening than the Swedish Government realized at the time. Charles XI had always, understandably enough, regarded Denmark as the principal danger to his realm's security. In 1689, as has been seen, he had been on the verge of war with her in defence of the Duke of Holstein-Gottorp. Denmark had then climbed down before English and Dutch threats, and the latter had guaranteed the Duke's possessions. They could therefore be relied upon to come to his aid if Denmark should attack again, and there was no particular cause for alarm when, in March 1700, news reached Stockholm of a fresh Danish assault on the Duchies. Much more disturbing were reports which had come in a few weeks earlier of the invasion of Livonia by Augustus, King of Poland and Elector of Saxony, and of threatening gestures by Tsar Peter of Russia. That all these moves were contemporaneous was no coincidence, for Sweden had at last to face a situation which all her diplomacy had for long been trying to guard against—a coalition of her immediate neighbours with the object of divesting her of her empire and partitioning it among themselves.

In 1699 and the early days of 1700, Saxony, Denmark and Russia had concluded a series of offensive alliances with just this end in view. Brandenburg, in spite of her ambitions in Pomerania—especially her desire for the great port of Stettin at the mouth of the Oder—refused to commit herself—for the time being. The policies of three new rulers[1] coincided, but they were also encouraged at this time by the accession to the Swedish throne of a young and inexperienced king, and by rumours of serious economic difficulties faced by his realm after a succession of poor harvests and of widespread unrest among the Swedish upper classes. The latter had little foundation as concerned the nobles of Sweden proper, but that there was discontent among the nobility of Livonia was attested by the activities of one of

[1] Peter I had taken over the government of Russia just before setting out on his first great European journey in 1697; Augustus had been elected King of Poland in the same year; and Frederick IV had followed his father on the throne of Denmark only a few weeks before the first of the alliances mentioned above was signed.

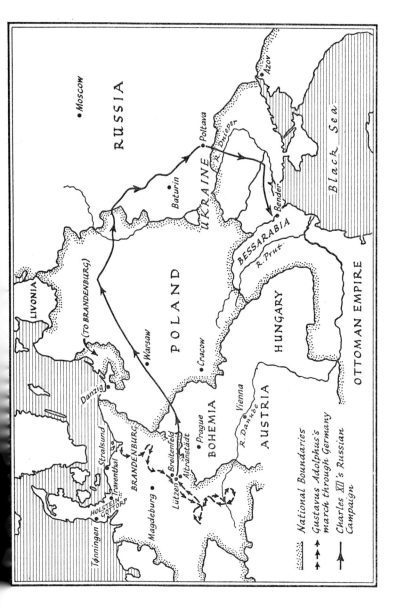

MOSCOW

RUSSIA

LIVONIA

POLAND

(TO BRANDENBURG)

Danzig

Warsaw

Cracow

Stralsund

Tönningen

HOLSTEIN-
GOTTORP

Traventhal

BRANDENBURG

Magdeburg

Lützen

Breitenfeld

Altranstädt

Prague

BOHEMIA

R. Danube

Vienna

AUSTRIA

HUNGARY

Baturin

UKRAINE

Poltava

R. Dnieper

Bender

BESSARABIA

R. Prut

Azov

Black Sea

OTTOMAN EMPIRE

National Boundaries
Gustavus Adolphus's
march through Germany
Charles XII's Russian
Campaign

5   The campaigns of Gustavus Adolphus, Charles X and
Charles XII

H

their number named Johann Reinhold Patkul. In 1692 this man had led a deputation to Charles XI to protest against the application of the *reduktion* to his province and the attacks on the rights and privileges of his class which accompanied the Crown's efforts, after the establishment of absolutism, to integrate its overseas possessions with the homeland. Far from gaining any satisfaction, Patkul had to flee the country to escape arrest, and was condemned to death for *lèse-majesté* in his absence. After failing to secure a pardon from Charles XII, he approached both King Augustus and the tsar with plans for the formation of a general coalition against Sweden. They welcomed the offer of his services in the negotiations which led up to their alliance in 1699.

The attack from Denmark was easily parried, and the war carried into the enemy's camp. In fulfilment of their treaty obligations, England and the Dutch Republic sent squadrons of warships to join the Swedes and enable them to land troops on Zealand. Much to Charles's chagrin—for, like his grandfather, he had hoped to be able to beat Denmark to her knees— King Frederick decided that resistance was hopeless, and, at the Peace of Traventhal, agreed to leave the Duke of Holstein alone and abandon his alliances with Saxony and Russia. Although far short of what Charles had hoped for, this did enable him to deal with the menace in the east, where he would have to rely wholly on his own resources. On reaching Livonia with his main army, he found the Saxons in retreat, but the Russians were attacking the important fortress of Narva on the border between Estonia and Ingria, and he immediately set off to relieve it. Although outnumbered by three to one, the disciplined Swedes soon put to flight the Russian troops, few of whom had as yet been trained on western European lines. Instead of attempting to follow up this victory, the king chose to deal first with the King of Poland.

The campaign which followed was in many ways a repetition of that conducted by Charles X nearly half a century before. The Poles and Saxons put up very little resistance to the Swedish advance, and by the end of the year both Warsaw and Cracow had fallen; Charles spent the winter in the latter town. But, as his grandfather had found to his cost, all this was far from implying that the country had been conquered; the force at his

disposal was far too small to provide an effective army of occupation, especially when a large number of men had to be
stationed near the Saxon border, behind which Augustus could
prepare for a counter-stoke. In 1704 Charles cajoled a meeting
of the Polish Diet in Warsaw to depose the elector and choose
as king in his place a young Polish noble named Stanislas
Leszczyński, who could be relied upon to co-operate with the
Swedes and would, it was hoped, be able to support them with
the Polish army, such as it was. It was not until 1706 that
Charles felt his hold on Poland secure enough to invade Saxony
itself, but when he did, Augustus gave in with hardly a struggle,
and by the Treaty of Altranstädt renounced his claim to the
Polish throne.

By this time, however, the menace from Russia was again
growing. In 1703 Peter had occupied the mouth of the River
Neva in Ingria, and had begun to build what he intended to
be his new capital of St. Petersburg. In the following year,
Narva and the university town of Dorpat in Estonia fell to him,
and Russian troops soon began to appear in large numbers in
eastern Poland. At Altranstädt Charles entertained a host of petty
princes and envoys from most of the leading European powers;
included among them was the Duke of Marlborough, who wished
to make sure that Sweden was not intending to come to the aid
of Louis XIV in the War of the Spanish Succession, then raging
in the west. But the Swedish king was mainly occupied in per-
fecting his plans for a knock-out blow against the tsar. This involved a march straight on Moscow in co-operation, it was
hoped, with the Turks and a host of Cossacks under their
leader Mazeppa.

By the summer of 1708 Charles was ready, and his army of
some 40,000 men was set in motion; it was planned to reinforce
it on the way with a further 16,000 from Livonia under General
Lewenhaupt and 8,000 more from Poland as soon as they could
be spared. The king, however, soon found himself faced with
much the same difficulties as those Napoleon encountered on
a similar route just over a century later; the Russians destroyed
everything in his path, and harried his supply lines as he
drew farther and farther from his bases. Eventually he was
forced to the conclusion that, under such conditions, he could
not hope to reach the Russian capital by the direct route,

and turned south in an attempt to approach it through areas as yet untouched by the tsar's 'scorched earth' policy, uniting with Mazeppa's Cossacks on the way. But from this point on he was dogged by misfortune. The movement was botched, and he found himself committed to wintering in the Ukraine. The Livonian army, whose march had been slowed to a snail's pace by the wretched Russian roads, was intercepted by the enemy, and had been reduced to 6,000 troops without supplies by the time it eventually reached him. Peter attacked the Cossack capital of Baturin, and Mazeppa was forced to flee to join Charles with only a handful of followers. There was no news of the corps from Poland, which never in fact started out. And, worst of all, the winter of 1708–09 was one of the severest on record. The privations suffered by the Swedish troops were vividly described by one of them in his diary: 'On Christmas Eve and the day before the cold was so intense that the whole road was littered with men and horses who had been frozen to death, and with abandoned baggage and hospital waggons, so that it was pitiful to behold. There wasn't a regiment in which some of the officers and many of the men were not injured or killed, and most of the drivers perished.'

The army survived, although by the spring it had shrunk to 23,000 combatants. Their situation was far from hopeless, as long as they could bring the main Russian army to battle quickly, and win a decisive victory. To entice Peter to risk an action, Charles's men lay siege to the small fortress of Poltava on a tributary of the River Dnieper, and the tsar rose to the bait; he drew near in June with a host twice the size of the Swede's. At Narva Charles had overwhelmed three times as many Russians, but Peter had taken that lesson to heart, and now headed a far more formidable body, largely trained on European lines and adequately supplied with artillery. Near Poltava his troops built themselves a large fortified camp, which the Swedes proceeded to assault. The king had been wounded in the foot just before the attack was launched, and was unable to supervise the battle adequately from his litter. In addition to this, some of the subordinate commanders were unaware of the overall tactical plan, and initial confusion was soon worse confounded. After suffering very heavy losses to no purpose, Charles was forced to admit defeat and to order a retreat south-

Charles XII and the Collapse of the Swedish Empire

wards towards the River Dnieper. Once there, he left the main
body of his army, and, with a small contingent, pushed on to the
Turkish frontier, which he reached safely, having left orders for
the rest, under the command of Lewenhaupt, to join him later
by a more circuitous route. How many realized at the time that
this was the beginning of the end for Sweden's empire? Certainly not the ever-sanguine king.

Charles now aimed to persuade the Turks to renew their war
with Russia, which had been interrupted by a truce in 1700.
This was on the assumption that he could offer them the help
of an army which, even after Poltava, still numbered over 14,000
men. But this army had ceased to exist soon after he had left it.
On the approach of the Russians, Lewenhaupt had surrendered
without making any attempt to escape and without firing a shot.
The Caroline warriors, destined to be the subject of so many
works of literature in the years to come, having already
faced so much with their king, were now to endure their greatest
ordeal without him, an ordeal which many (including, perhaps mercifully, Lewenhaupt) failed to survive.

For four years Charles XII stayed, by courtesy of the sultan,
in a camp outside the walls of the small town of Bender in
Bessarabia, while he tried to interest the Turks in his cause and
to persuade his councillors in Stockholm to form a fresh army
with which to launch a counter-attack in the Baltic. Here the
situation deteriorated rapidly. Encouraged by Poltava, Augustus, who had now re-established himself in Poland, and
Frederick of Denmark re-entered the fray. The participation of
both rulers in the war in the west against France had been rewarded by a more favourable attitude from the Maritime
Powers, and, in order to win even more approval from the latter,
they promised not to attack Sweden's possessions in Germany
unless she should use them as military bases. In 1710 Peter's
troops occupied the whole of Livonia and Estonia and threatened Finland. To match the worsening position abroad, Sweden
was faced by growing internal difficulties. A series of crop
failures, which could no longer, as in the past, be counter-
balanced by importing grain from Livonia, the granary of
Sweden's empire, and outbreaks of plague, which on one estimate carried off a third of the inhabitants of Stockholm, came
on top of a decline in agricultural production, caused by the

117

drafting of a large section of the male labour force into the army, and heavier and heavier taxation.

In spite of all this, there was little sign of open discontent in the country. But the *Råd* began to urge the distant king in stronger and stronger terms to reach a settlement with his enemies while something might still be salvaged; to accept England's offer of mediation; and to respect the neutrality of Germany. Charles, however, refused to consider peace on any terms which seemed likely to be offered, and ordered more and more peremptorily, the speedy formation of the new army which was to attack Poland from Pomerania. He refused to allow the Council, now led by Chancellor Arvid Horn, who had participated in the Polish campaigns, any initiative, but, when letters between Bender and Stockholm might take any-thing up to a year on the journey (if they arrived at all), it could obviously not submit every decision to him for ratification be-fore implementing it. It determined in 1710, for example, to share the responsibility for a situation which was becoming in-creasingly grave by calling together a committee of the four Estates. This was intended to discuss new means of raising revenue, but during its sessions the members made quite clear their desire for peace.

Charles's promise of a simultaneous Swedish assault on Poland finally persuaded the Turks to renew their war with Russia in 1711. They succeeded in surrounding the tsar's army on the River Prut but, since there was no news of the expected Swedish offensive, they agreed to make peace in exchange for the return to them of the Black Sea port of Azov (Peter's first conquest) and an undertaking that the Russians would withdraw from Poland; the enemy's troops were allowed to march home un-molested. Charles's last chance had gone, although he was not the man to admit it. Twice more the sultan declared war on Russia, but only to force Peter to abide by the terms of the Prut treaty, and on each occasion he was satisfied with Russian assurances. By 1713 he considered that he had obtained all the advantages he could expect from the king's presence in his dominions, and decided to get rid of his now embarrassing guest. But Charles (largely, it seems, to call the sultan's atten-tion to a local plot to betray him to the Russians), resisted the attempt made to dislodge him from the small town which he

and his companions had built outside Bender, and only surrendered after withstanding a regular assault. He was taken, a
virtual prisoner, to Demotika, near Constantinople, where he
received news which at last persuaded him that he could hope
for no more from the Turks.

Since he had refused to accept the offer of the Coalition to
neutralize Germany, his enemies had launched a full-scale assault
on Pomerania in 1711, while Danish troops occupied Bremen
and Verden. A Danish attack on the Swedish mainland was re-
pulsed by the new commander-in-chief, Magnus Stenbock, but
when, in 1713, having been forced by superior enemy forces to
retreat from Pomerania, he attempted an invasion of Jutland,
he was surrounded in the fortress of Tønningen in Slesvig and
compelled to surrender with his whole army. At the end of this
year, the tsar at last launched his long-awaited attack on Finland, the whole of which was soon under his control.

Charles did not complete his preparations for his return to
the Baltic until September 1714. After travelling incognito
through Hungary, Austria and Germany in less than two weeks,
he appeared outside the gates of Stralsund, the last vestige of
territory (with the exception of the port of Wismar) left to him
outside Sweden proper. It too was lost early in the new year, and
Brandenburg and Hanover, whose elector had just ascended
the British throne as George I, declared war on Sweden. Yet the
king still refused to entertain any thought of a peace which would
involve a surrender of his realm's status as a great power, and
prepared to continue the struggle from the homeland with the
help of Baron von Görtz. After his return he granted this able
but unscrupulous Holsteiner almost dictatorial powers under
himself. The whole Swedish economy was brought under his
control in an attempt to replace the revenue previously provided by customs dues levied at the mouths of the great Baltic
rivers, and to find the money for a new army which might yet
turn the tables on the foe. He made the export of all goods a
monopoly of the Government, which bought from the merchants at fixed prices and sold at the most advantageous rates;
bonds were issued on the scurity of State income, rather like
the *assignats* of Revolutionary France, and like them widely used
as currency; even token money was distributed for a short time,
but it soon declined sharply in real value. In 1716, Görtz

travelled to the United Provinces to try to secure a loan from Dutch merchants in exchange for commercial privileges in Sweden. Not only did he fail, but he was arrested by the Dutch authorities in response to requests from the English government, which was much concerned by his intrigues with Jacobite exiles; the papers of the Swedish envoy in London were seized at the same time and the envoy himself, Karl Gyllenborg, soon after.

These incidents are indicative of the strained relations which existed at this time between Sweden and the Maritime Powers. This was in part due to Charles's interference with the trade which both Britain and the Dutch were conducting with the Russian enemy. In this case again he overruled the advice of his Council, which wanted to continue the lenient policy towards neutral commerce which it had been pursuing in the king's absence. A British fleet under Admiral Norris was actually sent to the Baltic to protect British interests there, and the Coalition naturally hoped that it would be able to use these ships in the all-out attack on Sweden which was planned to take place in 1716. But the attack was never launched. Serious rifts had begun to appear in the ranks of Sweden's enemies, especially between Russia and the rest, who were coming to fear the outcome of the tsar's growing hold on Poland and his obvious interest in north Germany. This situation seemed to offer Charles a golden opportunity to split the Coalition completely by negotiating with its individual members, and even to turn them against one another. In 1718 talks were begun by Görtz, now released from captivity, with Russian representatives on the Åland Islands, and by September the two sides had reached agreement on the terms of a draft treaty. Sweden was to surrender her Baltic provinces to Peter in exchange for his promise to help her against any other power that should come to the aid of Denmark, from whom Sweden was to secure compensation in the shape of Norway. From all the evidence, it seems highly unlikely that Charles, even placed as he was, would ever have agreed to such conditions, but he never learnt of them, for in November he was killed during the siege of the fortress of Fredrikshald in southern Norway.

As soon as he returned to Sweden, the king had set about building up a new army with which to knock Denmark out of the war and perhaps repeat Charles X's *coup* of 1658, when the situation had been almost equally desperate. By 1718 he again had had an operation army of 40,000 men under his command, and in the autumn had begun to attack the forts covering Christiana. Fredrikshald was one of these.

Much ink has been spilt over the problem of whether or not Charles XII was murdered; his body has been exhumed several times to examine the fatal wound. But we seem today as far as ever we were from arriving at a conclusive answer. He could have been killed from the enemy lines, although these were nearly 200 yards away; he was notoriously reckless of his own safety. On the other hand, his death was certainly convenient for a large number of important Swedes, notably those who supported the claims to the throne of his younger sister Ulrika Eleanora, married to Frederick of Hesse-Cassel. These claims were opposed by the so-called Holsteiners or advocates of the rights of the young Duke of Holstein-Gottorp, the son of Charles's elder sister; and the leading Holsteiner was the highly unpopular Görtz, whose position depended wholly on the king's favour. The Hessians were also suspiciously well prepared to take advantage of the death.

Charles XII has become such a symbol in Swedish history that it is well-nigh impossible to arrive at a balanced judgment of him. For some he became the inspiration of all attempts to regain Sweden's imperial status—of the *revanchistes* of the eighteenth and nineteenth centuries, who preached war with Russia whenever such an enterprise seemed to offer any hope of success. For others—including most modern historians—his obstinacy in refusing to make peace while Sweden was still in a favourable position was largely responsible for the disastrous end of the Northern War, although it is generally admitted at the same time that, faced as she was by so many jealous neighbours, Sweden was probably not capable of retaining her position in the Baltic for very much longer in any case. To many—especially the philosopher and the romantic historian of the nineteenth century—he seemed a superman, warring against supernatural forces like some Norse god of old and perishing in a small-scale *Götterdämmerung*. His taciturnity and refusal to explain his motives even to his closest companions have made nearly every one of his moves during the Great Northern War the subject of great speculation. While we may condemn him as a king who led his people to destruction, he must still call forth our admiration as a man who refused to compromise with his beliefs, whose moral probity has never been questioned and who accepted full responsibility for all his actions.

With his death and the accession of his younger sister to the throne,[1] all the heart went out of Swedish resistance; the Norwegian campaign was abandoned, and, while the last vestiges of absolutism were swept away and the 'Era of Liberty' inaugurated, Britain's offer to mediate peace with the western members of the Coalition was eagerly accepted. Once this had been achieved, the Russian advance might, it was hoped, be halted and part at least of Sweden's position in northern Europe be retrieved with the help of the Western Powers, who were no more willing to see the Baltic turned into a Russian lake than they had been to see it become a Swedish one in the reign of Charles X. In 1719 therefore, Hanover left the war with the prizes of Bremen and Verden. In 1720 Brandenburg followed suit, for Stettin but only half Swedish Pomerania; France wished her old friend Sweden to maintain at least a toehold in Germany so that she might still enjoy a voice in the affairs of the Empire. Denmark made peace the same year, and was allowed to annex the Duke of Holstein's territories in Slesvig. Poland and Saxony received nothing. Only Russia now remained, and an alliance which Sweden concluded with Britain promised aid against the tsar. But, although Norris's fleet did give some limited assistance, Britain was unwilling to risk an open breach with Peter, whose best customer she was, especially as she was faced at this time with a serious domestic crisis caused by the bursting of the South Sea Bubble. She advised Sweden to make the best terms she could; and Sweden, with Russian warships harrying her coasts, had no choice. At Nystad in Finland in 1721, she surrendered Livonia, Estonia, Ingria and most of Karelia. Russia thereby took her place as the leading power in the Baltic.

[1] See p. 134.

CHAPTER XI

Sweden in the Age of Greatness

The later stages of the Great Northern War undoubtedly imposed a heavy strain on Sweden's economy, but her rapid recovery after Nystad shows that it had remained basically sound. Its very primitiveness may be said to have been its saving grace. For throughout most of the seventeenth century Sweden was as self-supporting as she had been in the Middle Ages. By about 1680, it is true, she was no longer able to grow enough grain to feed her population, and was beginning to rely on supplies from Livonia even when her harvests were good; at Nystad she was fortunate in being able to persuade the Russians to allow some corn to continue to be exported from the province without payment of customs dues. But otherwise she did not come to depend on any of her overseas possessions for her basic needs, and in some ways their loss was a blessing; it rid her of an expensive burden. No great industries were founded on imported raw materials at the mercy of the foreign supplier and enemy privateers.

The overwhelming majority of her people still made their living from agriculture, and conditions on the land in the seventeenth century were much the same as they had been for centuries past—and were to remain for many years to come. Most peasants still used wooden ploughs and harrows; lived in simple wooden cabins without chimneys or glass and furnished as sparsely as in the fifteenth century; and made all their own clothes. There were violent changes in the ownership of land during the period, and these, as has been suggested, deeply affected the status of many peasants. The alienation of Crown property encouraged some at least of the beneficiaries to build up compact estates such as were common in many other parts of Europe, but which had hitherto been rare in Sweden. On these, farming could be attempted on a more ambitious scale with the help of hired labour, and improved methods of cultivation could be tried out. And such demesnes were usually saved by the nobles who suffered from the *reduktion* policy of Charles XI and XII, for they were normally allowed to choose the land to be surrendered, and they naturally preferred to lose their small and scattered properties. All this had, however, little effect on the basic pattern of rural life or on the overall productivity of the soil, which remained low. The population of Sweden at the end of the Great Northern War probably amounted to about a million and a quarter souls; England then contained nearly five times as many.

After agriculture, mining had long been the country's most important occupation. And during the first decades of the seventeenth century copper was king. Indeed it can be claimed that Gustavus Adolphus fought his campaigns with the metal. This does not mean that exports of copper ever approached those of iron either in quantity or value, but Sweden enjoyed almost a European monopoly of it, and the Crown had acquired a substantial interest in the expanding industry. It was on the security of his realm's copper output that Gustavus raised the Dutch loans with which he redeemed Älvsborg from the Danes; and loans were similarly raised to pay for the German enterprise. The fine brass cannon which accompanied his armies were made wholly of Swedish copper. In an effort to restrict the amount of copper exported and so keep prices high on overseas markets, the king introduced a copper coinage for Sweden in 1625. But, although a bi-metallic (copper and silver) currency was retained until the later half of the eighteenth century,[1] the policy did not achieve the desired results; and the coins were so large and heavy that even small sums were difficult to carry, and large amounts needed carts for their conveyance. The productivity of the mine at Falun reached its peak in the middle of the century but then sank rapidly, and in 1687 the workings caved in; the crater which this produced can still be seen. Mining continued in spite of this, but the great days of copper were past.

Iron once more came into its own as Sweden's most important

[1] See p. 148.

product, and by the end of the century it accounted for well over half the value of her total exports, England being by far the best customer. Not only did production of iron increase five-fold, but its quality was improved by the introduction of new techniques, such as stone ovens of French design which could withstand much more intense heat than the older types made of earth and timber. Although Sweden did not enjoy anything like the mono-poly in iron which she did in copper, only Spanish iron could compete with hers for certain purposes, and the constant warfare of the period created a great demand for weapons made from high-grade ore. A College of Mines was set up in 1637, but, while the Crown retained its interest in the field, and sometimes attempted to limit production in order to maintain the level of prices, it generally left the disposal of the end-product to private individuals and rented or sold the mines on royal estates for ready cash. The industry was coming now to be dominated by the owners of the ironworks (*bruk*), where the pig iron, still pro-duced by small-scale craftsmen in Bergslagen, was turned into bars. They alone possessed sufficient capital to invest in the machinery needed for this operation.

For the development of her resources Sweden had always had to rely to a great extent on foreign capital and expertise. In the later Middle Ages these had been provided largely by Germans, but with the decline of Germany's economy in the sixteenth century, their place was taken more and more by Dutchmen and French-speaking Walloons from the southern Netherlands, then under Spanish rule. These arrived in the country in large num-bers at the end of the sixteenth and beginning of the seven-teenth century. The greatest entrepreneur of the period was one of them named Louis De Geer, from Amsterdam. He came to Sweden, where he already had considerable business interests, in 1627, and proceeded to build himself—with the help of lavish government concessions—a vast economic empire. There were few departments with which he was not concerned, but his fortune was made by supplying the needs of the Swedish army from his armaments works at Finspång in Östergötland, where he worked the ore from his own mines, and from his great cloth-factory at Norrköping; this town dates it importance as an industrial centre from this time, and was the port from which De Geer's own fleet of ships carried his products to foreign parts. No wonder that at his death in 1652 he was the richest man in the country. With these (and a few other) exceptions, however, Swedish industry remained on a small scale —too small even to encourage the development of craft guilds outside a few large towns.

These guilds were subjected to close government supervision, but it was upon trade that the State lavished most of its attention. Partly in an attempt to encourage the growth of an indigenous merchant class, Gustavus Adolphus tried to confine all trade to towns, where it could also be more easily controlled and more easily taxed. In 1636 all towns north of Stockholm were forbidden to participate in foreign trade, which it was hoped to limit to a few 'staples' in the south. Neither of these measures were new in concept; they can both be traced back to the Middle Ages. But never before had such vigorous attempts been made to put the ordinances into practice. Swedish ships after 1645 enjoyed a customs rebate, which might be as much as a third if they were of such a type that they could be used as men-of-war. On various occasions through the century, restrictions were placed on the residence of foreign merchants who refused to incur the burdens of Swedish burghers. But all these regulations had very little success. The State fought a losing battle against 'country trade'; the specifications to which a ship had to conform in order to claim customs privileges made it inefficient as a merchantman; and Sweden needed the capital which foreign merchants invested in her enterprises. It was found that Baltic trade had slipped out of the hands of the Hansa towns only to fall into the hands of the Dutch, whose vast merchant fleet the Swedes could never hope to match, and—especially in the later half of the seventeenth century—of the British with their lust for Swedish iron. Swedish tonnage did, however, grow in the last peaceful decades of the century, when the other maritime powers were at war with each other, and Swedish ships even found their way in considerable numbers to the Mediterranean. The volume of Baltic trade in general increased considerably after 1660. Not only was there a great demand for Swedish iron, but the navies of western Europe relied to a large extent on Swedish and Finnish tar and pitch and on Russian hemp and flax, which were exported through Sweden's Baltic provinces, to equip and maintain their fleets. Had it not been for the prosperity of this trade, Sweden could never have withstood the rigours of the Great Northern War as well as she did.

Internal communications in a country as large and as sparsley populated as Sweden was in the seventeenth century constituted a special problem for any government which wished to make its weight felt in every corner of the realm; to foster the economy; and to ensure the swift passage of troops from one province to another. And during this period serious efforts were made to level the main highways and fill in the worst potholes, so that coaches as well as single horses could use them: in 1664 an ordinanace imposed on certain peasants the obligation to maintain stretches of important roads. In addition to this, in the middle 1630's, inns, where horses could be changed and lodging found for the night, began to be set up at distances of about ten miles from each other along the country's main arteries; they were run by peasants who enjoyed exemption from taxation in return. But travel by land remained slow, uncomfortable and even hazardous; heavy rain and spring thaw often made it quite impossible, although a horseman might make reasonable progress in winter-time, when the mud was frozen hard. If possible one travelled by water, with which Sweden was well supplied.

About the same time that some peasants were placed in charge of the new inns, others were given the task of carrying mail along set stretches of the highway. By the 1660's there were seventy-eight of these post-masters, and letters for certain destinations were leaving Stockholm twice a week. Under Charles XII the inns became also post-houses, thus combining the two systems. The improvements in news-bearing and the great hunger for news during the Thirty Years War encouraged the growth of a primitive press, the Dutch having shown the way. The first newspaper published in Sweden appeared in 1645. It was an official journal edited by the chief postmaster in Stockholm, appeared once a week, and under the title of *Post- och Inrikestidningar* (Post and Home News) is still extant.

Interest in trade went hand in hand with interest in urban development and in colonies. Gustavus Adolphus had to re-found Gothenburg after the War of Kalmar, but it soon grew to be the second city of the kingdom with a population of nearly 5,000; it served as one of the main channels for Sweden's direct trade with western Europe and as *the* outlet for iron from the rapidly-developing mines and ironworks of Värmland. Charles XI, as has been seen, built a great naval base at Karlskrona. But these were only the most important of the towns created on royal initiative, and a host of other settlements—Borås in Västergöt-land, Sundsvall and Luleå on the Bothnian coast among them— also date from this period, although most of them remained very small. The growth of trade also led to the expansion of existing towns, especially of the capital, for which this was a boom time. The population of Stockholm rose from under 10,000 in 1600 to nearly six times that figure a hundred years later, and the whole city, including the growing suburbs to the north and south of the island, was replanned about 1640, when the old wall was pulled down. The plan was lavish enough to allow for growth over the next two centuries.

Sweden's activity as a colonial power outside Europe was limited and short-lived. A fort was built in the 1650's at Cabo Corso (now Cape Coast Castle) on the Gold Coast to serve as a base for the Africa Company founded by Louis De Geer, and a settlement was established on the River Delaware in 1638 and named New Sweden. But the former proved more of a liability than an asset and was abandoned to the Dutch in 1663, while in 1655 the latter, having failed also to live up to the Govern-ment's expectations, was absorbed by the adjoining Dutch colony of New Amsterdam (which became New York after its capture by the English less than ten years later). None of the motives which prompted Englishmen and Germans to emigrate to the New World in the seventeenth-century operated in Sweden, although the descendants of the few Swedes who did cross the Atlantic at this time played an important part in the develop-ment of the future United States.

The enormous strengthening of Sweden's ties with Europe in the course of the seventeenth century was reflected in her cul-tural development, which compares very favourably with that during the dark days of the fifteenth and sixteenth centuries. The University of Uppsala was to all intents and purposes re-founded by Gustavus Adolphus, who bequeathed to it his own collection of books to form the nucleus of its library; appointed its first chancellor; founded new chairs; and gave it financial independence by the extremely generous gift in 1624 of over

300 royal estates, the revenue from which still constitutes an important item in its budget. To serve the Baltic Provinces, he also, as one of his last acts, founded a university at Dorpat in Livonia; and eight years later Finland gained one at Åbo. As part of the attempt to integrate the newly-won provinces in the south with the rest of the kingdom and to wean their inhabitants from their former allegiance, a university was established in the old archiepiscopal see of Lund in 1668; it was even more generously endowed from the royal domain than Uppsala had been.

Lower levels of education were also catered for. The new school ordinance which was being discussed at the end of Charles IX's reign was finally published in 1611. It catered for two types of secondary school—a six-class cathedral school for intending clerics, and a four-class lay school in each province. But the latter—even when they were set up—did not cater adequately for the growing need of the Government for educated officials, since, for one thing, they taught, to a lower level, much the same subjects as the seminaries. In 1620, therefore, King Gustavus proposed the establishment of *gymnasia* similar to those existing in Germany, to teach 'modern' subjects like history and living languages, as well as the traditional ones, to a university level. The first of these was opened in Västerås in 1626, and others soon followed; those in Dorpat and Åbo formed the bases for the later universities in these towns. Both Axel Oxenstierna and Queen Christina paid particular attention to educational problems, and in 1649, with the assistance of the Pole Amos Comenius, the foremost educationist of the age, drew up Sweden's first true School Law. This made a clear distinction between the new *gymnasia* or grammar schools, which were coming to replace the old cathedral schools even for the clergy, and the more elementary 'trivial' schools. Primary education was not covered by this act, but the Church Law of 1686 bound every parish clerk to teach reading to the children of the parish and every parson to examine their literacy.

Revision of the existing church laws had long been discussed —notably during the early Regency period. But it was not until the squabbles of the various Estates had been hushed by the introduction of absolute monarchy that any progress could be made. The resulting code is still valid, although it has naturally been modified in detail over the years. Soon afterwards, a new psalm-book was published, and in 1703 there followed a revised version of the Bible in Swedish. All this activity in ecclesiastical affairs reflects Charles XI's belief in the important rôle the Church could play in unifying the nation, as well as in bringing enlightenment to the mass of his subjects.

For the latter there was much need. Especially in the more distant parts of his realm, superstitions of all kinds were rife, and in the early 1670's a particularly obnoxious one developed in some provinces into a veritable epidemic. In 1669 fifteen witches were burnt in Dalarna, and during the following decade hundreds more women were hauled before courts—especially in Dalarna, Bohuslän and Norrland—and accused by terrified peasants of consorting with the Devil and spiriting away children; even the capital was affected. The authorities fought hard against the tide, but could do little in face of the host of witnesses who usually appeared to testify against the accused. The Government finally set up commissions to investigate the phenomenon, and, as a member of one these, a doctor named Urban Hiärne convincingly exposed witchcraft and belief in the power of witches as the symptoms of sick minds. The malady did not suddenly disappear as a result, but persecution of those suspected of practising the 'black art'—by no means confined to Sweden in the seventeenth century—abated rapidly thereafter.

Pride in Sweden's new place among nations—together with the interest taken in and the support given to cultural activities by her rulers in the first half of the seventeenth century—helped to foster the growth of a genuine national literature and a scholarly tradition. The most outstanding representative of the former and the father of modern Swedish poetry was the favourite of Queen Christina, George Stiernhielm. But Stiernhielm was much more than a poet. Like so many men of his age, few fields of knowledge escaped his attention. Perhaps most characteristic of the spirit of the time were his concern to rid the Swedish language of its many foreign—especially its French and German —accretions and his interest in the hitherto-neglected literature in Old Norse and the rune-stones and other ancient monuments of his country. Other Swedes were also attracted to the study of such things. In 1667 a College of Antiquities was established in Stockholm with the job of recording and preserving

Sweden in the Age of Greatness

Sweden's rich heritage, examples of which the architect and later field-marshal Eric Dahlberg had just begun to picture in a series of masterly engravings, which were published after the Great Northern War as *Suecia Antiqua et Hodierna* (Sweden Ancient and Modern).

But the intense patriotism of the age reached its peak in the work of the greatest polymath of them all—Professor Olof Rudbeck (1630–1702). Besides his investigations into practically every branch of science then known (he discovered the lymphatics), Rudbeck published in 1679 the first part of the epitome of Gothicism, a doctrine which seemed far more credible in his age than it had done when it had first emerged in Union times. In *Atlantica*, as his book was called, he claimed that Plato's mythical kingdom of Atlantis could be identified with the ancient realm of the Goths which had its capital at Uppsala. His word was accepted (and not only by Swedes) for many years to come.

In the sixteenth century it had been only the king who could afford to indulge any taste for building and ostentatious luxury he might possess. But the political, economic and social developments of the early seventeenth century encouraged and enabled many of the nobles who benefited from the lavish grants of royal lands and revenues to ape their sovereign. The Swedish countryside began to be covered with distinguished seats, some of which—like General Karl Wrangel's Skokloster (between Sigtuna and Uppsala) and Magnus De la Gardie's Läckö on Lake Vänern (see plate 4)—rivalled the king's own. These were matched by the houses which the same nobles built for themselves in Stockholm. Some of them can still be seen there, although without the gardens with which they were once surrounded; Wrangel's palace on Riddarholmen is now the home of the Svea Supreme Court. Officers who fought in Germany were usually able to fill their rooms with treasures which they had brought back with them as booty; Wrangel bore back with him to Skokloster from Prague the great fourth-century Gothic translation of the New Testament known as the *Codex Argenteus* (Silver Book), which was later carried off by Queen Christina after her abdication and had to be bought back by De la Gardie.[1] Noble warriers like Wrangel might also

[1] It is now proudly displayed in the library of Uppsala University.

THE HOUSE OF VASA

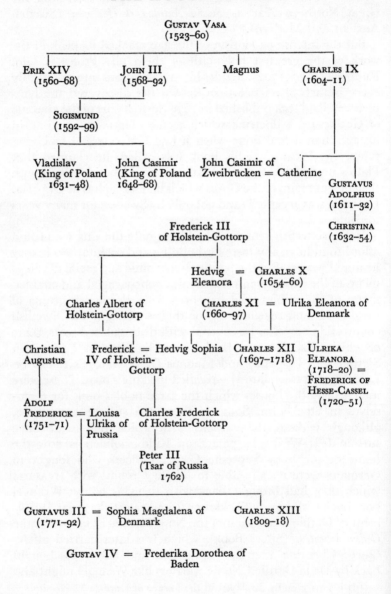

GUSTAV VASA
(1523–60)

ERIK XIV   JOHN III   Magnus   CHARLES IX
(1560–68)   (1568–92)   (1604–11)

SIGISMUND
(1592–99)

Vladislav   John Casimir   John Casimir of
(King of Poland   (King of Poland   Zweibrücken = Catherine
1631–48)   1648–68)   GUSTAVUS
                                                                   ADOLPHUS
                                                                   (1611–32)

                   Frederick III   CHRISTINA
                   of Holstein-Gottorp   (1632–54)

                              Hedvig   =   CHARLES X
                              Eleanora   (1654–60)

        Charles Albert of   CHARLES XI   =   Ulrika Eleanora of
        Holstein-Gottorp   (1660–97)   Denmark

Christian   Frederick = Hedvig Sophia   CHARLES XII   ULRIKA
Augustus   IV of Holstein-   (1697–1718)   ELEANORA
               Gottorp   (1718–20) =
                                                         FREDERICK OF
                                                         HESSE-CASSEL
ADOLF   (1720–51)
FREDERICK = Louisa   Charles Frederick
(1751–71)   Ulrika of of Holstein-Gottorp
            Prussia
                       Peter III
                       (Tsar of Russia
                       1762)

GUSTAVUS III = Sophia Magdalena of   CHARLES XIII
(1771–92)   Denmark   (1809–18)

      GUSTAV IV =   Frederika Dorothea of
                    Baden

132

import foreign manners, like eating with a knife and fork instead of with the fingers!

Meanwhile royal building went on. The palace of Drottningholm—happily not yet swallowed up in a Stockholm suburb—was begun for Charles X's widow in 1662 and betrays the French classical influence which was beginning to modify the exuberance of Baroque in the later half of the century. Dutch classicism made an even earlier appearance, notably in the Riddarhus intended to house the Estate of Nobles in Stockholm; this was completed in the early 1670's but had been designed some twenty years before.

Most of this work had still to be undertaken by imported foreign artists and craftsmen. The Riddarhus was planned largely by two Frenchmen—Simon De la Vallée and his son Jean, who was also employed by Wrangel at Skokloster. And the foremost painter working in Sweden in the period was the German David Klöcker, who arrived in Stockholm in the reign of Charles XI, and was appointed Court painter and ennobled with the name of Ehrenstrahl. Even the architect Nicodemus Tessin the Elder, whose family was to serve Sweden so well in both cultural and political life, had recent Flemish forebears; he worked with De la Vallée at Skokloster and designed Drottningholm. His even more famous son, to whom we owe the present Royal Palace in Stockholm, will figure in a later chapter.[1]

Many Swedes—then and later—regretted the luxury of the age, which, they claimed, was undermining the simple faith and high moral standards of former days. Whatever truth there might be in this, there can be little doubt that the often tasteless ostentation (in dress as well as building) of the richer nobles, which showed up even more glaringly in contrast to the puritan manners of Charles XI and his son, added to the social tensions which enabled the former to engage the help of the lower orders in humbling the magnates.

[1] See p. 182.

CHAPTER XII

The Era of Liberty

By the death of Charles XII in 1718, absolute monarchy as
a form of government had been thoroughly discredited
with most sections of Swedish society; only the peasants
favoured the retention of some degree of royal power as a
bulwark against the pretensions of the nobility. The noble
bureaucrats had become increasingly restive as they found
themselves deprived of all initiative by the absent king, and
were in a good position to engineer at least a return to the
constitution of the early seventeenth century as represented
by the Form of Government; this would give them a dominating place in political life through instruments already in existence.

A disputed succession strengthened their hand still further;
they could make a restriction of royal power a condition of their
allegiance. Of the two pretenders, Charles XII's sister Ulrika
Eleanora had a rather better claim in law, was more popular
than the young Duke of Holstein, and—of greatest importance
in the circumstances—was far better prepared to take over
power at the king's death. Even so, she had to agree to considerable limitations on the prerogative before the Council
would recognize her right to the throne, and then had to submit
her claims to the Estates. The latter proceeded to draw up a
constitution which put an end to the last traces of absolutism.
Ulrika accepted this, and was proclaimed queen, but she
still proved too independent for her subjects, and it was proposed that the crown should be offered to her consort on
condition that he would consent to modifications in the Constitution which would reduce still further the monarch's rights.
By the middle of 1720, while the Russian fleet was hammering

at Sweden's coasts, all was at last settled on these terms. The
Era of Liberty was born.

Under the Constitution, the composition of the *Riksdag* remained substantially unaltered. The lesser nobles succeeded in
1719 in procuring the abolition of the division of their House
into three classes, but it continued to be made up of about 2,000
heads of families or their proxies, of whom only a small proportion actually attended except on very important occasions. The
Estate of the clergy consisted of the bishops plus representatives
of the lower clergy from each diocese (no longer, as in earlier
times, from the cathedral chapters), to a total of around 50.
A majority of the 80–90 burghers who attended the *Riksdag* at
the beginning of the period were town officials and merchants;
Stockholm sent 10, Gothenburg 3, and the smaller towns one or
two according to size. The tax-paying peasants—that is those
who either owned the land they worked or were tenants of the
Crown—elected, usually indirectly, one representative for each
hundred—about 150 in all. The latter did not have equal status
with the other three Houses, for their chairman was chosen, not
by themselves alone, but in consultation with their 'betters'; and
they were generally excluded from the Secret Committee. This
was the most important of the committees, made up of members
of the Estates, by which much of the work of the *Riksdag* was
done, and which carried out its decisions; not only were the
peasants thought to be too ignorant to be able to make a contribution to the discussion of foreign and financial policy, with
which the Secret Committee was mainly concerned, but their
known royalist sympathies made them suspect. On all the committees the nobles had twice as many members as any of the
other Estates, a true reflection of their importance in political
life. But votes were taken, as in the *Riksdag* as a whole, by
Estates and not by head; the consent of three Estates was
necessary before any measure could become law. Under the
terms of the Constitution the Estates were to meet, for an undefined period, every three years, and could be called more
often in emergencies.

The size of the Council was limited to twenty-four members of
the nobility, who were excluded from their House as long as they
held office. Vacancies were to be filled by the King-in-Council
from a list of three candidates presented by the Estates, who

alone had the power to dismiss a councillor. The respective spheres of the Estates and the Council were never clearly defined. Although the latter was expected to carry out the instructions agreed upon by the Estates, and could be impeached as a body for not doing so, these instructions were often open to various interpretations, which might give a bold *Råd* much greater scope for initiative than it had been intended to have, and there was a multitude of matters on which it had been given no instructions to guide it. Much of the history of the following half century can be written in terms of a struggle between the *Råd* and the *Riksdag* for the dominant influence over policy.

Rarely did this struggle involve the Crown. Whatever the original intentions of the framers of the Constitution may have been, the king's power was reduced to a minimum. He was still free to appoint the Court officials, to fill the clerical livings in his gift and to confer titles of nobility. But the House of Nobles could decide whom it would admit, and all other important appointments had to be approved by the Council, where the sole privilege the king possessed was two votes. He had no truly independent authority at all. After attempting during the first few years of his reign to break his chains by courting popularity among the peasants, and being as a result threatened by the other Estates with dire consequences if he continued to do so, Frederick gave up; thereafter, for thirty years, he contented himself with being a mere titular Head-of-State.

The first twenty years of the reign were dominated by the Chancellor, Arvid Horn. But it was not until the *Riksdag* of 1726–27 that his position even seemed secure, and it never really was so. During the first few years he had to deal both with considerable social unrest, caused by the attempts of the nobility to profit from the situation to extend its privileges still further, and with the threat from the numerous supporters of the Duke of Holstein-Gottorp. The nobles secured a number of important concessions during the session of 1719, including the compulsory sale of all 'noble land' (that is land enjoying the tax-privileges granted to a noble) held by non-nobles and preferential treatment in appointments to even minor offices. But in 1720 the unprivileged Estates organized themselves for a counter-attack, which regained most of the ground lost; no more noble demesne land might be bought by non-nobles, but that already in non-

noble hands could remain so, and, while the nobles retained
their monopoly of high office, for lesser posts they would in future
have to compete on equal terms with their inferiors. So ended
the first of a series of social struggles which grew more intense as
the century wore on, and which played a large part in political
developments. The threat from the Holsteiners was made much
more serious by the international situation after Nystad, for the
Duke's claims were backed by the tsar, whose daughter he
married in 1725. Peter died in this year, but his wife, who
succeeded him as Catherine I, continued to support her son-in-
law, and for a time war threatened. But the Russian menaces
lessened support for the Holsteiners inside Sweden, and in the
Riksdag of 1726–27 Horn, who had adopted a rather non-
committal attitude hitherto, turned on them and had their
leaders expelled from the Council. With the death of Catherine
in 1727, Russian support for the Duke came to an abrupt end,
and the danger to Sweden from this quarter passed for the time
being.

Horn's power depended to a large extent on maintaining the
independence of the *Råd* without conflicting with the terms
of the Constitution. But this body was as unlike a modern cabinet as was that of eighteenth-century England; it always contained the Chancellor's enemies as well as his friends, enemies
he could not get rid of without the co-operation of the Estates.
He made no attempt to build up a party, but looked for support
largely to the higher ranks of the nobility and to the clergy,
whose struggle against the spread of the new Pietist Movement
within the Church[1] he supported. He was also favoured by the
economic prosperity which marked most of his period in office,
and by the war-weariness which fitted in well with his cautious
foreign policy.

Sweden made a remarkable recovery from the Great
Northern War, a recovery which contrasts strikingly with the
depression which followed it in Denmark, one of the victors. The
Chancellor himself took comparatively little interest in economic affairs, but his colleagues in the Colleges of Trade and
Mines applied a mildly protectionist policy, which contributed
much to the prosperity of the epoch. The merchant fleet grew,
until in 1734 there were as many Swedish as foreign merchant-

[1] See p. 180.

men sailing the Baltic, and in 1731 an East India Company was founded in Gothenburg, and flourished. The application of economy measures, including the writing-off of State debts, the farming out of customs dues and the reduction of the military establishment, brought some individual hardship and criticism, but resulted in a healthy financial situation and a steady ex-change-rate for Swedish currency abroad.

Horn's foreign policy was based on friendship with all the great powers of Europe, but especially with Britain, who was the best customer for Sweden's iron and who was, after 1716, allied to Sweden's old friend France. In the crisis on the Conti-nent which began in 1725 with the conclusion of an alliance between Spain and Austria in opposition to Anglo-French inter-ests and the formation of the Alliance of Hanover in reply to it, the Chancellor persuaded his colleagues to join the latter; the fact that Russia, at this time still backing the Duke of Holstein's claims to the Swedish throne, sided with Austria and Spain made it natural for Sweden to look to the Western Powers for support. Even so, it was not until 1727, when the crisis was nearly past, that Sweden committed herself. Horn did not mean to antagonize Russia more than seemed absolutely necessary for his country's safety, and with Catherine I's death the way was open for a *rapprochement*, of which he took full advantage.

What, however, was to be his policy when, in 1731, the Anglo-French alliance broke up and Britain gravitated towards Russia? He tried to retain the favour of both camps, but this became increasingly difficult, and his domestic enemies became increasingly vocal. A new generation was emerging, to which the horrors of the Great Northern War were mere history, but which was fully conscious of the position in Europe that Sweden had then lost; among its members the young noble officers were particularly vociferous. To them Horn's policy seemed timid and ignoble, wholly unworthy of their country's great past; and when war broke out in 1733 over the succession of the Polish throne, they regarded it as an ideal opportunity for Sweden to side with France against Austria and Russia, re-conquer the Baltic Provinces and so regain the dominance in the North which she had once enjoyed. These *revanchistes* were joined in their criticisms of the Chancellor by many of the burghers, who wanted even greater protection for trade and industry, and whom jealousy of Britain's maritime power made pro-French. In the *Riksdag* of 1734 Horn had to contend with strong opposition from both these Estates, who were encouraged by the French ambassador in Stockholm; the Secret Committee even recommended the conclusion of an alliance with France. The Chancellor's influence was, however, still powerful enough to prevent the Council from committing itself to any definite action.

The conclusion of peace preliminaries between France and Austria in 1735 helped to relieve the tension, but in the same year Horn renewed the alliance he had made with Russia in 1724 under pressure from the Holsteiners, and the French replied by refusing to ratify a subsidy treaty to which they had previously agreed. As a consequence, attacks on Horn and his followers, whom his enemies were beginning to refer to as 'Night-Caps' (soon abbreviated to 'Caps') because of their apparent sleepy neglect of the country's best interests, grew fiercer. The press and the stage were mobilized in a great propaganda offensive against them, and a regular election campaign of a new kind was launched in preparation for the meeting of the Estates in 1738. Horn's opponents organized themselves into a true party of 'Hats' (so called because of the tricorns worn by the young officers), and carried the Estates of the nobles and burghers. Horn, old and sickly as he was, gave up the struggle. He was allowed to retire from office on full pension amid the plaudits even of his enemies, who were compelled to acknowledge the very real services he had rendered the realm in a difficult period of her history.

His resignation did not, however, mean that his colleagues also had to withdraw from the *Råd*. The only way in which the complexion of this body could be changed was by judicial process, or the threat of it. Five of the Cap members were therefore charged by the Estates with having disobeyed their instructions by renewing the Russian alliance; and in face of this, four of them retired. But this was not enough for the Diet, which declared them—together with their recalcitrant companion— expelled from the Council for misdemeanour. In this way the dominance of the *Riksdag* over the *Råd* was reasserted, but the exact relationship between the two remained as loosely defined as ever, a fact which goes a long way to explain the bitterness of party politics in the years to come.

The five vacancies on the Council were immediately filled with nominees of the Hats, and the Hat Count Karl Gyllenborg, the envoy who had been arrested in London in 1717, was made Chancellor in Horn's place. The latter had already been forced before his fall to conclude a new subsidy treaty with France, and the new Government began at once to plan a war of revenge against Russia; a certain Major Malcolm Sinclair was sent to Constantinople to negotiate an alliance with the Turks. On his way back across Europe, in the middle of 1739, he was murdered by Russian agents, and the Hats naturally made full use of the incident to whip up Russophobia in Sweden to a new pitch of intensity. Unfortunately for them, France did not want a Baltic war at this stage and reacted coolly to Swedish proposals. But in 1740 the War of the Austrian Succession opened with an attack on Austria by the new King of Prussia, young Frederick II. Russia came to the aid of the empress, and France looked to Sweden to create a diversion against the tsar in the North. At the beginning of 1741 a new subsidy treaty was concluded which committed Sweden to declare war on Russia.

Militarily she was quite unprepared for war, but she hoped to benefit from a plot which she was helping to hatch in St. Petersburg with the object of replacing the reigning tsar by Peter I's daughter Elisabeth. When the *coup* proved successful and Elisabeth ascended the Russian throne, the slow Swedish advance on her capital was halted, and an armistice was arranged by the local commander in the expectation that the new ruler would show her gratitude for Sweden's support of her pretensions in a tangible way. But the tsarina turned on her helpers, renounced the armistice and, in June 1742, launched a full-scale attack on Finland. The thoroughly-demoralized Swedish army was rolled back to Helsingfors,[1] where it surrendered, and the whole country was soon in Russian hands; the Hats seemed doomed, and all the fears of Arvid Horn, who died just before the final disaster, to be justified. In the Estates which now met, the Caps, organized for the first time as a party with Russian support, captured the House of Nobles; the Hats were left with a majority among the burghers alone. Only by exploiting the question of the

[1] The Swedish form of the more familiar Helsinki.

succession to the Swedish throne were they able to save themselves.

Queen Ulrika Eleanora had died at the end of 1741 without children. Many officers had already come out strongly in favour of the claims of the new Duke of Holstein-Gottorp to be her husband's heir, and at the end of 1742 the Estates agreed to recognize him as such. The tsarina had, however, already adopted him as her own heir and intimated to the Swedish delegation suing for peace in St. Petersburg that his cousin Adolf Frederick would be equally acceptable to her as their king. When she backed this up with an offer to return part of Finland should he be chosen, the Hats agreed in the hope of reaching a swift settlement. There was, however, strong support among the peasantry for the candidacy of the Crown Prince of Denmark, and in the middle of 1743, while peace negotiations were still going on in Åbo, the peasants of Dalarna, who had been hard hit by the war, marched on Stockholm to force their choice on the Government. The Russians, fearful of a new Kalmar Union, responded by agreeing to restrict their territorial claims to the south-east of Finland, and this the Swedish negotiators accepted. News of the conclusion of peace put new heart into the *Råd*; the band of peasants, which was encamped in the streets of the capital, was easily routed and its leaders executed.

The mild terms of the peace and dissensions among the Caps saved their rivals, who were able to consolidate their power still further in the next few years. In the *Riksdag* of 1746 they recaptured the House of Nobles, and five of their number were elected to the Council. The policy adopted by Russia immediately after Åbo also played into their hands. Elisabeth had envisaged Adolf Frederick as her puppet. But he was encouraged by the Hats around him and by his ambitious wife Louisa Ulrika, the sister of Frederick of Prussia, to assert his independence of St. Petersburg, and in revenge the tsarina attempted to undermine his authority and even to replace him by a more tractable prince. But so open did her ambassador's interference in Swedish politics become, that even many Caps were alienated. The Hats were encouraged to strike at a number of Cap leaders, who were tried for entertaining treasonable communication with Russia. The king's physician, a Scot named Blackwell, was executed, and in 1748 the British envoy in Stockholm was expelled, ostensibly for trying to help one of the accused; Anglo-Swedish diplomatic relations were not resumed for another fifteen years. With the end of the European war in the same year, Russia was freed to make a fresh attempt to break the hold of the Hats, and gathered troops on the Finnish frontier. But, while France sprang to her ally's defence, Russia could find no support from other powers and was forced to climb down. In 1751 King Frederick died, and Adolf Frederick came to the throne without incident.

Meanwhile the Hats, led since the death of Gyllenborg in 1746 by the pleasure-loving architect Carl Tessin, had learnt their lesson. They turned from thoughts of revenge and military glory to the task of building up Sweden's defences, especially in Finland, where work was begun on the great fortress of Sveaborg outside Helsingfors. Their position seemed to be as secure as they could ever hope to make it, and the *Riksdag* of 1751–52 was the quietest since the adoption of the Constitution. But a new threat to their power was already beginning to make its appearance.

The new king would, if left to himself, have rested content with such powers as he had, but his able wife was determined to raise the prestige of the Swedish Crown to that enjoyed by her brother in Prussia, where there were no troublesome Estates to thwart his will. At first she hoped that the Hats might be sympathetic to her aspirations, but she was rapidly disillusioned, and set about forming an independent Court party, which appeared for the first time in the *Riksdag* of 1751. Only among the peasantry, however, did its claims find an echo. Tessin, it is true, was dismissed, but only to be replaced by another Hat, and the Crown lost to the Estates the power of appointing the Chancellor. The queen betrayed her frustration by openly insulting members of the *Råd*, and when the king's candidates were passed over by his councillors, she persuaded him to leave the posts concerned vacant. In face of this menace, the Hats and the Caps drew together, and in the *Riksdag* of 1755 agreed on counter-measures. New regulations governing appointments were passed which bound the king's hands more tightly, and the Council was even authorized to employ a rubber facsimile of the royal signature with which to by-pass the king's veto. Having failed to improve the Crown's position constitutionally,

Louisa turned with characteristic energy to extra-legal means. A *coup* was planned to take place in Stockholm, and money with which to bribe and to buy arms was raised on the security of some of the Crown jewels. But too many people became involved, and, in the middle of June, before even the date of the attempt had been fixed, the whole scheme was revealed to the Government. Eight of the ringleaders were arrested and executed; the royal couple was subjected to a rating from a delegation of the Estates; and an act was drawn up adjudging them worthy of deposition, with the implication that the sentence would be carried out if any similar attempt were to be made in the future. To guard further against such a contingency, the *Råd* was given the authority to assume full power in an emergency, and the governor of the capital and the colonels of the Guards regiments—key figures at such times—were to be appointed by the Estates. Never before had the Crown been so humiliated or rendered so powerless.

The Hats appeared once more to be firmly in the saddle, but in fact their power was about to enter a period of rapid decline, a decline which can be dated with fair precision from Sweden's entry into the Seven Years War in 1757. In spite of the weakening of *revanche* sentiment among the Hat leaders, they still valued their traditional ties with France, and when the latter called for help against Prussia, now her enemy, the Chancellor, Baron Anders von Höpken, was forced by his colleagues to consent, first to dispatch a large body of troops to Pomerania, and then to enter the war. Those who urged him on hoped that victory might once more bring Sweden control of the mouth of the River Oder. But, in spite of all the money which had been spent on the fortification of the frontiers, the army itself was even less well prepared than it had been in 1741, and on this occasion there was no enthusiasm at home for the war; the Court was openly pro-Prussian. Sweden did now have powerful allies in the shape of Russia, France and Austria, but these failed to co-operate effectively, and the Prussians repelled every Swedish attack. Spring after weary spring the Swedes would penetrate a few miles into Brandenburg territory, only to be forced to withdraw again every autumn having accomplished nothing; the Commander-in-Chief was replaced no less than five times without any consequent improvement in the situation.

Then, in 1762, Russia suddenly changed sides and Sweden hurried to make peace on the basis of the *status quo*. The disastrous course of the war was reflected in the composition of the *Riksdag* which met in 1760. Once more it was only among the burghers that the Hats had a firm majority; and Höpken had to retire. But the success of the Caps was limited. The Hats managed to throw all the blame for the disaster on two members of the *Råd*, who alone were dismissed and replaced by Caps.

The Hat's hold was, however, also being undermined by the failure of their economic policy. They had come to power with a programme which called for a stricter application of mercantilist principles, and these they had put into practice; industries were protected by ever higher tariff walls and encouraged by large loans from the State. But much of the money was lent to quite unsuitable enterprises on little or no security, and a reckless issue of notes by the Estates Bank caused a rapid inflation. This was becoming apparent even before the outbreak of the Pomeranian War, but it was the war which brought the crisis to a head. French subsidies were far from adequate to cover the cost of the military operations, and the Government had to resort to new taxes, more paper money, debasement of the coinage, and credit stretched to its uttermost. In the ten years after 1755 prices doubled; the value of the *riksdaler* on foreign exchanges was halved; and the national debt climbed to a height it had not reached since the Great Northern War. After the war, the situation was made still worse by a general depression in European trade.

In the course of many years of continuous Hat rule the régime had become stagnant. Reform projects were discussed only to be pushed aside; the *Riksdag* confined its discussions more and more to the business of appointments to public offices; and the Civil Service became independent and corrupt. The ground was thus well prepared for the emergence of a new and vigorous party of reform; and emerge it did at the end of the Seven Years War. Usually referred to as the Younger Caps, its members' links with the earlier group were rather tenuous, except in the field of foreign policy, where they again favoured friendship with Russia. Their economic policy expressed the growing criticism of governmental control to be found in many parts of Western Europe at this time. They wanted a lessening

—although not a complete withdrawal—of State aid to industry; freer trade; the ending of monopolies like the overseas trading companies and the handicraft guilds; and stricter economy in expenditure. This was a platform likely to appeal to the smaller independent manufacturers and merchants, who also supported, with the lower clergy and peasants, a new social policy. It would be misleading to call this democratic, but it did aim at the reduction of the nobles' privileges, especially their monopoly of certain offices and the tax-exemptions granted to their lands.

By the time the Diet met again in 1765, the Hats were completely discredited, and their rivals won control of all four Estates. The Chancellor and another Hat leader were compelled by threats to retire, and five more councillors were dismissed for their part in the decision to go to war in 1757. The abolition of censorship on all except religious works was, from a long-term point of view, probably the most striking measure adopted by the new régime, and placed Sweden among the few European countries in the eighteenth century who enjoyed completed freedom of expression. But the Caps' main concern was naturally the economic situation. Here the remedies they adopted unfortunately only made the disease worse. Sudden restriction of credit brought a general slowing down of growth, and the recall of loans by the Bank caused considerable distress; the leak of a plan to reduce the number of notes in circulation and increase their backing in silver until they could be redeemed at par led to hoarding; and unemployment figures soared. The hopes of the Court and the Hats rose once more, and they united to demand the calling of an extraordinary meeting of the *Riksdag* so as to exploit the discontent. When the Caps hesitated, the king, encouraged by the Hats, abdicated (though only for a few days) and refused to conduct any business. The Caps replied by threatening to use the rubber stamp, but the Civil Service, which they had failed to clear of Hat supporters, then went on strike.

There seemed no alternative between anarchy, which would benefit only the extreme royalists, and a surrender to the Hats' demands. The Estates were therefore summoned at the beginning of 1769, and met after a campaign in which foreign interference and bribery reached new heights. As was to be expected, the Hats won an overwhelming victory after exploiting to its utmost the Caps' blatant reliance on Russian aid. Adolf Frederick had hoped that the victors would support a restoration of at least some degree of royal power in gratitude for his help, but it soon became apparent that they had no intention of doing so, and by the king's death in 1771 the Court had broken with both parties.

The new king, Gustavus III, was in Paris at the time of his father's demise, but he returned with all speed to Sweden, determined to take advantage of the confusion there to limit the powers of the Estates. As long ago as 1767, when he had first begun regularly to attend meetings of the *Råd*, he had advocated a military *coup* to restore the balance and now had a firm promise of French support for any action of this kind which he might consider necessary. Internationally the situation was extremely favourable for him; Russia and Prussia, the powers most likely to interfere in defence of the old constitution, which they considered to be the best means of keeping Sweden weak, were occupied in planning the partition of Poland. In Sweden men of all classes had grown tired of the party squabbles of recent years and were prepared for the re-establishment of a strong executive to prevent their country's sharing the fate of Poland. The peasants were traditionally royalist; the merchants had been hard hit by the trade depression; the manufacturers and miners by the Caps' deflationary policy; the farmers by the restriction of credit; and the nobles were seriously alarmed by the Caps' social programme. After making what seem to have been genuine but vain efforts to reconcile the actions, Gustavus fell back on the idea of direct action. He drew up a plan under which military revolts on his behalf were to break out in Scania and Finland to be followed by a *coup d'etat* led by himself in Stockholm. The execution of the revolts was, however, delayed, and the young king was left to perform his part alone on 19th August 1772. With the help of the Guards, he did so with complete success, and without the shedding of a drop of blood. The Council was arrested and forced to resign. Then the Estates were hastily assembled and presented with a new constitution, which they obediently adopted.

CHAPTER XIII

The Reign of Gustavus III

The Constitution of 1772 was a compromise—an attempt to strike a balance between the extremes of the epoch which ended with Gustavus's *coup d'état* and the earlier Caroline absolutism. Under it the consent of the *Riksdag* was still necessary for the raising of extraordinary taxes and for the launching of an offensive war; it continued to have some say in legislation and could propose new laws; it retained control of the Bank. On the other hand, the speakers of the four Estates were in future to be appointed by the Crown, and the Diet to meet only when the king should choose to call it. Further, the Council was made responsible to him alone, needed to be consulted by him only in specified cases and became in practice a group of his supporters; these were often able men, but their influence on policy was limited. How long such a balance could be maintained would depend largely on the nature of the monarch's ambitions, for the wording of the Constitution left him ample scope to extend his powers still further. And it soon became obvious that Gustavus intended to take full advantage of every opening provided to increase his control. Opposition only made him more determined to do so.

After the stagnation of the later years of Hat rule and the chaos at the end of the 60's, practically every field of Swedish public life was crying out for reform, and Gustavus took up the task with genuine enthusiasm and concern for the welfare of his subjects, as well, it must be added, as for the enhancement of his personal glory. Much of the programme he adopted had been envisaged either by the Hats or the Caps, but they had lacked both the authority and the security which were needed to carry through the necessary measures. In this respect at least, the new king was the heir of the parties whose very names he outlawed.

A searching enquiry into the Civil Service was initiated, and many of the abuses which had become ingrained under party rule were swept away; incompetent officials were dismissed and a serious attempt made to raise standards of honesty and devotion to duty. Destitution in the countryside, following a series of bad harvests and made worse by a rapid increase in the population, was alleviated to some extent by wholesale imports of foreign grain and a ban on its use for the distilling of corn-brandy (*brännvin*), a drink which had grown rapidly in popularity since the middle of the seventeenth century. For the primary job of putting the realm's finances in order Gustavus was fortunate in having the assistance of his very gifted Secretary of Commerce, Johan Liljencrantz. He negotiated a foreign loan and used it to enable the Bank to buy up its notes at half their face value and to mint a new silver coinage; the copper standard introduced by Gustavus Adolphus was abandoned at last. In accordance with the new liberal doctrines being preached by the French physiocrats, Liljencrantz freed the internal trade in corn and removed many of the other State and instititutional controls which had been imposed on Sweden's economic life; entry into the handicraft guilds was made much easier. To ensure the country's independence, work on defence was given a high priority. A committee was set up to supervise reforms in both the army and navy; the great fortress of Sveaborg was at last completed, and the fleet built up to a strength of twenty-six line-of-battle-ships and twelve large frigates, many of them designed by Frederick af Chapman, the son of an Englishman who had settled in Gothenburg.

In other spheres Gustavus betrayed the influence on him of the ideas of the French *philosophes*—the godfathers of the so-called Enlightenment of the second half of the eighteenth century, who called for the establishment of a more rational and humane society; for the sweeping away of traditions which impeded progress; and for greater respect for the rights of the individual. Justice was made speedier and less corrupt; punishment was rationalized; the death penalty was lifted from certain crimes; and torture, in no period much employed in Sweden, was done away with altogether. Hospitals and orphanages were founded under royal patronage. Foreign non-Lutheran Christians were granted freedom of worship for the first time, and in 1782 Jews were allowed to settle—subject to certain restrictions —in some large towns, although the prospect of the wealth which both groups were expected to bring into the country was as strong a motive behind these measures as humanitarianism.

For a time all seemed to be going well for Gustavus. The previous régime had been thoroughly discredited, and the young king's popularity was enhanced by his personal charm and by the fact that he was the first monarch to have been born in Sweden since Charles XII; even his name helped him, by recalling periods of national prosperity and greatness. Before the *Riksdag* which he called in 1778 he gave a full account of his stewardship, and the Estates responded with fulsome professions of devotion. But appearances were deceptive; the storm-clouds were already beginning to gather.

Some causes of discontent were outside the king's control; a series of bad harvests began again in 1783 and helped to turn the peasants against the Government. But for others he must shoulder at least part of the responsibility. He chose the autumn of 1783 to set out on a long and expensive tour of Italy and France. Lavish outlay on the Court and, more excusably, on defence undid much of Liljencrantz's work in the earlier years of the reign, and some of the measures which were adopted to remedy the financial situation brought further criticism. The distilling of spirits had been made a monopoly of the State, and this involved widespread house-to-house searches for illicit stills, an invasion of their privacy which the peasants much resented. The clergy also condemned the step as an encouragement to intemperance; and they had grievances of their own—royal benefices were being sold for large sums, which went into courtiers' pockets.

But the most serious cause of unrest was Gustavus's growing absolutism; the *Råd* was increasingly ignored in favour of individual secretaries, *ad hoc* committees and favourites, and in the early 1780's several of the king's original advisers were replaced by still more tractable men. The class which was particularly sensitive to these developments was the most dangerous politically. The nobles felt themselves condemned to impotence in

State affairs; they seemed to be serving as mere decorations to add lustre to the monarch.

It is paradoxical that it should have been the Swedish aristocracy who became the king's bitterest enemies, for no one prized birth more than he. At Court it conferred absolute priority; officials who had given their country many years of faithful service had often to give way to young men who had nothing else to recommend them but membership of one of the old noble families. That Gustavus tried to make his Court, consciously modelled as it was on the French king's at Versailles, the heart of political life and an instrument of policy did little to assuage the resentment felt by many who attended it at being treated as courtiers and nothing more; everything was directed towards the enhancement of the royal status, and an elaborate etiquette was evolved to protect the dignity of the king's family. Many also resented the extravagance which all this involved, and criticized the love of pleasure and the frivolity which were encouraged.

A constant tightening of the censorship, which a new Press Law in 1774 enabled the Government to impose, made it more and more difficult for the Opposition to express itself. The only real outlet left to it was the *Riksdag*, but Gustavus proved singularly unwilling to call it; the Estates assembled on only four occasions during the twenty years of his reign. In an attempt, however, to replenish his store of popularity, which he realized was being rapidly dissipated, and to secure some help in the worsening economic situation, he did finally summon them to meet in 1786. He seems to have hoped that, in exchange for a few minor concessions and the sacrifice of the most unpopular of his favourites, he could persuade his subjects to grant him even wider powers than he already possessed. If so, he was soon sadly disillusioned. The noble bureaucracy was ranged solidly against him, and its example was followed by the unprivileged Estates. Most of the Government's proposals—for the introduction of a State tobacco monopoly; the abolition of the death penalty for infanticide; and various financial reforms, among others—were decisively defeated. New taxes were granted, but for four years only. It was a bitter humiliation, and Gustavus now determined to try to win over the clergy, burghers and peasants to his side and, with their help, to crush the recalcitrant nobles, whom he knew to form the heart of the Opposition. At the same time, he sought to restore his prestige by conducting a successful foreign policy.

The latter was always his chief interest, and during the 1780's it became more and more his one concern; reform, except in the sphere of defence, ground to a halt, and in some cases was even reversed. For several years after his accession, the king had been able, with the help of his experienced ex-Hat Chancellor, Ulrik Scheffer, to maintain close links with France, with whom a subsidy treaty was concluded in 1773, while remaining on outwardly friendly terms with potentially his most dangerous enemy—Russia. In 1780, during the American War of Independence, in which many Swedish officers fought as volunteers on the side of the colonists, Gustavus joined Catherine the Great's League of Armed Neutrality, which sought to protect neutral shipping from interference by British warships and privateers. He was helped also by the fact that the tsarina was embroiled with the Turks, and Prussia with Austria; Denmark was isolated, and the Opposition in Sweden deprived of any hope of foreign support.

Scheffer, however, resigned his office in 1783, and no successor was appointed. This left the king free to develop some ambitious schemes which had long occupied his mind. In many ways he was well-fitted to conduct relations with foreign states, but his incurable romanticism prompted him to try to imitate the exploits of his more illustrious ancestors and to regain a dominant place for Sweden in the Baltic, without taking sufficient account of the resources at his disposal. First he contemplated an attack on Denmark with the object of winning Norway from her, but when, on a visit to St. Petersburg, he sought from Catherine a pledge of her neutrality in such a war, he was sharply snubbed and had to abandon the project. His European tour already referred to was undertaken principally in search of new allies, but in this respect it was a failure; the international situtation was becoming less favourable for him. Even France was piqued that Sweden had not given her more active support in the American war, and was becoming more and more preoccupied with the internal difficulties which led to the outbreak of revolution in 1789; she did agree to conclude a new defensive alliance, but this involved only a third of the extra annual subsidy for which Gustavus had asked. Russia made peace with the Turks, and her relations with Sweden were soured by Gustavus's refusal to join her alliance with Denmark. He also suspected Catherine of encouraging the desire of a number of Finns for the independence of their country, and finally came to the conclusion that war with her was inevitable. The Russian ambassador in Stockholm subsidized the Opposition in the *Riksdag* of 1786.

When war broke out again between Russia and Turkey in September 1787, the king felt that his hour had struck. But his efforts to interest other powers in an attack on Russia came to naught, and Sweden was ill prepared for an armed conflict with such an adversary. The financial situation was most unsatisfactory, and in spite of the activities of the Committee of National Defence, the army was poorly equipped and incompetently led. Gustavus had, however, made up his mind. The provision in the Constitution of 1772 which obliged him to seek the approval of the Estates before launching an offensive war did not prove a serious obstacle. In June 1788 an incident was arranged on the Finnish border to make the Russians appear to be the aggressors, and an ultimatum was presented in St. Petersburg demanding the return of all Finnish territory to Sweden. This was of course rejected, and Swedish troops crossed the frontier. The plan was for the Swedish fleet to neutralize Catherine's and then for a landing to be made near the Russian capital. Everything thus depended on control of the Gulf of Finland. But this was never obtained. An encounter between the two navies ended indecisively, and the idea of a combined operation had to be given up. A group of noble officers then seized the opportunity to wreak their vengeance on Gustavus for all his sins against their class, and in August sent a letter to the tsarina offering to open peace negotiations. They followed this by a meeting on the estate of Anjala just behind the front line, at which they drew up a justification of their treachery.

But the Anjala conspiracy and collapse of the front in the east was not Gustavus's only problem. His main fleet was blockaded by the Russians in the harbour of Sveaborg; his realm was in the grip of an economic depression; and Denmark, when called upon by Russia to fulfil the terms of a defensive alliance, sent troops from Norway against Gothenburg. Deeply depressed as the king was by the disastrous beginning of the war, his reactions were swift and resolute; the Danish attack allowed him to appeal to the patriotism of his countrymen in the face of a traditional enemy and to rally them round the Crown. And the tide began to turn in his favour. Britain and Prussia, both unhappy at the prospect of a further extension of Russian power in northern Europe, exerted diplomatic pressure on Denmark, whose heart had never been in the struggle, and persuaded her to agree to an armistice under their mediation. Catherine contemptuously rejected the advances made by the mutineers in Finland, and their action caused a public revulsion against the nobility as a whole, which enabled Gustavus to deal the blow which he had been planning since the humiliation of 1786. At the end of 1788 the situation was such that he could, with high hopes, do what the Opposition had been demanding he should do only a few months earlier—call a *Riksdag*. It met in January 1789.

As was to be expected, criticism from the nobles was as fierce as ever, but they now found themselves completely isolated; the Government carried all the other Estates. This was due not only to Anjala, but also to Gustavus's successful wooing of the unprivileged orders since the previous meeting. The clergy had been granted a fairer system of promotion; the peasants were once more allowed to distil spirits; and the abandonment of the plan to create a State tobacco monopoly helped to pacify the burghers. At the opening of the session, the king proposed the appointment of a secret committee to examine the situation, and when the nobles tried to limit its powers, he called all the Estates into his presence, harangued the recalcitrants and dismissed them. He then proposed to the clergy, burghers and peasants an amendment to the Constitution accompanied by a reduction of the nobles' privileges. The result was the Act of Union and Security, which swept away most of the constitutional safeguards which had remained after the *coup d'état* of 1772, and imposed on Sweden a new form of absolute monarchy.

The Estates were to lose all initiative in legislation, and while new loans and taxes were still to require their consent, grants were to be made for an indefinite period; in practice the king was left ample means for raising money without consulting his subjects. He was also empowered to launch an offensive war on his own initiative and to appoint and dismiss officials as he saw fit. The judicial powers vested in the *Råd* were transferred to a new body, the Royal Supreme Court, and the size of the *Råd* itself was to be determined by the Crown. The unprivileged Estates approved the Act without demur, but in spite of the arrest of its leaders, the House of Nobles refused to be cowed. Finally Gustavus had to declare the measure law without its consent. This he was entitled to do by the terms of the Constitution, but he had been guilty of several irregularities in carrying out what amounted to a new *coup* and these did little to enhance his reputation. But for the time being the continuance of the war with Russia muffled criticism among the unprivileged orders, especially as he faithfully carried out his promises to them and embarked on a comprehensive programme of social levelling similar to that envisaged earlier by the Caps, and not unlike that being imposed at this very time by the French bourgeoisie on King Louis XVI. All official posts, except those at Court and the very highest in the bureaucracy, were thrown open to all classes; commoners' promotion prospects in the Civil Service were considerably improved; the right of non-nobles to purchase Crown lands, of which they had been deprived in 1772, was restored; and half the judges of the Supreme Court were in future to be drawn from their ranks.

Both sides soon grew weary of the war, from which neither seemed able to draw any benefit; Catherine had her difficulties too. The Swedish fleet managed finally to break out of Sveaborg and win a notable victory in the summer of 1790, which enabled Gustavus to make peace with some honour at Värälä soon after. The territorial *status quo* was restored.

During the last years of his life, Gustavus became more and more preoccupied with the progress of the revolution in France. While many European monarchs had welcomed it when it first broke out as weakening France's power and diminishing the part she could play in international affairs, the King of Sweden had forecast from its inception that it would lead eventually to the abolition of the monarchy and become a threat to all rulers. The plight of Louis XVI and his family touched him deeply, and he assisted Queen Marie Antoinette's Swedish favourite Axel von Fersen to plan the ill-fated flight to Varennes. This took place while he was paying a visit to Aachen, where were gathered a large number of French noble *émigrés*. The king discussed with them his plans for the launching of a general crusade against the revolutionaries. But other monarchs whom he approached were not interested in such a project at this stage. Catherine of Russia, although as horrified by the events in France as he was, refused to commit herself beyond expressions of sympathy; she was too busy with the second partition of Poland. And the emperor proved equally unco-operative. Gustavus continued to toy with various schemes to restore the French king's power, but no attempt was ever made to put them into practice.

The Act of Union and Security and the end of the war with Russia did not solve his domestic difficulties. Foremost among these was the economic situation, which the war had made even more critical; an excessive issue of paper money brought inflation as bad as in the days of the Hats. To deal with this the king called what was to prove to be his last *Riksdag* at Gävle in 1792. The meeting passed quietly enough. But the events of 1789 had merely driven the Opposition underground. A large body of nobles, many of them influenced, paradoxically enough, by the ideas expressed by the revolutionaries in France, regarded Gustavus as little better than a tyrant; others were simply incensed by the loss of their privileges. Many registered their disapproval merely by absenting themselves from Court, but a few, who included members of old Cap families, decided to take more drastic action—to do away with the king altogether. They hired Jakob Anckarström, an ex-Guards officer who entertained a personal grudge against Gustavus, to attempt his assassination. And on 16th March 1792, in the course of a masked ball in the Stockholm Opera House, Anckarström mortally wounded the king, who died a fortnight later at the age of forty-six.

The complex character of Gustavus III has fascinated writers ever since his death. And the placing of the emphasis on one or other of his conflicting traits has given rise to widely differing interpretations of the man and the ruler. The brilliant cultural life which marks his reign[1] and which he fostered so assiduously brought lavish praise from artists who lived through the dark days following his death. Others were dazzled by the personal charm with which he was so handsomely endowed. There

[1] See pp. 182–3.

has come down to us, on the other hand, a host of diaries and memoirs written by disgruntled members of his Court, who condemn—and not without justification—his shallowness, dissimulation and unreliability. Those who see the Era of Liberty as an age of licence rapidly degenerating into anarchy see the *coup d'état* of 1772 as a salutary measure, necessary to restore stability and save Sweden from Poland's fate; others condemn it as putting an end to a promising constitutional experiment. There seems much evidence to support those historians who have detected a moral degeneration in the king's later years—an over-confidence in his own abilities following his early successes; a growing contempt for legal forms; and an increasing reliance on men whose only recommendation was a willingness to flatter the royal vanity. That Gustavus was genuinely concerned for the welfare of his country and its inhabitants can hardly be doubted, but his patriotism was too often warped by vainglory and lust for power. His shrewd realism was accompanied by an excessively vivid imagination which led him too frequently into the realms of fantasy.

CHAPTER XIV

The French Revolution and Napoleon

T
he seventeen-year-long reign of Gustavus III's son was a gloomy period in Swedish history, although made to seem gloomier than it really was by the cultural brilliance of the years preceding it and by the rapid revival in national fortunes which followed. Gustavus IV was only thirteen in 1792, and his father's last wish was that the realm should be governed during his minority by a council made up of the most intimate colleagues of the old king. This constituted a snub for the new king's uncle, Duke Charles; in an earlier settlement he had been named Regent, but his brother's growing distrust of him had now caused his powers to be reduced to those of one member of a committee. He was not the kind of man to be content with such a subordinate rôle, and as soon as Gustavus III was dead, he had himself restored, with the connivance of the Council, to what he regarded as his rightful place at the head of the administration. He gained the Council's support for this *coup* by promising to keep it in being, but his promise was soon broken, and in revenge for his brother's treatment, he proceeded to replace Gustavus's intimates with his own. He himself had little interest in the day-to-day running of affairs and was happy to devolve this responsibility on Gustav Reuterholm.

Reuterholm appealed to the Regent both as a fierce critic of the former king and as a devotee, like Charles, of the occult, especially of the teachings of the Rosicrucians and the Freemasons. He never occupied a post higher than that of President of the Exchequer Court, but he was nevertheless the real ruler of Sweden for the next four years. He possessed a considerable capacity for hard work, but his real abilities fell far short of his conceits, and he was fortunate that a temporarily favourable economic situation dampened discontent. Nicknamed 'The Grand Vizier', he was soon made aware of his unpopularity when, in an attempt to prove his enlightenment, he eased the restrictions which had been imposed on the press. They had to be quickly reimposed. Many looked forward to the king's coming of age, for he never succumbed to the favourite's influence, and as the end of the regency approached Reuterholm realized that he could not hope to stay in office much longer. He resigned voluntarily and left the country just before Gustavus took up the reins of government himself in 1796.

The king had several good qualities. He was undoubtedly upright, methodical and, unlike his father, genuinely pious. Unfortunately, he had inherited none of Gustavus III's charm; he carried method to the point of pedantry and beyond; and he failed to win the friendship or even the confidence of any of those around him. Inwardly passionate, he offered the world a cold, aloof exterior, while he lacked the ruthlessness and intellectual ability which might have compensated for it; it was soon apparent that his nervous system would be unlikely to withstand the strain of a prolonged crisis. He refused to allow his ministers any initiative in the making of policy and thus took upon his own shoulders a burden they were unable to bear. But for a time all went well. The year after the end of the regency, he married Frederika of Baden, a sister-in-law of Grand Duke Alexander of Russia, later Tsar Alexander I. The marriage was a happy one, and the birth of two sons seemed to ensure the future of the dynasty. Economies at Court even enabled the Government to produce a surplus in its budget. But the economic situation was now becoming less favourable. The harvests of 1798 and 1799 were poor; inflation continued; and the dislocation of trade caused by the European war, combined with the rapid development of the British iron industry, brought a sharp decline in Sweden's vital iron exports.[1] Ominous riots broke out in several towns, and the king was advised that the only solution was a full-scale redemption of the rapidly-depreciating paper currency like that which had been carried through in the early years of his father's reign. But this required the consent of the Estates, who were summoned to meet in Norrköping in 1800.

[1] See also p. 170.

The result was a shattering experience for Gustavus. It is true that a majority in all the Estates supported the monarchy, and that a plan for the redemption was approved. But violent opposition to the scheme, which involved a new tax on land, came from certain radical members of the lesser nobility who wished to embarrass the Government; some of them even carried their protest so far as to renounce their titles. Such defiance, even if from only a small group, confirmed the king in his absolutist convictions, and he resolved never to call the Diet again. The financial plan approved at Norrköping proved unworkable, but the Government had also been granted the power to make such changes in it as should be found necessary, and, as a result, and entirely new scheme could be introduced in 1802; it was partly financed by the mortgaging of the town of Wismar (one of the last remaining footholds owned by Sweden on the Baltic coast of Germany) to the Duke of Mecklenburg for a hundred years.

The financial and economic situation certainly improved during the next few years, which also witnessed the beginning of considerable changes in the Swedish countryside. As a result of decrees issued in 1803 and 1807, much land in the southern and central provinces was enclosed for the first time, and Scania, in which the king himself took a particular interest, began to be transformed into the great agricultural area it is today.[1] Attempts were also made at this time to integrate the part of Pomerania still held by Sweden more closely with the homeland. In 1806 the German nobles there lost their special privileges; their great estates were broken up; serfdom was abolished; Swedish law was introduced; and a constitution on the Swedish model was approved by an assembly of four Estates. But the sands were rapidly running out for Sweden in Germany.

Developments in Revolutionary France continued to be watched in Sweden with interest and by some, especially students and a number of nobles, with sympathy. But the Government remained as firmly opposed to the ideals being trumpeted abroad from Paris as it had been in the previous reign; the censorship was considerably tightened up in 1798, and in 1804 the import of all French books was banned. Sweden, as a neutral whose prosperity depended to a large extent on her

[1] For more about the enclosure movement in Sweden, see p. 175.

overseas trade, was placed in an extremely delicate position by the war. Britain was her best customer, but, as in previous wars, her ships were constantly harassed by British warships and privateers searching for contraband goods on their way to French ports. In 1794 she had concluded an agreement with Denmark to protect her trade, as she had done at the time of Britain's war with her American colonies. Partly as a result of this, British pressure was relaxed for a time, and France became the greater menace on the seas. Indeed, when Gustavus IV concluded an alliance with Russia in 1799, it seemed as if he might be on the brink of joining the new anti-French coalition then being formed. Napoleon's swift victories, however, broke this up before Sweden could go any further, and Britain again began seriously to interfere with her trade. Both Denmark and she sought protection for their merchantmen from Tsar Paul, and in 1800 the three countries concluded a new League of Armed Neutrality, which was later acceded to by other neutrals. Britain's answer was to bombard Copenhagen, an act which forced the Danes to withdraw; Sweden was saved from similar treatment only by the intervention of the new tsar, Alexander I, Gustavus's brother-in-law. The League was largely ineffective, but in 1803 Britain did agree to pay compensation for the Swedish ships which she had seized and taken to her ports for examination.

Meanwhile, Sweden's relations with France were growing increasingly strained, in spite of the king's attempts to effect a *rapprochement* with the Consulate. His marriage to a south German princess and his possession of part of Pomerania inevitably gave him a keen interest in the affairs of the Holy Roman Empire, and he became more and more alarmed by Bonaparte's bullying of the German princes. While on a visit to his wife's relations in 1803, French agents, in flagrant violation of international law, kidnapped the young Duc d'Enghien from Baden and carried him back to France, where he was condemned to death on the flimsiest evidence for having conspired against Napoleon, and shot. The incident made a profound impression on Gustavus, and, in spite of his ministers' opposition, he determined on war. At the end of 1804, Sweden concluded a convention with Britain which allowed the latter to use Swedish Pomerania as a base for military operations in Germany in exchange

5a. *Charles XII* by J. D. Swartz.
Svenska Porträttarkivet

5b. A seventeenth-century farmhouse (Älvosgården in
Härjedalen). *Nordiska Museet*

6a. *Gustavus III* by Sergel. *Svenska Porträttarkivet*

6b. *The English Park at Forsmarks Bruk* (Uppland) by
R. N. Heland (1765–1814). *Nationalmuseum, Stockholm*

for subsidies. This was followed by an alliance with Russia and, in the autumn of 1805, by a declaration of war on France.

British troops were sent to Pomerania, but they were able to do little when they got there. Austria and Prussia were swiftly crushed by the French emperor (which title Napoleon had now adopted), and in the spring of 1807 Sweden signed an armistice. Russia now not only made peace with France, but at Tilsit concluded an alliance with her against Britain and her other enemies. Gustavus's foreign policy lay in ruins. Yet, in spite of the fact that the British troops had to be withdrawn from Pomerania, that the Swedes quickly followed them and that Denmark was forced into the conflict on the French side by Britain's seizure of her fleet, he determined to fight on, denounced the armistice and made a new subsidy treaty with Britain. At their Tilsit meeting, Napoleon had given Alexander the task of forcing Sweden to join the Continental System and to close her ports to British ships and goods. When Gustavus refused to do this, the tsar, in February 1808, attacked Finland, which he had determined to annex. Denmark declared war on Sweden the following month, and a French army under the command of Marshal Bernadotte began to gather on Zealand in preparation for an assault on her from the south.

The Swedish army numbered about 66,000 men. This figure was raised to nearly 100,000 by universal conscription, but the quality of the troops enrolled in this way was doubtful, and commissariat and medical services left much to be desired. The king, once more against the advice of his ministers, who feared to weaken the defences of Finland, decided to concentrate his forces to withstand the expected Danish and French attacks from south and west. These were, after all, directed against Sweden proper, and in this area British sea-power could enable a really decisive blow to be delivered against the enemy; having accomplished this, all resources could be switched to meet the Russians. But the threat from the west and south failed to develop. British warships guarded the Sound; the large number of Spanish troops in Bernadotte's army deserted on hearing of the revolt against the French in their homeland; and this revolt turned the attention of both Britain and France away from northern Europe. In June Gustavus sailed to join his soldiers in Finland.

Here the Commander-in-Chief, overestimating the strength
of the enemy, had withdrawn in good order towards a base in
the north from which he could launch a counter-attack in more
favourable circumstances. In spite of the fact that his losses were
slight and no major defeat was sustained on the way, the retreat
did much to lower his troops' morale; many of the officers were
imbued with the feeling that defeat was inevitable and that
Sweden's best hope of salvation lay in close co-operation with
France. It was such a mood which helped to bring about the
greatest disaster which befell the Swedes before their king
arrived. The fortress of Sveaborg was bound to play a key rôle in
any counter-offensive; beneath its walls lay a good proportion
of the fleet, and its garrison of 7,000 men was well supplied with
food and ammunition. Yet, at the beginning of May, its commander, an admiral who underestimated the strength of his
position, was pessimistic about Sweden's future in Finland and
influenced by some members of his staff who were in Russian
pay, agreed to surrender it to the Russians after putting up only
a token resistance; and with it went all its stores and 110 galleys.
In spite of this grave set-back, the counter-attack was launched
soon after Gustavus landed, and had considerable initial success;
Swedish troops swept down the Finnish coast, while the Russian
fleet was bottled up in an Estonian port. But the victory was
short-lived. The Russians reinforced their army, and with the
first set-back, the timid Swedish commander ordered a retreat.
Not only was the ground which had been recovered lost again,
but no effort was made to stand again in Finland, and by the end
of the year the whole country was in Russian hands.

Dissatisfaction in Sweden itself was growing. Britain refused
to increase her subsidies, and the cost of the war could only be
met by the imposition of new taxes, which the peasants particularly resented in view of the poor harvests from which they
were suffering. The nobles, who still filled the higher ranks of
the Civil Service, shared the pessimism of their military equals
and supported their monarch with a lethargy little short of
treason. They were, however, too disunited to be able to do
anything positive; it was left to the army to take the initiative.
Here there had been talk of a *coup d'état* to depose the king
as far back as 1807. It was not, however, until, as a punishment
for the supposed cowardice of some of their number in Finland,

he attacked the most influential families in the land by depriving officers in the Guards of the privileges granted to them by his father, and not until he made it quite clear that he was determined to continue the struggle against Russia into 1809, that decisive action was taken. In March of that year, Lieutenant-Colonel Georg Adlersparre of the army facing Norway occupied the town of Karlstad in Värmland and gathered there a force with which to march on Stockholm. As soon as Gustavus realized the seriousness of the situation, he began to make preparations to leave his capital at the head of its garrison and march south to join the army in Scania, which he believed to be loyal. This at last stung the bureaucrats into action. They arrested him before he could escape, and persuaded Duke Charles, who had long been on bad terms with his nephew, to act as regent until the Estates could decide what was to be done next.

There was no general agreement among the conspirators and their supporters on a future course of action, except that peace should be made as soon as possible and that the king must go. While some argued for the retention of the Gustavian system of government with Duke Charles acting as regent for the king's son, others wished Charles to take the crown. Among those who favoured the latter solution, some wished to bind the royal hands with a new constitution; others, including the all-powerful Adlersparre, were willing to allow the Duke to ascend the throne without any limitations on his power. The Estates, when they met, decided to make the Duke king, but not until he had accepted a constitution drawn up by his future subjects. Within a month such a constitution was prepared, accepted by the Estates and agreed to by Charles, who was duly proclaimed king as Charles XIII. Having failed to save the succession for his son, Gustavus left Sweden for ever, to spend the rest of his life wandering about Europe, growing more and more mentally unbalanced; he died as Colonel Gustafsson in Switzerland in 1837. He has been harshly judged by posterity and certainly lacked the stuff of which leaders are made, but it must be remembered that he had to struggle throughout his reign against defeatism and disloyalty in many of his servants.

The new constitution, on which the modern Swedish constitution is based, was a compromise between executive and legislative authority similar to that attempted in 1772. The four Estates were retained, in spite of some support for the idea of a bicameral system. The king remained head of the executive with power to appoint the members of a council of nine, and only two of his ministers (those for foreign affairs and justice) had to be admitted to the Council, but all were made responsible to the *Riksdag* and could be impeached by it. The latter was to be called at least once every five years; had the right to reject the budget; and could veto legislation in the same way as the king. Freedom of the press, speech and worship were guaranteed, and the private citizen was protected from the bureaucracy by a so-called *ombudsman*, elected by the Estates to hear and investigate complaints against abuses of power by public servants. The peasants failed to carry the measure which most interested them—equal taxation for all land—but the nobility did surrender all the exclusive claims to office which still remained to it, as well as its privileges with regard to the purchase of real property.

The constitutional question was thus settled with surprising speed; but the problem of the succession remained, for Charles XIII had no children. Adlersparre favoured the claims of Christian August of Augustenborg, the Danish commander-in-chief in Norway, who had allowed him to carry out his *coup* without fear of the Danish army's taking advantage of an undefended frontier. An even weightier consideration than gratitude was the hope that Christian would bring Norway with him to counter-balance the loss of Finland to Russia, which now seemed unavoidable. Christian was duly elected by the *Riksdag*, but he accepted the offer only on condition that peace with Denmark should be made immediately.

With the Swedish defences in the north collapsing and appeals to Napoleon to use his influence with the tsar coldly pushed aside, the Swedes had to agree to their main enemy's demands, which were enshrined in the Treaty of Frederikshamn, concluded in September 1809. Finland and the Åland Islands passed to Russia, together with a small strip of Sweden proper in the far north. With this loss of territory, part of which at least she had ruled over for 500 years, a completely new epoch in Sweden's history had dawned.

Agreement with her other enemies was soon reached. Denmark, in whose ambitions neither Russia nor France had any interest, had to content herself with the restoration of the *status quo*. Early in the new year Napoleon agreed to return Pomerania, although at the same time he insisted on the closure of Swedish ports to all British goods with the exception of salt, which was still a necessity for the Swedish peasant. Christian August kept his promise, and came to Sweden to take up his duties as heir apparent. In May 1810, however, while attending a military review in Scania, he fell from his horse and died. Although it was a heart-attack which reopened the whole succession question, in the agitated atmosphere of the time, wild rumours of poison received wide currency, and the public's hatred turned against the intimates of the ex-king and his father. At the crown prince's funeral in the capital, a mob seized one of these, Axel von Fersen, the friend of Marie Antoinette, as he rode in the procession, and tore him to pieces before the impassive gaze of the hundreds of troops present. Such deeds have fortunately been rare in Swedish history.

The *Riksdag*'s next choice for heir was Christian's brother, still in the hope of gaining Norway. But on this occasion it was thought wise to secure the approval of Napoleon, now at the height of his power, and a messenger was sent to Paris for this purpose. In addition to the official envoy, the Government sent a certain Lieutenant Mörner with duplicate dispatches in case the originals should go astray. Mörner was one of a number of Swedish officers who favoured flattering the emperor still further by offering the succession to one of his marshals. Among the latter, Bernadotte, Prince of Pontecorvo, who had married Bonaparte's ex-fiancée and was the brother-in-law of Louis Bonaparte, was particularly popular after his generous treatment of Swedes taken prisoner in north Germany. Bernadotte, having fallen out with his master, was living in semi-retirement in the French capital, and as soon as Mörner arrived there, he went to see him. The Marshal agreed to allow his name to be put forward, and Napoleon, although he publicly approved the *Riksdag*'s choice, also gave his consent to the candidature. Mörner thereupon returned to Sweden to win over the Estates. He was helped in this task by Bernadotte's own agent, the French vice-consul in Gothenburg, who suggested that a French loan might be arranged and hinted that the emperor would be very pleased if the *Riksdag* changed its mind—which it duly did.

Bernadotte arrived in Sweden in October 1810, and, having been received into the Lutheran faith, adopted the name Charles John. Many members of the Swedish aristocracy had been understandably doubtful about the future sovereign in view of his humble birth and Jacobin associations, but they were soon won over by his dignity and charm, which led some even to compare him with Gustavus III. He immediately took charge of his adopted country's destiny; the king was no more anxious to accept responsibility for it than he had been while regent for Gustavus IV. Charles John had to acquiesce in the emperor's demand that Sweden declare war on Britain, but he had no intention of acting as Napoleon's pawn, and realized that his reputation with his future subjects would depend largely on his conduct of foreign policy; to win their hearts he must either regain Finland or secure Norway as compensation. Of these two alternatives, the latter seemed the more likely of attainment and from a military point of view the more desirable, but it was only after Napoleon had refused to countenance the idea of Finland's return to Sweden that the crown prince turned to Russia.

Russia's relations with France had grown so strained since Tilsit that by 1811 war between the two powers seemed almost inevitable. But Bernadotte had to move with the greatest caution, not only for fear of French reprisals before his *volte-face* was completed, but also out of deference to those Swedes who still believed that their country's best hope lay in a close alliance with the emperor, those Swedes indeed who had been most responsible for his election. Bonaparte, however, played into his hands when, at the beginning of 1812, he occupied Swedish Pomerania and took prisoner a large part of the garrison in revenge for Sweden's failure to enforce the blockade against British goods. This action came as a rude shock to Swedish francophiles, and Charles John felt ready at last to proclaim his country neutral and then, in April 1812, to conclude an alliance with the tsar, who promised his support for Swedish claims on Norway; if Denmark agreed to desert France, she was to be given compensation in Germany. The extent to which the crown prince had made himself master in his future realm was clearly demonstrated at a meeting of the *Riksdag* in Örebro. In spite of a series of poor harvests and high prices, extra taxes

were voted with little complaint and conscription for all men
between 20 and 25 agreed to. In addition, the press, freed from
control by the Constitution of 1809, was again muzzled by
granting the Government the power to seize any periodical
which it considered was printing news or views contrary to the
national interest. This was the later-notorious *indragningsmakt*.

Sweden played no part in the campaign of 1812, but in
March of the following year, with the *Grande Armée* in full retreat after the Russian débâcle, Charles concluded an alliance
with Britain; she promised subsidies, support for the acquisition
of Norway, and the French West Indian island of Guadeloupe,
in exchange for the assistance of 30,000 Swedish troops in Germany. When Russia and Prussia concluded an armistice with
Napoleon three months later, it seemed that Sweden might find
herself faced with another Tilsit, but the war broke out again,
and Charles was largely responsible for planning the offensive
which followed. He himself took command of the northern army
of Swedes, Prussians and Russians, but did not join the great
drive on Paris which followed the French defeat at Leipzig in
October 1813. This was partly because he wished to finish with
Denmark, who remained allied with Napoleon to the bitter end,
but also partly, it seems, because of the hopes he entertained of
the French throne; he did not want to kill any more of his future
subjects than he could help!

The first of these ambitions was soon achieved. The Danes
accepted the inevitable and, by the Treaty of Kiel in January
1814, agreed to exchange Norway for Swedish Pomerania[1] and
a cash payment. But the Norwegians, with some encouragement from the Danish king, refused to submit meekly to such a
fate. A month after the signing of the treaty, a representative
body of them met at Eidsvold to the north of Christiania (the
modern Oslo) and composed a constitution for an independent
monarchy with the Danish viceroy, Prince Christian Frederick,
cousin and heir of Frederick VI of Denmark, as its king. Without outside help their cause seemed lost, and Britain, on
whom they had counted most, stood by her Swedish ally and
enforced a blockade of the Norwegian coast. In July, Charles
John was ready to invade Norway with an army larger and

[1] Denmark then exchanged this with Prussia for Lauenburg to the south
of Slesvig-Holstein.

167

much better equipped than anything the Norwegians could hope to raise. But after a few skirmishes he agreed to an armistice and to the opening of negotiations; he wanted a quick settlement which he could present to the great powers, whose word he did not wholly trust. He offered to accept the Eidsvold Constitution, with certain amendments made necessary by the union of the Norwegian and Swedish Crowns, and to this the Norwegians then agreed. As a result, they gained a considerable measure of autonomy, although some aspects of the partnership were left obscure, which led to serious disputes later in the century. The foreign policy of both countries was to be determined in Stockholm, and the king was to appoint both a viceroy to represent him in Norway and the members of the Norwegian council in Christiania. But the only control he possessed over ordinary legislation passed by the *Storting* was a suspensive veto valid for six years (in Sweden his veto was absolute).

Sweden did not obtain with Norway her former dependencies of Iceland, The Faroes and Greenland; these remained under the Danish Crown. With the exception of the small island of St. Barthélemy in the West Indies,[1] she had now lost all her territory outside the Scandinavian peninsula; Guadeloupe was returned to France under pressure from Britain, who paid Sweden compensation (used to pay off part of the national debt), and the town of Wismar, although in theory only mortgaged to Mecklenburg, never returned to its former allegiance. The Swedes, having fought their last war, had to turn, in the words of their poet Esaias Tegnér, to 'making the fatherland great within more restricted bounds'.

[1] See p. 170.

CHAPTER XV

Swedish Economic Life and Culture in the Eighteenth Century

The recovery of Sweden's economy after the twenty years of continuous warfare which ended in 1721 was remarkably rapid, and particularly so in the field of overseas trade. Only for a brief period during the war had this been seriously interrupted, and the loss of the possessions in the southeast Baltic by the Peace of Nystad did not cause any dramatic change in its character. Its expansion in the later decades of the seventeenth century continued well into the eighteenth, and a favourable balance between imports and exports was speedily attained. The growth of Sweden's merchant marine, which numbered no fewer than 572 vessels in 1762, enabled her to carry on an increasingly greater proportion of her trade in her own ships, a development helped (although it is difficult to tell exactly to what extent) by the *Produktplakat* of 1724. This, like the English Navigation Acts of the seventeenth century, on which it was modelled, forbade foreign ships to carry to Sweden any goods not produced in the ships' country of origin or its colonies. Iron remained Sweden's most important export (about 75 per cent of the annual total for much of the period), and the bulk of it continued to go to Britain. A very large number of her merchant ships sailed every year to southern Europe to collect salt, but over half her imports was made up of colonial goods like sugar, coffee and tobacco, and of corn, in which she was no longer self-supporting.

But Sweden failed to keep pace with the rapid expansion of European trade which occurred during the century, of which Britain and France were the main beneficiaries, and the political dominance which Russia had gained in the Baltic was matched by her increasingly important economic rôle in the area. By 1750 Sweden had lost the monopoly of tar and pitch which had been hers in the seventeenth century, and St. Petersburg had become more important than Stockholm as an outlet for iron. By 1800 only a fifth of Europe's iron came from Sweden, although the high quality of that which did made it highly prized for certain purposes. The invention in England in 1784 of the 'puddling process', which enabled her to use her vast resources of coal (in the form of coke) for smelting instead of charcoal, made that country less dependent on Swedish iron, exports of which fell sharply as a result.

As in most other countries at this time, trade was the subject of detailed government regulation. No port north of Gävle was, for example, allowed to engage in overseas commerce before 1765, when more liberal economic doctrines were beginning to have some effect on policy; and even after this date there was still a ban on any ship calling north of Stockholm. Direction was made easier by granting a monopoly of a large part of extra-European trade to great chartered companies like the East India Company, founded in 1731 by a group of Gothenburg merchants, including a Scot named Colin Campbell. In spite of its name, the activities of this enterprise were confined to the Chinese port of Canton, whence it imported tea, silk and porcelain for the delectation of the Swedish upper classes. For some thirty years it was a brilliant success but a decline in its fortunes set in around 1770, until in 1813 it had to be wound up. The Stockholm Levant Company of 1738 was much less favoured; it lasted less than twenty years. One of the fruits of Gustavus III's visit to Paris in 1784 was his country's acquisition of the French West Indian island of St. Barthélemy, and two years later a West India Company was formed to exploit this as a base for the African slave trade; it survived until 1805. In Stockholm, these and similar ventures were largely controlled by about twenty families who constituted the capital's burgher *élite*, referred to as the *Skeppsbroadel* or nobility of Skeppsbro, where most of them lived.

It was not only external trade which the State attempted to control. The ancient ban on 'country trading' continued in principle throughout the period, although it was gradually modified to exclude most foodstuffs, and all the peasants' own produce was exempt. It was a difficult measure to enforce, especially in remote areas, where the itinerant salesman was depended upon for news of the outside world as well as for the articles he supplied. 'Country trading' was further encouraged by the tolls levied by towns on all goods passing through their gates, which lasted until as late as 1810.

But even if there had not been such restrictions, internal commerce would still have been considerably hampered by the poor state of Sweden's roads, although those in many other countries seem to have been worse. One solution to the problem was to exploit Sweden's excellent water communications by building canals to link her lakes and large rivers. Gustavus Adolphus had built a canal uniting Lake Hjälmaren with Mälaren, and several attempts were made in the course of the eighteenth century to join Lake Vänern to the Kattegat by using the waters of the River Göta. But it was not until 1800 that the Trollhätte Canal provided such a highway for the export of iron from central Sweden through Gothenburg, which benefited greatly from it. Six years later, Mälaren was given a new outlet to the Baltic through Södertälje, and in 1810 work was begun on the great Göta Canal, which was eventually to span the country from coast to coast.

As has been suggested, the health of Sweden's economy in the eighteenth century depended to an even greater extent than before on her production of iron ore. The industry was dominated by the *brukspatroner* or iron-masters, who controlled the *bruk*. These were self-supporting communities of miners and foundrymen, settled near rivers in the forest regions of middle Sweden though generally outside Bergslagen, which was now the home of small-scale producers of pig iron for the hammers of the *bruk*. Most *brukspatroner* ruled their domains with a firm patriarchal hand. Their employees were often cared for in sickness and old age, but were at the same time liable to suffer harsh corporal punishments for any misdemeanours. Skilled foundrymen might live well, but the underground and unskilled worker was much worse off. The masters, who formed a very influential pressure-group in political life, were organized in a society which met every three years to elect the officials of the Iron Office. This was a government-sponsored body, set up by the

Hats in 1748 to regulate the trade in iron in order to maintain the level of prices, and to grant loans for mining and smelting operations. The Great Copper Mountain at Falun, which had played such a large part in Sweden's economy in the early seventeenth century, had by the eighteenth been reduced to a very minor rôle, but its output remained stable until the 1790's, when it began on its final decline. Particularly associated with the development of mining techniques in the late seventeenth and early eighteenth centuries is the name of Christopher Polhem (1661–1751), Sweden's first real engineer and an inventor of genius. His most famous discovery was a means of conveying the energy generated by waterfalls over long distances, but there were many others; he was involved in all the early projects for a Trollhätte Canal.

Surprising as it may seem today, it was not until the nineteenth century that there was any extensive exploitation of Sweden's forests for timber;[1] a small amount of wood was exported, but high transport costs precluded serious competition with Norway. Norrland remained most important for its furs and skins, and in the central provinces trees were used to shelter the peasants' cattle or feed the furnaces of the *bruk*; fears of a shortage which would cripple the iron industry led the State to restrict cutting for other purposes.

By far the greatest part of Sweden's iron was exported; little was used in her industrial life proper. Here, as in England, it was textiles which led the way, and of these it was wool which took pride of place. Most cloth for sale was produced by the domestic system, under which the wool was provided by an entrepreneur, worked up by the weaver in his own home and then sold back to the entrepreneur who put it on the market. But, especially on the south side of Stockholm and in Norrköping, there grew up during this period true industrial complexes of small factories with a number of looms. An industrial proletariat began to make its appearance, helped by the relaxation of guild regulations after 1739. Its living conditions were generally wretched, especially in the capital; wages were low, a working-day of sixteen hours was by no means uncommon, and child labour the rule. But it constituted only about 1 per cent of the total population (compared with the 3 per cent

[1] See p. 207.

associated with mining and the 2 per cent occupied in urban crafts).

Mercantilism—the economic doctrine of the age—taught that the Government must encourage industry in every possible way—by subsidies, tax concessions, loans and favourable legis-

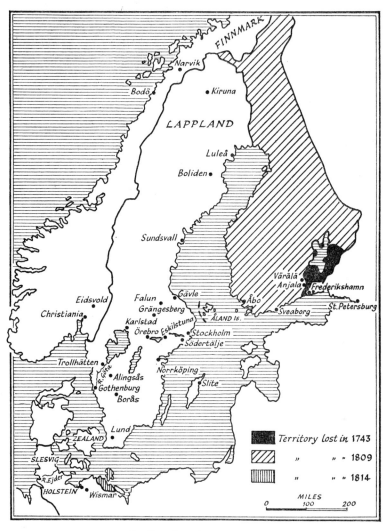

6   Sweden since 1721

lation—and the Hats in particular embraced the idea with enthusiasm. A large number of enterprises owed their existence to
State policy, and none were more favoured than those run by
Jonas Alströmer. Alströmer returned to Sweden in 1724, after a
long sojourn in England and Holland, with ambitious plans to
establish a mill which would employ the latest English techniques and even English workmen. His project attracted the
attention of the Government, which granted special privileges
to the textile factory he built in his home-town of Alingsås,
north-east of Gothenburg, and equipped with looms smuggled
out of Holland; loans were made available, and the religious
restrictions usually imposed on foreigners who settled in Sweden
were waived for the workers he imported. With the even greater
help given to him by the Hats when they came to power,
Alingsås grew to be a considerable industrial centre, but when
the subsidies and other concessions began to be withdrawn in
the 1760's, the edifice collapsed. Its importance has often been
exaggerated, for its disappearance had little effect on Sweden's
industrial life as a whole.

The urban handicrafts retained their guild organization, and
indeed guilds spread in the eighteenth century to many small
towns which had not known them before. But their character
was changing. They were rapidly becoming closed oligarchies
of masters, who used their position in the *Riksdag* to make it as
difficult as possible for outsiders to enter their circle. A larger
and larger number of apprentices never attained a higher rank
their whole lives through, and never expected to do so; they
married and lived away from their master's house. The great
majority of craftsmen, however, remained outside the guild system altogether. On the isolated farm the peasant himself made
most of the tools he needed and in most villages there was room
for only one specialist in each of a limited number of skills,
although an area might become famous for a particular product.

Industry was growing, but very slowly. Over three-quarters of
all Swedes before 1815 were engaged in full-time in agriculture,
and a good many more, like the miners and other workers of the
bruk, and even a considerable number of town dwellers, relied
to a greater or lesser extent on the land. Up to the middle of the
century, life in the countryside still differed hardly at all from
what it had been in the Middle Ages. In central and southern

Sweden at least, most of the cultivated land was divided into strips apportioned among the members of the village community, and a two- or three-field rotation of crops was practised. It was a system which militated against change and experiment and which kept productivity low, especially as the rapid rise of population which occurred in the early eighteenth century necessitated constant subdivision of holdings.

By 1750 there was a growing demand for change among enlightened nobles who knew something of the improvements being carried out on the land in England and the Low Countries, and of the increased profits which these produced. The Estates gave them their support by passing, as a first step, a series of ordinances in and after 1757 aimed at consolidating and reducing the number of separate strips owned by individual peasants, which might amount to forty or more. Such an amalgamation needed the consent of a certain proportion (although not necessarily the majority) of the members of the community concerned, and progress was slow; there was much opposition even to this mild reform, which did little or nothing to disturb the fundamental character of rural life. Large landowners had greater freedom of action when dealing with their tenants, but even they were bound to a considerable extent by the custom of the parish. In 1783, one of them, Rutger Maclean, a member of a Scottish family long settled in Sweden, began to carry out full-scale enclosure on his estate at Svaneholm in Scania; he resettled his tenants on single compact blocks of land, which they could deal with as they chose. The results were so encouraging that other landowners of the province followed his example, and ordinances of 1803, 1804 and 1807 attempted to apply the solution to the whole of Sweden outside Norrland and Dalarna, where the older, less radical movement begun in 1757 went slowly on. By the end of the Napoleonic Wars, however, only Scania, the richest, most progressive and most densely-populated province in Sweden, had benefited from the changes to any great extent. Here, and on the estates of enlightened landowners, complicated crop-rotation systems were being tried out with a resulting increase in yields. But yields were also rising in many other parts of the country, and the food supply was further increased by the growing of potatoes (which Alströmer seems to have been the first to introduce to

Sweden) on land which had previously been left fallow or which had never been cultivated at all.

On the poorer lands, especially in the north and the thickly-forested regions of the country, livestock was still often at least as important a source of livelihood as cereals, but in this field there was little progress in these years. Indeed, in the decades immediately after the Great Northern War, there appears to have been an actual decline due to attacks of murrain and a deterioration in the climate; a period of cold winters and late springs known as 'The Little Ice Age' lasted into the nineteenth century. Although men like Alströmer pressed for the application of scientific breeding methods (and he himself tried to introduce high-grade sheep to provide wool for the textile industry), the average peasant preferred to keep a large herd of small cows, whose milk yield was only about a quarter of that of their twentieth-century descendants, rather than raise a smaller number of good quality cattle. He fed his best fodder to his horses, but even these were much smaller and weaker than those used today.

In the middle of the eighteenth century, about half the peasants of Sweden owned their own land, and the proportion of the country which belonged to them was growing. Much of this increase resulted from the sale of Crown property, but even while there was a ban on the purchase of noble (i.e. tax-free) land by non-nobles, a considerable amount of this also passed to the freehold peasant by means of various legal fictions. Conditions, however, varied a good deal from one part of the realm to another; while in the north nearly all land was held by those who worked it, in the Mälaren district a majority of the holdings remained in the hands of the nobility. The rising standard of living enjoyed by the well-to-do yeoman is reflected in his aping of the aristocracy by building a two-storey house and giving his children two baptismal names.[1] But with the rise in size of the population (from about a million and half in 1720 to nearly two and a half million a century later) the proportion of such men was reduced; the bulk of the increase was made up of industrial workers, tenant farmers and cottagers. The latter cultivated

---

[1] Family names proper, as distinct from the surnames formed by adding -*son* to the Christian name of the father, were, however, rare in this class before the nineteenth century.

7a. *Portrait of the Artist's Wife* by Alexander Roslin (1763).
Nationalmuseum, Stockholm

7b. *Charles XIV* by François Gérard (1810).
Svenska Porträttarkivet

8a. Shopping centre in Vällingby, near Stockholm.
Swedish Tourist Traffic Association

8b. *The Orpheus Fountain* by Carl Milles,
in front of the Concert Hall, Stockholm.
Swedish Tourist Traffic Association

small plots which had been carved out of either marginal land
or the common land of the village or the demesne land of a
noble, to whom rent and labour services were owed. There was
also a large army of landless servants, who lived in their employers' homes and might become cottagers in old age. And
below these were paupers supported either by the parish in a
workhouse or by 'outdoor relief', by private charity or by wandering from estate to estate within a well-defined area. Sweden
had as yet no effective poor law such as England had possessed
since the days of Elizabeth I to make every parish responsible
for its own unfortunates, although from 1788 parishes were entitled to refuse entry to anyone they considered unfit for work
and thus likely to become a burden to them.

At the other end of the social scale, the Swedish nobility constituted a very much smaller proportion of the total population
than in many other European countries; it made up about one-
half of 1 per cent in the middle of the century, and this percentage sank steadily thereafter. But until 1789 it retained extensive privileges. The highest offices in central and local government were reserved for it, and it had a monopoly of the higher
ranks in the armed forces; in the Great Northern War many
non-noble officers had had to be employed, but these were
purged once the fighting was over and, for a time, even most
lieutenants and captains were of noble birth. Even before 1789,
however, the position of the nobles was being undermined. As
has been seen, their lands were falling into the hands of men
outside their class, and they were losing their hold on the
bureaucracy; little new blood was admitted to their ranks, for
new creations were comparatively few in the eighteenth century.
The nobility was never a closed caste, and after 1723, when it
was decreed that a morganatic marriage did not involve the
loss of aristocratic privileges, the number of such unions rose
rapidly. But the extent of social mobility, although greater than
in many other countries, must not be exaggerated. The son of a
peasant could not rise very high on the social scale unless he
were of outstanding artistic or intellectual ability, although, if
he entered the Church, his son had a much better chance of
success. The Swedish parsonage was as prolific of notables in
the arts and sciences as was that of England or Scotland.

Nobles, traders and craftsmen, clergy and freehold peasants

all enjoyed a recognized place in society through their representation in the *Riksdag*, while the bulk of the rural population had been made up of tenant farmers and cottagers from time immemorial. But rapid technological change and the growing sophistication of civilization had greatly increased the number of men and women who could not easily be fitted into any of these traditional categories. The industrial proletariat, unorganized and leaderless as it was, was as yet a minor problem, but the true burghers and the nobles were coming to rely more and more on professional men—lawyers, teachers and doctors, who, while often as rich as the members of the Estates, did not officially belong to any of them. Long before the Estates system was finally swept away in the second half of the nineteenth century it had lost all touch with social realities.

The loss by Sweden of her great-power status at the beginning of the eighteenth century tended to isolate her culturally from the rest of Europe to a greater extent than had been the case during the previous hundred years; she became more provincial in her outlook. Yet she could never revert to the condition in which she had found herself in pre-Vasa times. Her diplomatic ties with France, who remained the cultural leader of Europe she had become under Louis XIV, and her commercial ties with Britain brought intellectual stimuli to her from both these centres, while her German possessions provided a bridge over which flowed a host of new ideas from central Europe. Eighteenth-century culture was cosmopolitan, with French as its common language; it was as yet unhampered by the nationalism which was to burst forth with the Romantic Movement in the early 1800's. Many young Swedish nobles made the grand tour, and other Swedes, including some of the most distinguished representatives of their country (the great botanist Linné and the theologian Swedenborg, for example) travelled far and wide; some, like Alströmer, went to England, Scotland and Holland, but many more were drawn to France and to Germany, whose Protestant universities welcomed a good number of Scandinavian students.

In spite of her political power, Sweden had failed to produce during her Age of Greatness any figure in the arts or sciences with a European reputation; St. Bridget had remained unique in this respect. But in the eighteenth century, when her political

178

power had gone, a number of her citizens acquired a fame which radiated far beyond her borders. The most outstanding of these was undoubtedly Carl von Linné. The son of a poor parish priest of Småland, he published in 1735, after journeys through Lappland and Dalarna, his *System of Nature*, in which he described a classification of plants by genera and species still used, with certain modifications, by botanists today. As a professor at Uppsala from 1741 until his death in 1778, he gathered together a number of able and enthusiastic disciples, who travelled all over the world seeking further specimens of living things; one went with Captain Cook on his voyages of discovery in the Pacific.

But Linné was by no means the only Swedish scientist with an international renown at this time. The nephew of his teacher, Anders Celsius, originated, while Professor of Astronomy at Uppsala, the use of the centigrade scale for measuring temperature which even Britain is at last beginning to adopt. Carl Scheele, a native of Swedish Pomerania, isolated oxygen quite independently of Joseph Priestley, and, as discoverer of chlorine and a host of other substances, has been called the greatest experimental chemist of his age. In the same field, Jöns Berzelius in 1818 produced his first periodic table of chemical elements, using the symbols now familiar to every schoolboy. As early as 1739, the Swedish Academy of Sciences was founded in Stockholm to exchange reports of discoveries with similar bodies in other countries, including the Royal Society of London.

One of the most remarkable applications of the scientific spirit in eighteenth-century Sweden was the royal decree of 1748 organizing the first full-scale census in Europe, the results of which were published. In 1756 a Statistical Commission was set up to analyse the information sent in by the local ecclesiastical authorities, who had long acted, as in England, as registrars of births, marriages and deaths. It was originally intended to demand annual returns, but they were soon made triennially and from 1775 every five years. At the same time, however, they were providing more and more information, invaluable not only to the contemporary administrator but also to the modern historian, who, while he may often complain of faulty calculations, can refer with more confidence to Swedish population trends in the eighteenth century than to those of any other major country. Britain's first census was not taken until 1801.

Emanuel Swedenborg (1688–1772) began his career as a 'natural philosopher', being for a certain time Polhem's assistant in the College of Mines, and he evolved scientific theories far ahead of his age in many subjects, especially those of physiology and psychology. It was through these that he passed to the theological speculations for which he is much better known. Although he never intended to found a new sect, his mystical teachings led to the establishment by his followers of the so-called New Church, which made its greatest impact in northern England in the later part of the century and thence spread to the United States; it was appropriate therefore that Swedenborg, a great traveller, should die in London.

In his own country, where his beliefs never enjoyed much popularity, he had to contend with the bigotry of the established Lutheran Church, which frowned on any attempts to ease the lot of non-Lutherans in Sweden, and opposed any new movements within itself. The most important of these was Pietism, an attempt, which had originated in north-west Germany in the last decades of the seventeenth century, to restore some of the original moral fervour and evangelical spirit to what had become the rather arid formulae of Lutheran theology. It acquired a strong hold on Swedish prisoners of war in Russia after Poltava, but was hard hit by the Conventicle Act of 1726, which forbade all prayer meetings in private houses not confined to members of the resident family, and by the middle of the century its force in Scandinavia was largely spent. But English Methodism later exercised a considerable influence on certain pious upper- and middle-class circles, and prepared the way for the religious revival which was set in motion in the Napoleonic period in association with the Romantic Movement.[1] The intolerance of the official hierarchy, together with the declining part it played in education, weakened the Church's hold on society, but a bishopric was still considered an acceptable reward for services in fields other than the religious, and the social status of the ordinary clergy was rising.

The decline of the Church's influence, especially among the nobility, was also an outcome of the reception in Sweden of

[1] See p. 227.

rationalist ideas from England and France, especially the latter. The foremost exponent of these in the literature of the first half of the century was Olof von Dalin. Although his output in all forms of verbal expression was considerable, he will always be best remembered for his weekly magazine *The Swedish Argus*, which first appeared in 1732 and was closely modelled on *The Spectator* of Addison and Steele; the clarity of its style made it the foundation stone of modern Swedish prose. During the rule of the Hats (whom Dalin attack in many of his works) and with the encouragement of the cultivated Queen Louisa Ulrika (who was his patron), French influence grew, as can be seen in the productions of the members of the salon which met in Stockholm in the 1750's at the house of the accomplished lyric poetess Hedvig Nordenflycht, the widow of a naval chaplain. But it reached its height under Gustavus III, whose librarian and secretary, Johan Kellgren, was probably the most 'finished' poet of a generation so rich in talent; he co-operated with the king on the librettos of a number of operas, in the performances of which Gustavus himself took part.

But in the eyes—or rather the hearts—of all Swedes, these figures pale into insignificance before that of Karl Michael Bellman (1740–95), whose 'day'—July 26th—is still celebrated with festivities in the capital he loved. For he is above all Stockholm's poet. His *Fredman's Epistles*—odes he himself set to music (often adaptations of popular melodies) for the lute—portray, as nothing else could, the low life of the city, in the midst of which he spent most of his time, while other poems picture the beauties of the surrounding countryside. Every corner of the Old Town 'between the bridges' is associated with him in some way or other, but especially the *Gyllene Freden* (Golden Peace), a tavern where he would often sing his latest compositions to a crowd of cronies. Unfortunately he is so Swedish, although by no means immune from foreign influences, that he defies satisfactory translation.

In painting, sculpture and allied arts, Sweden generally followed the trends prevalent in western Europe. The baroque and classicism of the seventeenth century evolved into the rococo of the eighteenth, which was succeeded in its turn by the neo-classicism of the French Revolutionary period. Here it was undoubtedly France who was the predominant pace-setter.

Alexander Roslin, probably Sweden's greatest portrait painter, (see plate 7), lived most of his life in Paris and died there in 1792, although he paid frequent visits to his homeland as well as to other countries. And many other Swedish artists joined him in the French capital for briefer stays. French artists contributed extensively to the Royal Palace in Stockholm, designed by Nicodemus Tessin the Younger to replace that burnt down in 1697, but not completed until 1757. From them Sweden's foremost sculptor, Johan Sergel (1740–1814), learnt much of his skill, although his classical style was largely the outcome of a long sojourn in Italy, whence he was recalled by Gustavus III; in 1790 he cast the bronze statue in honour of his patron which now stands at Skeppsbron.

Stockholm, however, contains comparatively little of the eighteenth century, whose spirit is more easily recaptured in the Swedish countryside, in the presence especially of the numerous extant mansions built at this time by nobles on their estates, or by *brukspatroner* on the edge of their *bruk*. These are much more modest affairs than the proud edifices put up by the seventeenth-century magnates; they are generally of wood and of two stories. But they are always handsomely proportioned and often surrounded by the artificially-natural 'English parks' which were so popular in this period (see plate 6); some retain in addition a more formal 'French garden'. As much care was lavished on the decoration of the interior as on the planning of the structure; and it was not only the upper classes who so indulged themselves. The introduction of enclosed fireplaces into many peasant homes encouraged the painting of their inside walls with pictures, usually illustrations of biblical stories in eighteenth-century costume. Such folk art, which is particularly associated with the province of Dalarna, reached its peak in the later eighteenth and early nineteenth centuries, before it was overwhelmed by the urban influences which flowed in with improved communications.

The reign of Gustavus III witnessed a brilliant flowering of Swedish culture. Despite claims that the king's interest in the arts was rather shallow, his attempts to embellish his Court and make it the cultural as well as the political centre of his realm certainly acted as a great stimulus to the writers, painters, musicians, sculptors and architects of his time; even Bellman was found a post in the State lottery. Gustavus helped found the Swedish Academy in 1786 to act as an arbiter of literary taste, and he took a special interest in the theatre. He acted in as well as wrote several of the plays performed in the theatre at the palace of Drottningholm (now once more in use after over a century's neglect) or in the one he himself had built in Gripsholm Castle. Under his patronage, the Royal Opera House was opened in Stockholm in 1782 and the Royal Theatre in 1788 (the original buildings have unfortunately not survived). While several future Swedish kings were to show great interest in the arts and even to practise them, none was able to play Maecenas on such a scale.

CHAPTER XVI

A French Prince

T he Constitution of 1809 left the King of Sweden as active head of the executive with extensive powers, and Charles John was not the man to neglect any opportunity to exploit either the legal rights of Charles XIII before his death in 1818 or his own as Charles XIV. He appointed his own ministers throughout his reign, but, even so, acted on occasion over their heads. He vigorously opposed all attempts by the *Riksdag* to assert its control over finance or to make the Council responsible to it rather than to the Crown. And he silenced criticism whenever possible by means of an efficient secret police and of the *indragningsmakt*, which remained in force even after the crisis which had given rise to it had passed. His intolerance of criticism was rendered all the fiercer by the feeling of insecurity which dogged him throughout his life; he never felt quite safe on his throne, and dealt particularly harshly with any who were suspected of maintaining relations with the house of Vasa.

Such conduct naturally provoked growing discontent among the more liberal of his subjects. These were not confined to any one social stratum, but they were particularly well represented amidst the wholesale merchants and manufacturers, who wanted a freer economy, the richer peasants, and the professional men and intellectuals who together made up Sweden's middle class. But for a number of years after the end of the European war, criticism was sporadic, poorly organized, and directed mainly against the Government's financial policy, over which the Constitution gave the Estates most power.

Finance was undoubtedly the most serious immediate problem with which Charles John had to deal, for the situation in this field had improved little since the crisis of Gustavus IV's reign; the conversion of 1802 had proved to be only a temporary palliative. Between 1807 and 1812 the number of bank-notes in circulation had doubled; prices had nearly doubled; and the exchange rate of Swedish currency on the international markets had worsened proportionately. Wages also rose, and while some large farmers benefited from the increased costs of their produce, the majority of the population, especially those on a fixed income, suffered; many tenants were evicted. After 1812 conditions became somewhat more stable, but the exchange rate continued to deteriorate, while the price of corn, following a series of good harvests and a decline in foreign demand, fell; and trade was hit by the general post-war depression.

A committee set up by the *Riksdag* of 1815 to investigate the problem recommended the adoption of a rigorous protectionist policy to restore the balance of trade. Its findings were accepted, and a ban was placed on the import of 300 and the export of some 50 articles. This did not have the desired effect, but there was considerable disagreement on what further measures should be adopted. Charles John had an exaggerated idea of his own financial acumen, and blamed the situation on foreign enemies and unpatriotic elements in Sweden. He intervened in the dispute by buying up a large quantity of bank-notes at a loss to prevent speculation, and then urged the Estates to adopt an inflationary policy aimed at giving all notes in circulation their full value. He failed, however, to win wide acceptance for this scheme, which seemed to many members too reminiscent of the disastrous line adopted by the Hats. The only decision reached was to maintain the quantity of notes at its existing level for the next five years. This was a minor victory for the deflationists, who looked forward to a further conversion and a return to the silver standard, which had in practice been abandoned; and by the end of the *Riksdag* of 1828-30 all the Estates had been won over to their point of view. But it took much longer to obtain the reluctant agreement of the king. Not until 1834, after half the existing notes had been bought up, did the principles of 'sound finance' and 'hard money' triumph and the rate of exchange become stable once more.

This victory over the king marks an important stage in the struggle of the Estates for control of policy, but the Opposition

was still far from united in its aims, and had made disappoint-
ingly little progress during the 1820's. The most vigorous critic
of royal actions and attitudes was a noble, Colonel Anckarsvärd,
but his main interest was in securing a reduction of Government expenditure, and his constitutional ideals looked back to
the Era of Liberty rather than forward to parliamentary
government. Far more like a modern party leader was the
spokesman of the peasants, Anders Danielsson. He agreed with
Anckarsvärd on the need for economies, and did succeed in
getting some cuts made in the budget of 1823, but at the same
time he pressed for greater equality in the tax burdens imposed
on the various classes of society. As a body, however, the
peasants remained royalist in sympathy and in 1827 voted
against the abolition of the *indragningsmakt*. This was becoming
an increasingly important weapon in the Crown's armoury, for
the most sweeping criticisms of its policy now came not from
inside the Estates, but in liberal newspapers led by the *Argus*,
which had been founded in 1820 by Johan Johansson, a former
ally of Anckarsvärd who had grown impatient with the Baron's
eighteenth-century outlook.

It was not only Charles XIV's autocracy, naïve financial
theories and social conservatism which the Opposition attacked.
There was also considerable dissatisfaction among liberals and
conservatives alike with his foreign policy, especially its apparently pro-Russian character. It is true that Bernadotte realized
the importance of maintaining as friendly relations as possible
with the power which could do his realm most harm, but his
'1812 Policy' (named after the Russo-Swedish alliance of that
year) did not imply that Sweden should agree blindly to the
tsar's slightest whim, especially if this whim might antagonize
Britain. Good relations with that power were vital both for economic reasons and because the British navy would be essential for
Sweden's defence should war break out in the Baltic. This pull
between East and West is apparent in all the minor crises in
international relations with which Sweden found herself faced
in the decade after the Napoleonic Wars—the Danish Debt Dispute; the Bodö Affair; and the 'Ships Question'.

When Norway was transferred from the Danish to the
Swedish Crown, it was agreed that she should shoulder a fair
share of Denmark's public debt. No figure was, however, speci-

fied, and subsequent Dano-Swedish negotiations failed to produce a settlement, in spite of considerable pressure exerted on
Charles John by the great powers. Not until the attitude of the
latter, especially of Russia, became menacing, and Britian
threatened to impose economic sanctions, did the king, in 1819,
accept the latter's mediation. Under this, a solution was finally
reached, but by it Norway still paid only half the sum Denmark
had originally demanded.

A further conflict between Britain and Sweden arose in the
same year. An English merchant, who had been imprisoned by
the Norwegian authorities for smuggling goods through the new
town of Bodö in the far north of the country, claimed compensation for wrongful arrest, and was backed by his Government.
The claim was rejected, and the diplomatic atmosphere grew
tense, until in 1821 Charles finally agreed to pay part of the
amount asked for. This was accepted, but the king's action
brought forth vigorous protests from the Norwegians, who were
already sorely discontent with Britain owing to the tariffs she
had imposed on her imports of their timber.

But the most dramatic crisis in foreign affairs which Charles
had to tackle in these early years of his reign—and the one which
lent most ammunition to the Opposition in Sweden—arose as a
result of the struggle being conducted at this time by the Latin
Amercian peoples to free themselves from Spanish rule. While
Britain, largely for commercial reasons, supported the rebels
and, in 1825, recognized their independence, Russia, as part of
her policy of defending the cause of 'legitimacy' throughout the
world, called on the monarchies of Europe to help the King of
Spain to force his subjects to return to their allegiance. While
the Swedes did not dare to go so far as to recognize the new
republics, they did agree to sell some of their obsolete warships
to Colombia and two new ones to Mexico. The Government's
motives in making this decision were mixed. The king was himself very interested in the commercial possibilities of closer con-
tacts, for his realm's trade with America was growing steadily
at this juncture. But he also joined his anglophile Foreign
Minister, Count Gustav af Wetterstedt, in hoping that the sale
would strengthen Sweden's ties with western Europe, while one
of the prime movers of the scheme, Admiral Rudolf Cederström,
hoped to spend the proceeds on modernizing and strengthening

the fleet. The proposal brought fierce protests from Russia, and Britain, who did not wish for any complications in the Baltic area at this time, advised Charles to give way. Very reluctantly he did so. The sales were stopped; compensation was paid to Mexico for breach of contract; and the warships intended for Colombia were sold in New York at a substantial loss. The king was accused by the Opposition of having kotowed to Russia, but he had in fact stubbornly defended his freedom of action in St. Petersburg and run the risk of an open breach with the tsar.

In spite of his resentment at Russia's attitude during the 'Ships Crisis', in the years following, he drew nearer to his eastern neighbour and gave his critics more justifiable cause for complaint; in 1831 he even had his grandson christened Nicholas after the tsar, who acted as one of the godparents. One of the reasons for this change of attitude seems to have been the death of Alexander I in 1825, which weakened the link binding the Vasas and the Romanovs (Alexander, it may be remembered, was the brother-in-law of Gustavus IV). But another was the outbreak in 1830 of a number of liberal-nationalist revolts in various parts of Europe, in particular the rising of the Belgians against the King of Holland, under whose rule they had been placed by the Vienna settlement of 1815. This might, it was felt in Stockholm, set a bad example to the Norwegians, who the previous year had rioted when the Government banned celebrations in Christiania to mark the anniversary of the declaration of Norway's independence in 1814. But the growing effectiveness of liberalism in Sweden itself was also making the king even more conservative than he had been before, and thus more sympathetic of the tsar's attitude.

The revolutions of 1830, especially that of the Poles against their Russian masters, gave a great fillip to Swedish liberalism. At the end of the year it at last gained an effective mouthpiece in the paper *Aftonbladet*, founded—and for the next twenty years edited—by Lars Johan Hierta, the scion of a noble family who nevertheless voiced the aspirations of the progressive middle class, and gathered round him a number of able collaborators. Older Opposition journals like *Argus* quickly succumbed, and in five years *Aftonbladet*'s circulation reached the then record figure of 4,000 copies. The modern Swedish press was born.

The great improvement in the strength of the Opposition was reflected in the elections to the *Riksdag* of 1834. The Government retained a firm hold over the nobles and the clergy, but it lost its majority in the Estates of the burghers and peasants. Such an equal balance prevented the latter from achieving any very positive reforms except in the budget, which was cut, but the liberals' new self-confidence manifested itself in a stream of petitions calling for the repeal of the *indragningsmakt* and reform of the Estates system, and attacking the part supposed to be played in government by the king's favourite, Count Brahe, Adjutant-General since 1828. In 1838, the liberals were further heartened by the adoption of certain parts of their programme by the great poet and historian Gustav Geijer,[1] who had previously supported the Crown and a conservative policy; his former allies never forgot his 'apostasy'.

In spite of the reformers' apparent lack of achievement in the 1830's, it was obvious from the outcome of some of the measures which the Government took to defend itself that it was being forced more and more on to the defensive, and was becoming more and more embarrassed by the attacks launched against it. In 1832, one of Hierta's associates, Anders Lindeberg, was condemned to death for personal attacks he had made on Charles XIV. Not even the most reactionary Swede really wished such a sentence to be carried out, but it was the only one laid down for the crime of *lèse-majesté*, and the judges had no choice in the matter once guilt had been established. The king intervened to reduce the punishment to three years' imprisonment, but Lindeberg decided to make things as awkward for the ministers as possible by insisting on suffering the full rigour of the law. The Government was finally compelled to resort to the device of proclaiming an amnesty for all political prisoners, of whom there was only one in the country—Lindeberg himself! When further proceedings were instituted against him a few years later, the increasingly influential Crown Prince Oscar persuaded his father to withdraw the charges in order to avoid the risk of fresh ridicule; August von Hartsmansdorff, the Lord Chamberlain and chief organizer of the conservative forces in the Estates, resigned his office in protest at what seemed to him such an abject surrender. In 1838 another fierce critic of the régime, Magnus

---

[1] For more about Geijer see p. 220.

Crusenstolpe, a journalist and short-story writer who had deserted the conservative press four years previously, was also arraigned for *lèse-majesté*. The law had been hastily changed after the Lindeberg case so as to make it possible to impose a mere three years' imprisonment for the offence, but the application of even this penalty led to riots in Stockholm in which two people were killed. Meanwhile, the Government was having as little success with its use of the *indragningsmakt* against liberal publications. Hierta, who was the chief target, constantly outwitted it by republishing his newspaper after confiscation under a slightly different title, such as *New Aftonbladet* or, finally, *Twenty-sixth Aftonbladet*.

In the *Riksdag* of 1840–41, the longest of the reign, the Opposition at last achieved something of a breakthrough, although still on a rather narrow front. The only Estate with a decided liberal majority was that of the peasants; the burghers were divided, and the clergy and nobles supported the Government. But the latter house contained a larger number of liberals than ever before, and superior organization enabled the reformers to capture the various committees at the beginning of the session. The *Råd* was so alarmed by this success that it offered to resign as a body, an entirely unprecedented move. The king refused to allow it to do so, but he did agree to put into operation a reform of the administration which had been pending since 1835. This involved the abolition of a number of offices (including those of Lord Chamberlain and Adjutant-General), and, even more important, the transformation of the Council into something like a modern cabinet of seven ministers, each at the head of a department, together with three without portfolio. It did not, however, bring any appreciable change in personnel and did little to mollify the Opposition. As before, this enjoyed most success in the field of finance, cutting taxation while increasing expenditure on such items as education. But more significant for the future was the proposal of the powerful Constitutional Committee, which could, in certain circumstances, impeach a minister, to make a drastic reform of the legislature itself. It voted for no less than the replacement of the Estates by two houses elected on a common and wide franchise as existed in Norway, the ideal of many Swedish liberals at this time. Unfortunately, by the time the project came before the whole *Riksdag*, Hartmansdorff had been able to rally his followers and it was rejected. The old system was to survive for a further quarter of a century.

The forces of conservatism remained extremely strong. But this does not mean that they resisted all change during these years. The king and his ministers were no die-hard reactionaries, and carried through important reforms in spheres which did not involve the royal prerogative. This was especially true in the late 1830's and early 1840's, when the aging Charles bequeathed more and more of the burdens of government to his more liberal son. Restrictions on trade were lifted; as early as 1828, many of the articles whose import had been banned were once more admitted into the country, although they were made subject to heavy duties. Considerable attention was paid to agriculture; the enclosure movement was speeded up by an ordinance of 1827. In 1842 another ordinance, embodying recommendations put forward by the Estates, ordered the setting up of an elementary school in every parish, to be attended by all children until they had reached a certain level of proficiency.

Sweden's foreign policy after 1830 continued to reflect the opposing pulls of East and West to which she was exposed. When war threatened to break out in 1833 between Russia on the one hand and Britain and France on the other over the Eastern Question, and the former began ominously to increase her military activity on the Åland Islands, only some sixty miles from Stockholm, the Swedes took counter-measures to protect their capital. The following year, they joined the Danes in issuing a declaration of neutrality which permitted foreign warships the restricted use of Scandinavian ports. The tsar immediately protested at what he regarded as an unfriendly act; since he had his own naval bases on the Baltic, only his enemies could benefit. The crisis passed, but soon afterwards Russia was further disturbed by news of Swedish plans to turn the small harbour of Slite on Gotland into a free port. Again it was Britain who was the most likely to profit; her interest in the trade of the Baltic area had increased considerably since the opening in 1832 of the Göta Canal linking Gothenburg and Stockholm. On a sudden visit to Sweden in 1838, Nicholas persuaded Charles to postpone the project, which was finally dropped. The tsar later complained also of the anti-Russian character of many of the joint meetings held by Scandinavian students after 1839, and of the tone of the articles in Swedish newspapers which supported their call for closer co-operation between Denmark and Sweden. The king had little sympathy with this 'Scandinavianism' and throughout his life remained extremely suspicious of the intentions of Denmark, who was its main sponsor. He was therefore happy to oblige his fellow sovereign so far as to issue, in 1842, a series of statements specifically disassociating himself from the movement.

The following year he celebrated his silver jubilee amidst widespread rejoicing. The liberals' successes in the recent *Riksdag*, however limited, and the reforms which the Government itself had carried out had between them taken some of the sting out of the Opposition. In a world where the middle class was becoming increasingly conscious of its strength, it could in any case afford to be generous to an 80-year-old monarch, whose ideas were growing more and more anachronistic. But there was more to it than this. Charles John's reign, which ended the next year, was the longest in modern Swedish history, and yet it was the first one not to be troubled by foreign wars; by his skilful diplomacy before he came to the throne he had done much to retrieve the honour of his adopted country; though no thanks to him, the financial situation at his death was more stable than it had been for half a century; and the future of all classes looked reasonably bright. Sweden in 1844 had much to be thankful for, and Charles XIV, whose last words were 'no one has had a career like mine', deserved well of them.

CHAPTER XVII

Liberalism and Scandinavianism: 1844–66

The passing of Charles XIV attracted more attention than had the death of his predecessor, but it did not constitute any more of a turning-point in Swedish history. For several years before it, the Government's policy had been betraying the influence of his son's more liberal views, and, as the Opposition in the *Riksdag* had hoped, the accession of the 45-year-old Oscar I brought with it an intensification of the work of reform.

Among the first measures of the new reign were the formal abolition of the already dormant *indragningsmakt* and a reduction in the life of the Estates from five to three years. In 1845, the first victory was won in what proved to be a long struggle for the emancipation of Swedish women; daughters in the countryside were given equal rights of inheritance with sons, something which their urban sisters had long enjoyed in accordance with town customs. This came about as a result of a proposal in the *Riksdag*, which was carried by all the Estates except that of the nobles. But it was the Government itself which, the following year, did much to free the economic life of the country by abolishing most of the remaining restrictions on the exercise of a craft in towns; the guilds were replaced by much looser associations. There had long been a demand for such a move from the liberal burghers, who had been strengthened in the *Riksdag* of 1828–30 by the admission into the Estate of five representatives of the industrialists, but it met with considerable opposition from the smaller craftsmen and retailers, who were alienated from the ministry by this policy. In 1847 Sweden at last received a Poor Law which obliged towns and parishes to care for their less fortunate members. The king had a special interest in this question, and played a leading part in the composition of the ordinance. As crown prince he had also campaigned vigorously for a sweeping reform of the Law Code (now over a hundred years old) and of the judicial system, but the Estates would agree to only minor changes which simplified procedure and to reduce the severity of the punishment for some offences. Finally, in 1849, a new Education Act unified the system of public instruction by associating the various secondary schools, whose students were no longer to be obliged to read Latin, Greek or Hebrew, with the elementary schools provided for by the Act of 1842, although this was still far from being fully implemented.

By 1848, however, it had become evident to many liberals that they had expected far more from Oscar than he was willing to give, and even that which had already been granted had alienated many members of his Government. He showed no inclination to surrender any of his constitutional powers, and was decidedly luke-warm on the burning question of reform of the *Riksdag*. The establishment of a republic in France in February 1848 led to upheavals in many parts of Europe, and Sweden did not wholly escape the contagion. Riots broke out in Stockholm, in which radicals calling for the introduction of universal suffrage and even for the abolition of the monarchy were joined by craftsmen who feared the effects on themselves of a freer economy. The windows of reactionaries like Hartmansdorff were broken, and when troops were finally called out and fired on the assembled crowd, about thirty citizens were killed; Swedish radicalism had its first crop of martyrs. In face of all this, and of the growth of criticism from both Right and Left, the king's reforming zeal began rapidly to evaporate. He never in fact had much love for the noisy, pushing *bourgeoisie*, and was becoming more and more apprehensive of the danger from socialism, although the movement had as yet little following in his realm.

He allowed his Cabinet to resign, and reconstituted it on a more conservative foundation. Conditions were ripe for the emergence of a right-wing group of nobles known as the Junker Party, led by Count Henning Hamilton and Baron Carl Otto Palmstierna. These men were very close to Crown Prince Charles and acquired great influence through their skilful use of the press. In 1851, Palmstierna was appointed Minister of Finance, and Hartmansdorff found himself pushed more and more into the background. The only important reforms of the early 1850's (often referred to as Oscar I's 'conservative period') were largely extensions of those passed earlier; in 1854 permission was given to Jews to settle wherever they chose in the country, and the following year further restrictions on internal trade were removed.

Of the issues which concerned liberals most—electoral and parliamentary reform—little was heard for several years after the defeat of a Government project in the *Riksdag* of 1850–51. This was a rather more radical version of the proposal made by a committee of the Estates in 1847 for the replacement of the four Estates by two houses enjoying equal power—an upper house elected on a franchise with a high property qualification and with a third of its members chosen by the Crown, and a more popular lower house. Such a solution had satisfied no one, not even the members of the committee which drew it up, only one of whom accepted it without reservations. The plan of 1851 removed the royal nominees and widened the franchise for the lower house, but Oscar let it be known that he was opposed to its adoption, and it was consequently thrown out by all the Estates except that of the burghers. The conservatives' case against the introduction of a bicameral system was somewhat strengthened—although their influence was at the same time undermined—by changes which had recently been made in the composition of the Estates aimed at giving representation to certain groups of the middle class hitherto excluded. The clergy admitted four members for the universities in 1823, and, as has been seen, the *brukspatroner* were entitled after 1830 to send four of their number to sit with the burghers. By 1844 peasants owning tax-free land, who had previously been unrepresented, were allowed to vote for members of their Estate. But such piecemeal —and often grudging—reform could do no more than shore up temporarily a tottering structure which was growing more out of touch with social realities with every year that passed. The remaining privileges of the nobility were under constant attack; the laicization of education and society in general was undermining the influence of the clergy; and a freer economic life was making the status of the burgher an anachronism.

In the final destruction of the conservative edifice foreign affairs played an important part. King Oscar had as crown prince taken no trouble to conceal his sympathies for Scandinavianist aspirations, nor his desire to strengthen Sweden's ties

THE HOUSE OF BERNADOTTE
(Some less important members of the family have been omitted for the sake of clarity)

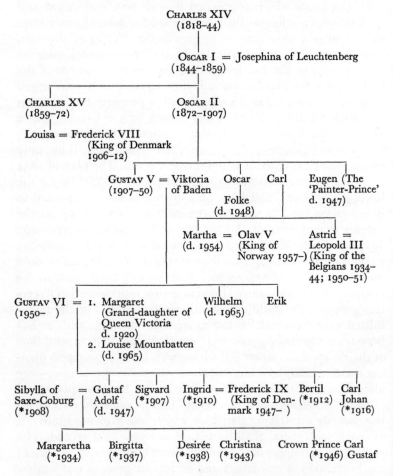

CHARLES XIV
(1818–44)

OSCAR I = Josephina of Leuchtenberg
(1844–1859)

CHARLES XV
(1859–72)

OSCAR II
(1872–1907)

Louisa = Frederick VIII
(King of Denmark
1906–12)

GUSTAV V = Viktoria   Oscar   Carl   Eugen (The
(1907–50) of Baden   'Painter-Prince'
                       Folke   d. 1947)
                       (d. 1948)

Martha = Olav V   Astrid =
(d. 1954) (King of   Leopold III
         Norway 1957–) (King of the
                       Belgians 1934–
                       44; 1950–51)

GUSTAV VI = 1. Margaret   Wilhelm   Erik
(1950–)   (Grand-daughter of (d. 1965)
             Queen Victoria
             d. 1920)
          2. Louise Mountbatten
             (d. 1965)

Sibylla of = Gustaf Sigvard Ingrid = Frederick IX Bertil Carl
Saxe-Coburg   Adolf   (*1907) (*1910) (King of Den- (*1912) Johan
(*1908)   (d. 1947)   mark 1947–)   (*1916)

Margaretha   Birgitta   Desirée Christina   Crown Prince Carl
(*1934)   (*1937)   (*1938) (*1943)   (*1946) Gustaf

with the West to protect her against Russia. Scandinavianism and Russophobia were, as St. Petersburg knew full well, very closely allied; fear of the giant in the east was one of the main motive-forces behind the campaign for closer co-operation between Denmark and Sweden-Norway and for eventual political union which began in Denmark in the late 1830's. The King of Sweden could obviously not afford to antagonize Russia too much before the movement had more positive achievements to boast of than pious outpourings at student gatherings, and his reactions to the approaches which came from Denmark early in his reign were cautious. In 1848, however, an opportunity offered itself to demonstrate his friendship for his southern neighbour without offending his eastern one. In that year, the German-speaking inhabitants of the Duchy of Holstein rebelled against Frederick VII, demanding independence, union with the partly Danish-speaking Duchy of Slesvig to the north, and the entry of both Duchies into the nation which their fellows in Germany proper were attempting to weld from the multitude of small states of which it then consisted. The latter granted the Holsteiners military support against Denmark, and in face of this threat, the Danish king welcomed Oscar's offer of 4,500 Swedish troops to help him defend his territories. The tsar, opposed as he was to all nationalist aspirations and any movements by subjects against their rulers,[1] also supported Frederick, and the German forces were compelled to withdraw from the Duchy. An armistice was then signed under Swedish mediation, and the Swedish troops returned home. Fighting broke out again, but this time the *Riksdag* proved less willing than before to grant subsidies for military operations, and Sweden took no further part in the war. By the terms of the peace preliminaries signed in July 1849, however, her troops were to occupy northern Slesvig until the conclusion of a definitive settlement, which came the following year; and in 1852 she joined other interested powers in signing the Treaty of London, which guaranteed the *status quo*.

Although he was certainly attracted by the prospect of wearing the Danish crown and reviving the Union of Kalmar, King Oscar in fact placed more reliance on Britain and France as a bulwark against Russia than on Denmark, with her comparatively meagre resources. And the Crimean War, which broke out in 1854, seemed to him a golden opportunity to secure the pro-

[1] He was also interested in the question as a descendant of Tsar Peter III, who had been Duke of Holstein.

tection he wanted on favourable terms. The Baltic was one of only two gateways into Russia for her enemies, and British and French warships were immediately sent there, and negotiations opened for Sweden's active participation in the conflict. Oscar, however, overreached himself. The Allies found his terms, which included large subsidies and Austria's entry into the war on their side, too high, especially after they had decided to launch their main attack, not in the Baltic against St. Petersburg but in the Black Sea against Sevastopol. The king decided eventually to climb down, and in 1855 sent one of his own group of friends, whom he was in the habit of employing on diplomatic missions without the knowledge of his too-cautious ministers, to sound Napoleon III. He failed to gain from the emperor a promise of military support sufficient for an attack on Russia, but he had some success when he turned to Britain.

Lord Palmerston, who had become Prime Minister at the beginning of the year, had long been alarmed by reports (in fact unfounded) of Russian plans to use claims to fishing rights off the coast of northern Norway to secure a warm-water naval base on the Atlantic. Playing on this fear, Oscar obtained from Britain and France, by the so-called November Treaty, a guarantee against Russian aggression, not only for Finnmark but for his whole realm. Although the agreement was a purely defensive one, it constituted a definite break with the '1812 Policy' initiated by Charles XIV; and there can be little doubt that his son saw it as the first step towards belligerency, for which he was prepared in 1856. He secretly encouraged the 'activists' (joined by *Aftonbladet* after a 'palace revolution' in the editorial office at the end of the year), who were calling for a crusade against Slavic barbarism to liberate Finland, while he skilfully gave the impression of yielding to their pressure. At the beginning of 1856, however, Russia accepted the Allies' terms, and all Oscar's plans collapsed. All that the Swedish delegation to the peace conference in Paris was able to secure was the demilitarization of the Åland Islands.

Whatever might be said in defence of the king's foreign policy at this time (which was certainly disapproved of by his military advisers, who were very dubious about Sweden's preparedness for war) there can be little doubt that its net effects were to increase his unpopularity at home and weaken his position abroad.

The activists formed a comparatively small, if vocal, group, and the majority of Swedes were opposed to foreign adventures; they valued too highly the peace which Charles John had given them and the growing prosperity which it had brought. Some liberals feared—so far had their earlier hopes of the king been shattered —that he might try to use a war to introduce some kind of military dictatorship. His ministers resented the way he had acted over their heads. Sweden's relations with Russia were naturally strained without any compensating intimacy being established with the Western powers. And the way in which Denmark had been practically ignored throughout the proceedings considerably lessened the chances of achieving closer Scandinavian cooperation. It is significant that, while in the 1840's the initiative for this had come largely from Denmark, immediately after the Crimean War the rôles were reversed. The press in Sweden was by then overwhelmingly Scandinavianist in sentiment; in 1856 Oscar ostentatiously entertained the leaders of a Scandinavian student assembly at Drottingholm; and the following year he offered Denmark a defensive alliance, which she turned down as being too limited in scope.

In June 1857 Oscar fell too ill to perform his duties, and his 31-year-old son became first regent and then king as Charles XV on his father's death two years later. The comparatively brief reign of this very popular monarch, who befriended artists in all fields and himself wrote poetry, is an important landmark in Swedish history. It saw the end of personal monarchy as Charles XIV and Oscar I had attempted to practise it and the triumph of cabinet government, not so much because the new king was less ambitious than his predecessors (although he did once declare that he aimed to be 'a man first and a king second') as because conditions were no longer favourable for royal power; the behaviour of Oscar I had, for one thing, opened men's eyes to the abuses to which it might be put. These years also witnessed the triumph of free trade in Sweden; sweeping reforms in local government; the replacement at last of the four Estates by a Parliament of two Houses like that which existed in most other European countries; the death of Scandinavianism in its nineteenth-century, political form; and a crisis for the Swedo-Norwegian Union from which it never really recovered.

A committee formed at the end of Charles John's reign,

which published its report just after his death, had recommended the strengthening of ties between Sweden and Norway by the appointment of a council of twenty-four drawn from the *Riksdag* and the *Storting* to discuss matters of common interest, but this advice was not accepted; Oscar had done no more than grant equal rights to the flags and coats-of-arms of the two nations. The hopes expressed by the Swedish activists during the Crimean War for a reunion of Finland with Sweden alienated many Norwegians, who feared the possible effects on themselves of such an access of Swedish power. And their fears seemed justified by the reactions in Sweden to Charles XV's proposal in 1859 to placate them by abolishing the office of Governor of Norway (an actual viceroy was appointed for only two brief periods in the nineteenth century). With his encouragement, the *Storting* did so, but this brought forth such a storm of protest from the Cabinet in Stockholm, which threatened to resign, that the king had to veto the resolution. In such circumstances, the chances of achieving a closer union were very slender, although Charles did not give up hope, and a new committee to consider the question was set up in 1865. By this time Scandinavianism had suffered an even more serious—indeed a fatal—blow.

There was a great deal of liberal agitation in Sweden in 1863 on behalf of the Poles, who had once more rebelled against Russian rule, and the king dreamed for a time of launching a new crusade in the east in alliance with France, where sympathy for the Polish cause was also strong. But the days of royal diplomacy had passed with the fiasco of Oscar I's attempts, and the Council was decidedly cool to the idea of giving any practical aid to the rebels; it appealed to the tsar to avoid unnecessary bloodshed, as Charles John had done during the previous uprising, but turned back a group of Poles who arrived in Malmö on a British steamer hoping to make Gothenburg a base for anti-Russian operations.

The Government was equally unenthusiastic about the Danish king's declaration the same year that the Duchy of Slesvig was an integral part of his realm, thus breaking its ties with the predominantly German-speaking Duchy of Holstein to the south; the ministry in Stockholm recognized the *fait accompli*, but failed to give the Danes the support they had hoped for when the German Confederation threatened to intervene to restore the *status quo*. Declarations of Nordic solidarity were confined to Scandinavianist activists. Since 1860, these had been strongly represented among the Sharp-shooters, a kind of militia with over 40,000 members, which had little military value but a strongly nationalist and anti-Russian character. The king shared their feelings and, when the Germans issued an ultimatum to Denmark in July, he visited King Frederick in Copenhagen on his own initiative, and promised Swedish help in defending the line of the River Ejder, which divided Slesvig from Holstein. His Foreign Minister, Christoffer Manderström, refused, however, to back up this promise with any written agreement, and was supported by his colleagues, Louis De Geer, Minister of Justice and, as such, Premier, and Baron Johan Gripenstedt, Minister of Finance. Only if either Britain or France could be drawn in were they prepared to consider an alliance with Denmark, and of this there was little prospect. When German troops crossed the Ejder at the beginning of 1864, some Swedish volunteers were allowed to join the Danes in the brief war which ended in Denmark's loss of both the Duchies to Austria and Prussia; but Sweden made no official move to help her neighbour. The windows of Gripenstedt's and Manderström's houses in Stockholm were broken, but the heart had already gone out of Scandinavianism, and it could hardly be expected to withstand this final shock.

It was Gripenstedt, the 'strong man' of the brilliant ministry formed after Charles XV's accession, who was largely responsible for the triumph of free trade in Sweden with the Franco-Swedish commercial treaty concluded the year after the Slesvig-Holstein débâcle; like the Cobden Treaty made between Britain and France in 1860, it considerably reduced the tariffs imposed by each country on the other's goods. There had been a powerful movement in favour of free trade for several years in Sweden, and a Free Trade Association, strongly influenced by the English Anti-Corn Law League of the 30's and 40's, had been founded in Gävle in 1846. The economic situation favoured it, and King Oscar lent his support to the campaign, which enjoyed considerable success in the *Riksdag* of 1853–54. The Crimean War greatly benefited Swedish agriculture by eliminating the competition of Russian wheat, and in 1857 it was agreed to make permanent the hitherto-temporary abolition of import duties on grain. Although a trade crisis followed hard on the heels of this decision, and a reaction set in, the Government stood firm.

Another field in which the liberal character of the late 50's and the 60's is apparent is that of religious toleration. The freedom of settlement accorded to Jews in 1854 has already been noted, and in 1860 they were also given the same rights to own property as other Swedes, although they were excluded from the *Riksdag* and public office for a further ten years. King Oscar was particularly interested in the question of toleration for Christian minorities, as his wife, Josephina of Leuchtenberg, was a Roman Catholic, and just before his death a bill was passed which allowed non-Lutherans to hold public services, although only on certain, rather restrictive, conditions. In 1860, the punishment of exile for apostasy from the State Church was abolished and Lutherans allowed to enter recognized dissenting bodies.[1] It is notable how far Sweden was behind Britain—and many other European countries—in this respect, but it must be remembered that there is, on the other hand, nothing in her history to compare with the Marian persecutions, the panic of the Popish Plot or the hunting down of the Covenanters, and also that religious minorities have never formed more than a very small proportion of the total population.

Important as were such questions as free trade *versus* protection, and religious toleration, it was that of reform of the *Riksdag* which dominated Swedish politics in the 1860's. Feeling in favour of reform had been growing again for several years; the Sharp-shooters were behind it, and the size of the petitions pressing for it was impressive. By 1862 De Geer realized that the problem could be shelved no longer. He had already drawn up his own project, and now threatened to resign if the king did not accept this as the official proposal. Charles XV had some doubts about it, but finally agreed to his Prime Minister's demand. The plan was accordingly presented to the Estates in January 1863. It provided for an upper and a lower House. One-ninth of the former was to be elected annually by the city and county councils set up as part of an extensive reform of local government the year before: members had to be at least thirty-five, own a considerable amount of property or enjoy a substan-

[1] For Dissent in Sweden, see pp. 227–8.

tial income, and were to be unpaid. The members of the lower
House, who were to be elected every three years, had to be at
least twenty-five and have a reasonable income, but they were to
be paid, and chosen by all men over twenty-one who possessed
the same property qualifications as themselves. The *Riksdag*
composed of these two Houses was to meet every year.[1]

The new system of local government, which in 1862 paved the
way for parliamentary reform, granted the smallest unit in the
countryside—the township or commune—much greater freedom than before in such matters as the apportioning of taxes,
and allowed all towns of over 3,000 inhabitants to elect a
council. The communes and urban councils were responsible
for the election of an entirely new body—the *landsting* or county
council, one for each of the twenty-four counties (*län*) into
which the country was divided, under a chairman appointed by
the Crown. For some time the powers and responsibilities of all
these organs remained ill-defined except in the spheres of
poor-relief and health, but as the State came to concern itself
more and more with social matters, an increasing burden was
placed on their shoulders.

It was left to the *Riksdag* of 1865–66 to decide whether or not
to accept De Geer's plan, and as the time appointed for its
meeting drew near, the press and pamphlet war grew fierce; the
liberals, while not particularly happy about the proposal,
generally backed it for fear of getting nothing at all, but conservatives and radicals were less inhibited in their criticisms.
The crucial vote was taken in December 1865. The burghers,
who, as a result of reforms of their order carried through in
1858, now represented all urban property owners and trades-
men, voted in favour by a large majority, and the peasants
imitated them. The clergy resolved to await the decision of the
nobles, which thus became all-important. The debate in the
Riddarhus lasted four days, at the end of which, in spite of the
oratory of Henning Hamilton in opposition to the bill, it was
passed by 361 votes to 294. The clergy obediently fell into line,
and in June 1866 the four Estates were dissolved for the last
time.

[1] The precise size of the two Houses was not fixed until 1894, since when
the Upper House has contained 150 members and the Lower 230.

CHAPTER XVIII

Industrialism, Defence and the End of the Union with Norway: 1860–1905

The four decades between the abolition of the four Estates in 1866 and the dissolution of the union with Norway in 1905 witnessed a transformation of Swedish society hitherto without parallel in the country's history, a transformation which may be summed up in the one word 'industrialization'. Like most similar developments, industrialism reached Sweden considerably later than north-west Europe, and it cannot really be said that she ever underwent an Industrial Revolution in the same way as did Britain, Belgium or Germany, nor that she ever became an industrial power in the same class as these. But the fact that, while in 1850 over 90 per cent of all Swedes lived in the countryside, only 75 per cent did so fifty years later is a graphic indication of the changes which were gathering momentum throughout the period. Behind this phenomenon, which profoundly affected Sweden's political as well as her economic and social life, lay a great improvement in communications with the rapid spread of railways, the amelioration of inland waterways and the replacement of sail by steam on rivers and sea-lanes; the introduction of the telegraph and telephone, and the growth of banking and in the complexity of industrial organization which these encouraged; the mechanization of agriculture; the application of steam—and, at the very end of the period, electric—power to old industries, and the foundation of new ones.

The first railway line in Sweden was a twelve-mile stretch from Örebro north to Ervalla, and was opened in March 1856. It was the result of the private initiative of Count Adolf von

Rosen, who had long been campaigning, with only limited success, for the development of a national rail network. But it was built with the help of a Government subsidy, and three years previously the *Riksdag* had approved a plan for the construction of a series of main lines under State control to link the chief cities of the country. Only a few months after Rosen's line began operating, the first part of this plan, whose execution had been placed under the direction of Colonel Nils Ericson (brother of the American inventor John Ericsson (*sic*)), bore fruit in short tracks connecting Gothenburg with Jonsered and Malmö with Lund. By 1862 it was possible to travel by train from Gothenburg to Stockholm, and by the end of the century Sweden could boast a greater railway mileage per head of population than any other country in Europe. The competing merits of private and State enterprise in this field formed the subject of frequent debates in the *Riksdag* after 1852; Gripenstedt was the leading spokesman for the latter, while Rosen called for a fully independent system. The outcome was a compromise, by which the individual entrepreneur and the Government competed on roughly equal terms, with the latter taking responsibility for the main network and the former concentrating on branch lines to serve the smaller centres of population. This mixture has remained typical of Sweden's economic life in general to the present day,[1] although communications have recently come more and more into public ownership, and over 90 per cent of her railways are now run by the State. Some private lines, like that uniting Gothenburg with Malmö, were taken over by it, while others, like that from Luleå on the Gulf of Bothnia to the Norwegian border, were State-extended. One of the most important results of the creation of a railway system—and one of the primary aims of the original planners—was the opening up of Norrland and other isolated areas of the country; the threat of a famine like that which swept through the north as late as the 1860's was thereby exorcized.

The railway undoubtedly constituted the most important advance in transport in nineteenth-century Sweden, but it was by no means the only one. Much was done to improve the road system during the period; State subsidies for the building of new and the betterment of existing highways (especially in Norrland)

[1] For more about this see pp. 231, 260.

were made available after 1840. The first motor car did not appear on them until 1891, and it was not until six years after this that a Swedish model began to be manufactured on a modest scale. But the bicycle arrived in the 1860's and, together with horse-drawn trams in the larger cities, enabled an ever-larger number of workers to live in more salubrious surroundings, often at considerable distances from their factories, shops and offices. Sweden's excellent water communications enabled her to exploit rapidly the small paddle-steamer, first introduced into the country by the English immigrant Samuel Owen in 1818. Ten years later a service was initiated between Malmö and Copenhagen, but it was probably the northern part of the realm which benefited most from the invention. The tempo of business life—and of life in general—was appreciably increased by the spread of the electric telegraph after 1853, when a line was opened between Stockholm and Uppsala, and of the public telephone system after 1880, when the Bell Telephone Co. built an exchange in Stockholm with American capital. The first was under Government control from the beginning, but in the second field the State had to compete with several private enterprises until the end of the First World War, when it acquired a virtual monopoly. The postal system was completely reorganized after the introduction of the postage stamp and a single rate for all inland mail in 1855.

Industrial expansion presupposes an efficient credit system, and it was indeed largely lack of capital which held the Swedish economy back for so long. Private banks issuing notes in competition with the Estates or *Riksbank* were not permitted until 1824, and for several decades after this date the most important source of capital remained the great trading houses of Stockholm and Gothenburg. Only after 1856, when *Stockholms Enskilda Bank*, the oldest of the present 'Big Five' of the Swedish banking world, was founded, were they seriously challenged, but their decline in importance thereafter was rapid. By 1908 there were 84 private banks operating in the country, although only the *Riksbank* was allowed to issue notes after 1904.

In spite of the fact that Sweden had to import nearly all her coal,[1] steam power greatly helped her existing industries to

[1] There are some very small deposits in Scania.

expand in the latter part of the nineteenth century. Probably the most dramatic developments took place in the production of timber. The steam-driven saw, which could be set up on the coast near the mouth of the river used for the flotation of the felled trees, was first introduced in 1849. It began to be used in Sweden on a large scale in the 1860's, and, together with the improvements in communications and a rising demand on the British market at the same time, enabled the great resources of the northern provinces, so neglected in the past, to be exploited to the full. Up to this time, it had been the west of Sweden which had been the leading timber-producing area, but by the end of the century, when Sweden had become the world's leading exporter of wooden planks (about 40 per cent of the total), Norrland was providing 80 per cent of production. There was for long little attempt made to control the rapid depletion of the fir-forests which all this activity brought about, and soon after 1900 the industry's limit of expansion was reached. But already a use had been found for trees, such as spruce, which were unsuitable for sawing. Some of them had been pulped for paper-making since the middle of the century, but it was not until the 1880's that the perfection of various chemical processes enabled a satisfactory quality to be obtained. Exports of pulp then rose sharply, until they eventually overtook those of timber proper in value.

While Sweden's timber resources had been neglected in the past, her deposits of iron ore had long been recognized as among her most precious assets. The late eighteenth and early nineteenth centuries were periods of crisis for the iron industry; Britain's demand sank as the use of coke furnaces spread, and war interfered with exports. Although the position improved somewhat after 1815 and the United States provided a new market, Sweden's share of European iron production, which had been as high as 30 per cent fifty years before, now sank to a mere 3. From about 1840, however, prospects improved. Rapid strides were made in the techniques of smelting, which considerably cheapened the process, and enabled both greater concentration of output and the exploitation of deposits hitherto unusable because of impurities in the ore. The so-called 'Lancashire process', which demanded less fuel than its predecessors, was first employed on a large scale in the 1850's, and remained dominant until the end of the century in the manufacture of pig-iron. But the most striking advances in the field came with the introduction, at the end of the same decade, of the Bessemer process, another English discovery, which enabled steel to be made in quantity for the first time, and of the Thomas-Gilchrist method in the 1880's. The latter allowed the mining of the huge deposits of ore at Grängesberg in Bergslagen and round Kiruna in the far north, which had previously been useless because of their high phosphorus content: the building of a railway between the latter and the Norwegian port of Narvik in 1902 greatly facilitated export from the area. Side by side with these purely technical improvements went a modification of the extreme decentralization which had characterized the old *bruk* system; in the middle of the eighteenth century, there had been about 500 *bruk*, but by 1913 their number had been reduced by amalgamation to 140. Partly as a result of this, the old patriarchal government was replaced by more impersonal supervision of the workers.

Previously, most of Sweden's iron had been exported, but during the last decades of the nineteenth century a rising proportion of it was used to feed her own industries. With the spread of the railway and the mechanization of agriculture, engineering, which before 1870 played a very minor rôle in her economic life, leapt into prominence; in thirty years the number of engineering firms increased fivefold, and the number of workers employed by them sixfold. While factories and work shops were widely scattered, the town of Eskilstuna became the 'Sheffield of Sweden'. And Norrköping became her Manchester, for this and Borås in Västergötland were the leading textile centres of the country. Expansion here was not so dramatic, but twice as much cotton was spun in 1900 as in 1870. In addition to these key enterprises, a host of other forms of manufacture either, like the chemical, electrical and cement industries, appeared for the first time, or were greatly expanded during the period.

In spite of the rapid development of Sweden's industry and the concentration of her inhabitants in towns which accompanied it, she was still at the end of the nineteenth century primarily an agricultural country; three-quarters of the populations still lived on the land. In 1860 farming methods were fundamentally little different from what they had been in the seventeenth century; large parts of the forest regions had not yet been enclosed, and even the rotation of crops was by no means universal. The following decades, however, brought a great transformation. Iron ploughs and harrows began to be widely used, and harvesters and other mechanical devices were rapidly adopted. The use of chemical fertilizers and the improvement of seed by selection raised the productivity of land already under cultivation while many marshes were drained and wasteland made fertile. Scania continued to lead the way, especially in the growing of wheat; production of this crop expanded to such an extent that by the end of the century wheaten bread had ceased to be a luxury throughout the realm. The same is true of sugar; the growing of sugar-beet spread at a remarkable rate, and its refining became a major industry, concentrated in Scania. The farmer was at last persuaded to reduce the size of his herds of cattle and concentrate on quality by selective breeding; the heavier new tools also called for stronger horses to pull them. In dairying, the use of the mechanical cream separator, invented by the Swede Gustaf de Laval in 1878, greatly increased the output of butter, which again became one of Sweden's major exports. Agricultural co-operatives appeared in Sweden much later than in Denmark, and the idea spread more slowly there, but co-operative dairies were operating in the 1880's.

These spectacular changes on the land came partly as a result of the serious crisis which Swedish farmers, in common with many of their fellows in other parts of Europe (including Britain), had to face between 1870 and 1900 as improved communications began to flood the market with cheap Russian and American cereals; they had to improve their methods and organization, or go under. But the depression had two other important effects. It drove an unprecedented number of Swedes to seek their fortunes abroad, especially in the United States; and it led to a long and heated political debate over the desirability of protecting agriculture—and to a lesser extent industry—against foreign competition by means of tariff barriers.

A small number of Swedes were attracted by the open spaces of North America as early as the 1840's, but a fair proportion of these belonged to nonconformist religious groups who had been driven out by the intolerance of the State Church. After 1850, the pressure of a rapidly-growing population (by over 10 per cent between 1840 and 1860) on a still primitive economy and the easier transport facilities available for crossing the Atlantic caused a significant increase in the number of emigrants who left for purely secular reasons. Most of these settled in Minnesota, whose countryside of woods and lakes was reminiscent of that of their homeland, and 3,000 Swedes fought for the North in the American Civil War. But it was in the 1880's, at the height of the agricultural depression, that the movement reached its peak. During the decade, no fewer than 325,000 Swedes out of a total population of some four and a half million made their homes in the United States, many more than all those who had gone before. With the return of prosperity in the 1890's, the figures slumped, but it has been calculated that in 1910 every fifth Swede was on the other side of the Atlantic. The loss was greatest from the southern and western provinces, and was largely made up of younger sons and daughters and landless labourers, but urban workers were also driven away by the long hours and low wages which then prevailed in most industries. Although a third of the increase in the population during these years disappeared by emigration, it was not until the very end of the century that the Government began to show concern over this loss of manpower and its possible effect on the economy; it was argued, with some justification, that the movement was ridding the country of many potential malcontents.

For fifteen years after the conclusion of the trade treaty with France in 1865, the doctrine of free trade met with no serious opposition in Sweden. But the sharp fall in corn prices after 1880 caused criticism to mount. A Protection Association was formed, and the first shots of the coming battle in the *Riksdag* were fired in 1882, when proposals were put forward for a new commercial agreement with France. The newspaper *Svenska Dagbladet*, founded in 1884, became the leading mouthpiece of the protectionists, who won their first success two years later, when, by a small majority, the Upper House approved the imposition of duties on imported cereals. This was, however, rejected by the Lower. The elections of 1887 gave the free-traders a small majority in the latter, but this was lost when one of the members for Stockholm was found to have tax arrears and all the lists on which his name had appeared were declared invalid. This meant the unseating of all the twenty-two successful free-trade candidates in the capital and their replacement by their protectionist opponents. After this, duties were laid on corn, meat and other foodstuffs together with some industrial products; but a fully protectionist ministry was not formed until 1889, and the elections of 1890 again gave the free-traders a majority in the Lower House. The tariff on corn was reduced in 1892, but the expiry of the second French treaty enabled new duties to be laid on manufactured goods, and a particularly severe, if short-lived, agricultural crisis in 1894 forced the Government to yield to pressure from the farmers and restore the original protection to their wheat. All Europe, apart from Britain and one or two small nations like Holland, was by this time rapidly abandoning free trade, and Sweden could not resist the tide. Opposition to protection dwindled considerably in the 90's, and the question slipped once more into the background of political affairs.

Political life in general after the abolition of the four Estates was dominated by a struggle for power between an Upper House largely controlled by the old noble families and a Lower House where the farmers formed the largest and best organized section. The reform of 1866 had not given the influence to the liberal middle class expected by De Geer and his colleagues, and, as in England after 1832, the aristocracy continued to play a leading part in Swedish politics for many years; Carl Thyselius, the first commoner Prime Minister, was not appointed by the king until 1883. Nor did the reform lead to the formation of clearly defined parties on the British or American pattern, rather to the evolution of a number of groups after the French model. The picture is extremely confusing, as combinations in the *Riksdag* split up and amalgamated again under different names. Sectional interests, such as those of urban and rural areas, combined with different views on key issues, such as free trade and protection, to dictate the composition of these political formations, which it would be tedious to enumerate in any detail.

The parliamentary conflicts of the late 60's and early 70's were fought mainly over defence, which the successive defeats of Denmark, Austria and France by Prussia in these years made a particularly acute problem. The highly-organized German conscript army, equipped with new weapons made available in large numbers by industrialization, had revolutionized warfare, and successive Cabinets, all representative of the more conservative elements in Swedish society, pressed incessantly for an increase in the length of the military training which every citizen was expected to undergo; the thirty days which had been imposed after the Crimean War now seemed wholly inadequate. But the farmers in the Lower House demanded just as vigorously that any increase should be compensated for by reductions in the land-tax and radical modifications of the *indelning* system[1] which they had to support. A compromise, which could obviously be only temporary, was reached in 1885, when the tax was cut by a third and military service extended to forty-two days. Protection was now the burning question, but it was closely associated with defence, for the free traders feared that the protectionists would strengthen their case by claiming that the income from higher tariffs was needed to meet the costs of army reform. Not until the power of the free-traders was on the wane, in 1892, could a further advance be made. In this year, the farmers were persuaded by Erik Boström, one of the most able of Sweden's parliamentary leaders, to agree to ninety days' service in exchange for a gradual abolition of the land-tax. Tsar Alexander III's attacks on Finnish autonomy after 1895, combined with the growing strain in relations with Norway,[2] played further into the Premier's hands, as did the considerable improvement in the Government's financial position during his exceptionally long ministry (1891–1900). But it was left to Boström's successor to reap the harvest. In 1901, against the background of the Boer War, a bill was passed by both Houses under which military service was extended to eight months and the *indelning* system abolished.

A radical group known as the New Liberals appeared in the *Riksdag* in 1868 with a programme of full cabinet responsibility and universal suffrage. But it lasted only a few years, and it was not until the election of 1884 that the radicals of Stockholm, led by Sven Hedin, emerged as an important political factor. In the early 1890's, they formed the People's Party, the first group to attempt to reconcile the interests of town and country, and

[1] See p. 108.
[2] See pp. 216–7.

benefited from the steady shift to the left which marked subsequent polls. But of greater significance for the future was the entry of four Social Democrats into the Lower House in 1902.

The first socialist meeting was held in Stockholm in 1881; a socialist association was formed in 1884; and a socialist paper, *Socialdemokraten*, appeared in 1885. In the following year, its editorial board was joined by a 26-year-old professor's son who was to be the acknowledged leader of Sweden's social democratic movement for several decades and her first socialist Prime Minister—Hjalmar Branting. In 1889 he helped found the Swedish Social Democratic Workers Party to fight for an eight-hour day and universal suffrage, and finally, in 1897, secured election to the Lower House, though, like Britain's first Labour M.P.s, on a Liberal ticket.

The steady growth of an industrial proletariat, the increasing support for radical ideas and the example of the 'State Socialism' of Bismarck's Germany, which attracted many Swedes on both right and left for different reasons, prompted the Government to pay more attention to the needs of the lower classes of society. In 1881, regulations of 1846 banning the employment of children under twelve in certain industries were tightened up, and night work was forbidden to those under eighteen. In 1900 more industries were included, and it was made illegal to send women underground or allow them to work during the first four weeks after childbirth. But these and certain other measures on behalf of the old, the sick and orphans could be interpreted as products of eighteenth- and early nineteenth-century humanitarianism rather than as concessions to socialism; nothing was done to regulate the hours of adult male workers, and little to improve the conditions under which they laboured. Proposals for old age and sickness insurance were put forward by Boström in the late 1890's but immediately ran up against opposition from *laisser-faire* liberals and from the farmers, who feared that the cost involved would mean increased taxation. All that could be accomplished in this period was the granting of State subsidies to voluntary insurance organizations and a scheme for insurance against accidents in factories (in 1901). Sweden was thus far behind several other European countries—especially Germany —in laying the foundations of a Welfare State.

By the terms of the franchise introduced in 1866, less than a quarter of all adult males in Sweden were entitled to vote, and the position did not change until after the period dealt with in the present chapter. This meant that the voice of organized labour failed to obtain a fair hearing within the walls of the *Riksdag*, but by the end of the nineteenth century it had undoubtedly become a voice to be reckoned with. The compositors of Stockholm formed an association which had some affinities with a modern trade union in 1846, and the success of a bricklayers' strike in the capital in 1869 encouraged many other craftsmen to organize in the same way. Ten years later, the first great 'industrial dispute' in Sweden broke out at Sundsvall, the centre of the timber industry on the coast of Medelpad. The strikers were crushed with considerable brutality; a large number of them were driven from their homes by troops, and replaced by workers imported from other parts of the country. But far from being discouraged by the affair, Swedish trade unionism made a breakthrough in the decade following. In 1883, the Stockholm unions elected a central committee to co-ordinate their activities and campaign for a ten-hour day, and in 1886 the compositors again led the way by establishing the first union to cover the whole country. Finally, in 1898, by which time most industries had been organized, a congress of unions was held in the capital, and a Confederation of Trade Unions established. While no serious attempt was made to stop the workers forming unions, the extent of their right to strike long remained uncertain. In 1899, however, after a series of disputes, legislation was passed which imposed a penalty of two years' imprisonment even for peaceful picketing, and, with certain modifications, this remained in force until 1938.

One of the points in the programme adopted by the Stockholm trade union committee in 1883 was in favour of temperance, and strong links existed almost from the beginning between the movements campaigning for the rights of the labouring class and for restraint in the consumption of alcohol. The Swedes' addiction to *brännvin* rose alarmingly during the later decades of the eighteenth and early years of the nineteenth century, until in the 1830's a Scanian pastor named Peter Wieselgren, appalled by the condition of many of his parishioners at divine service, began a crusade for partial abstinence (i.e. the renunciation of spirits, but not of beer). This had considerable success, and led to the passing of a law in 1855 which aimed to tax the small peasant-stills out of existence and confine all production of potato- and corn-brandy to factories as well as to restrict its sale; much the same as had been done to curb gin-making in England a hundred years earlier. In 1865, the authorities in Gothenburg made the retailing of spirits a municipal monopoly, the profits from which were to be devoted to the welfare of the citizens. Other towns followed the example, and between them the two measures did bring about an appreciable reduction in consumption, and formed the basis for further controls imposed after 1905[1]. But many were still not satisfied. In the 1870's, a new campaign was launched by missionaries from the United States—for total abstinence. A Swedish lodge of the Order of Good Templars was founded in 1879, and the membership of it and similar associations increased apace. With the considerable funds at the disposal of the movement, it was able to embark on ambitious educational and cultural activities, and acquired an influence in many fields which it still enjoys.

A further movement which sprang into prominence in this age of popular movements was that for women's rights. Here the pioneer was the authoress Frederika Bremer. In her novel *Hertha*, published in 1856, she compared the position of her sex in Sweden very unfavourably with that which it enjoyed in the United States, whence she had recently returned. Among early victories for her cause were the act of 1863 by which unmarried women over twenty-five were no longer to be treated as minors, and their admittance the same year into the postal and telegraph services: those women who possessed the necessary property qualifications could vote in local elections on the same terms as men after the reform of 1862, and thus, after 1866, take an indirect part in the choice of members of the Upper House of the *Riksdag*. But the struggle was a long and painful one, especially when it involved the property rights of married women, although some progress was made even in this respect before 1900. In 1884 the Frederika Bremer Union was founded to advance feminine culture and intellectual life.

In spite of all the changes outlined above, the monarch's personal influence in politics remained considerable. Oscar II succeeded his brother, who had no sons, in 1872. He shared

[1] See p. 240.

Charles XV's interest in literature, was a persuasive speaker and proved an equally popular ruler. But he was also just as anxious to maintain as far as possible the prerogatives which the Constitution had left to the Crown. He was to a large extent responsible for bringing the defence debate to a temporary conclusion in 1884, and his views on foreign policy and on relations with Norway were of great significance.

The former field in particular was one in which the king was reasonably free to exercise his talents, for few members of the *Riksdag*—few even of the ministers—took much interest in international affairs. But after the temporary settlement of the Slesvig-Holstein question in 1865, Scandinavia was not involved for many years in any major European problems; during the Austro-Prussian War in 1866, the Franco-Prussian War in 1870–71 and the crises in the Balkans in 1877–78 and 1885–86, Sweden observed a strict neutrality. Oscar, however, hoped that the mighty German Empire, whose rise to dominance on the Continent he had welcomed as providing an additional bulwark against the traditional Russian foe, would support him in the quarrel with his Norwegian subjects, a quarrel which became more and more acute as the century approached its close.

Soon after the new king's accession, the Norwegians disputed his right to impose an absolute (as distinct from a suspensive) veto on constitutional amendments passed by the *Storting*. Then, when, in 1882, the Left (the farmers' party) gained a majority in the Christiania Parliament, and Oscar refused to dismiss the Conservative Prime Minister, they proceeded themselves to get rid of him by means of an impeachment. The king replied by appointing another ministry of the Right. But even many Swedes condemned this high-handed action, and the Cabinet in Stockholm advised him to give way. Finally—though with a bad grace —he did so; Norway at least had won parliamentary government. Eight years later, the *Storting* reopened the issue of their relations with the Crown by voting for the establishment of a separate Norwegian consular service, to which, in view of the enormous growth of Norway's merchant marine in the later nineteenth century, she seemed to be entitled. When the king vetoed the measure the Norwegians refused to contribute any longer to the existing service. Swedish opinion now began to swing to the side of the monarch and to support the stand which he was taking. A majority in the *Riksdag* favoured the establishment of full equality between the two countries with the abolition of the customs privileges enjoyed by their neighbours, and agreed themselves to pay the subsidy which the *Storting* had refused. Negotiations for a revision of the terms of union broke down, and the situation grew even more tense; rumours of the mobilization of a Norwegian army exercised a considerable influence on the defence debate in Sweden.

In 1903, Boström, back in office for a second term, agreed in principle to a Norwegian consular service, but by the beginning of 1905 negotiations on its introduction had reached deadlock; the Norwegians demanded far wider powers for their consuls than the Swedes were willing to concede. The *Storting* then passed a new Consular Ordinance, and, when the king refused to sign it, declared his powers suspended. The united front presented by the Norwegians took most Swedes completely aback, and few of them wished to attempt to settle the problem by force; the powerful influence of Crown Prince Gustav, who had earlier favoured resistance, was now exerted in the cause of moderation. The Swedish Cabinet therefore asked the *Riksdag* to agree to a dissolution of the Union, but the *Riksdag* demanded the fulfilment of certain preliminary conditions. In face of this, the ministers resigned, and their successors, who formed the first completely new ministry in their country's parliamentary history (and the first one to contain a farmer), persuaded the Norwegians to hold a referendum, one of the conditions on which the *Riksdag* had insisted. As had been expected, this revealed an overwhelming majority in favour of independence. Further negotiations between the two nations on their future relations ran into serious difficulties, and there were even troop movements on either side of the frontier. But the international situation favoured a settlement; the German emperor had just thrown down the gauntlet to the other great powers in an inflammatory speech at Tangier and was unable to promise Oscar any support, while the British Government was not willing to back the Norwegians to the extent they had hoped. In October, the so-called Karlstad Convention formally ended the 90-year-old experiment; all frontier fortifications were to be destroyed, and all future disputes to be settled before the International Court in The Hague. The Norwegians first offered the new throne to a Swedish prince, but Oscar's ministers refused their consent, and it was Prince Carl of Denmark, the grandson of the Danish king and son-in-law of the English Edward VII, who, as Håkon VII, became the first king of an independent Norway since 1380.

The way in which the Union was dissolved is a tribute to the common sense of both Scandinavian peoples. The Swedes lost some prestige, but they gained more of greater value by the move. The Norwegians had never been wholly happy even with the considerable degree of autonomy they had been granted in 1814, and in the course of the nineteenth century, as economic prosperity grew and the leaven of the Romantic Movement did its work, nationalist sentiment, represented by men like the writer Bjørnstjerne Bjørnsen, had grown more and more powerful and had poisoned relations between two countries who had so much in common. Swedish and Norwegian politicians could now turn to the pressing social problems which existed within the respective states.

CHAPTER XIX

Nineteenth-Century Swedish Culture

The cultural brilliance which marked the reign of Gustavus III did not long survive his death. Bellman and Kellgren both died in 1795, and, although three other leading Gustavian poets—Carl af Leopold, Thomas Thorild and Johan Oxenstierna—lived on into the new century, their best work had been written by 1792. Roslin and his most serious rival, Carl Pilo, disappeared from the scene in 1793. Only Sergel, who lived long enough to witness the revival of his country's fortunes under Bernadotte, maintained her reputation in the plastic arts which he himself had done so much to establish.

But already during the reign of Gustavus IV the seeds of a renaissance were being sown. The main impulse for this came from the Romantic Movement, which swept through Europe after the collapse of the *ancien régime*, and which attained its most perfect expression in Germany. In Sweden, the revolution of 1809 was followed significantly by the foundation of two associations wherewith to broadcast the new doctrine, with its emphasis on feeling and the mystery of life, and its search for national identity in the past: the Aurora Society of Uppsala (the ancient university town which was to be the country's leading cultural centre for several decades) was initiated in 1810, and the Gothic Association of Stockholm in 1811. The first of them was a purely literary gathering presided over by Per Atterbom, the poet-editor of its monthly magazine *Phosphorus*, and later the author of one of the most perfect expressions in verse of the Romantic spirit in the Swedish language, *The Isle of Bliss*. The second, recalling the Gothic Movement of the sixteenth and seventeenth century, had rather wider aims and included among its members Per Ling, a poet who sought to create a nation healthy in body as well as spirit by means of his world-famous system of gymnastics. But also associated with it were the two greatest figures of Swedish culture in the early nineteenth century—Gustav Geijer and Esaias Tegnér.

Geijer was the son of a Värmland *brukspatron*. Although his visit to England in 1809 produced a charming and sympathetic description of its people at the height of the Napoleonic Wars, the main influences on his work, as on that of most of his contemporaries, came from Germany. He is best known as the writer of what is usually considered the first modern history of Sweden, which appeared in the 1830's when he was a professor at Uppsala; while strongly marked by the patriotism which the Gothic Association had been formed to foster, it was more objective than most of its predecessors, and was based on a wealth of source-material. But Geijer was also a philosopher, and his small output of poetry is worthy of note. His conversion in 1838 from his earlier conservatism to an individual brand of liberalism has been noted earlier in another context. Tegnér came from the same beautiful and, in the early nineteenth century, remote province which has been so rich in literary talent. But his background—as the son of a poor parson and the grandson of a peasant—was very different. Although he occasionally wrote in prose, Tegnér was above all a poet—perhaps the greatest whom Sweden has produced. His best-known work, *Frithiof's Saga*, which appeared in the 1820's, is based, in typical Romantic fashion, on Old Norse legend and, like most of his output, reflected the powerful nationalism of his school. He was the chief mouthpiece of the Russophobia which gripped so many Swedes after the loss of Finland; while most of his colleagues became reconciled to their country's new status in the Baltic, and in time came to recognize the wisdom of Charles John's '1812 Policy', Tegnér was never able to shake off his fear and hatred of the 'barbarians in the East'. After occupying a chair at Lund, he died in 1846 as Bishop of Växjö.

Greater educational facilities and cheaper books for a growing population had, by the 1880's, created a considerable reading public in Sweden. Romanticism had by then yielded place to Realism, and German influence had to a large extent been replaced by French, still at that time the second language of the educated Swede. The transition can be traced in the novels of

Viktor Rydberg, a radical journalist who turned to poetry fairly late in life, but who, by his death in 1895, was recognized as his country's leading exponent of the art in succession to Tegnér. The most prominent member of the new school was, however, August Strindberg. More familiar to the outside world as a dramatist, he first made his name in 1879 as the author of a novel, *The Red Room*, which expressed vividly the radicalism of the capital, once more the main focus of cultural life; and he continued throughout his life to write short stories and longer prose pieces set in Stockholm or its archipelago. Theatre audiences know him best for the stark realism of such plays as *The Father* and *Miss Julie*, written in the 1880's, but much more influential in the development of European drama have been his impressionist and symbolist pieces from the 90's and early 1900's—*To Damascus*, *Easter* and *The Dance of Death*. The bulk of his even less well-known historical plays—*Charles XII*, *Christina* and *Gustavus III* among them—also belong to this period.

The weakening of the Realist Movement in Sweden in the last decade of the nineteenth century can also be seen in much of the work of Strindberg's younger contemporaries; from commenting on current social problems they turned to the task of providing a more personal and intimate interpretation of life in the spirit of the Romantics. Nationalism was once more in full flood throughout Europe, and Sweden was by no means immune from it, although she remained largely free of the crude imperialistic form which affected several other countries including Britain. The aristocratic socialist Verner von Heidenstam took up with enthusiasm the call to patriotic endeavour after a long sojourn abroad; his collection of tales about the Great Northern War entitled *King Charles's Men* and his *One People*, a poetic cycle written a few years later, in 1902, would have gladdened the heart of any member of the Gothic Association.

Another feature of this 'Neo-romanticism' was the provincial literature which it produced. Heidenstam composed pieces set in his native Östergötland, but pride of place among writers in this genre must go to the Värmlanders Gustav Fröding and Selma Lagerlöf. Fröding has often been compared to Bellman as one of Sweden's greatest lyric poets, and he shares with the latter a genial good humour for long lacking in his country's verse (this in spite of an increasingly tragic life which ended in

1911 in insanity). After Strindberg, Lagerlöf is the best-known Swedish writer outside her own land. Although she lived until 1940, it was around the turn of the century that her reputation was firmly established; she was awarded the Nobel Prize for Literature in 1909, and in 1914 became the first woman member of the Swedish Academy. *Gösta Berling's Saga*, her first novel, published in 1891, reveals that love of fantasy which marks so much of her work, and which is most delightfully expressed in *The Wonderful Adventures of Nils*, a child's introduction to the geography of Sweden.

The Romantic Movement in painting and sculpture did not produce any Swedes to match Geijer and Tegnér in literature. Indeed, a country which had given birth to Sergel in the eighteenth and was to boast Carl Milles[1] in the twentieth century was barren of really great sculptors for the whole of the nineteenth century; the Romantic Bengt Fogelberg, whose statue of Birger Jarl now stands on Riddarholmen in Stockholm, and the Realist Per Hasselberg, most famous for his charming nudes, are not in the international class, able craftsmen though they were. But it must be remembered that the sculptor has always—in modern times at least—been something of a *rara avis* everywhere among the host of writers and painters. And of talented, if not brilliant, painters Sweden had her fair share at this time, especially after the arrival, in the 1880's, of waves from the Impressionist revolt in Paris. The movement was taken up with enthusiasm by the so-called 'Opponents', a group of Stockholm artists who held an exhibition in the capital in 1885, and who formed the Artists Union in the following year. Most famous of these was Anders Zorn, whose scenes of Dalarna peasant life are the equivalent in paint of the work of provincial writers like Fröding and Lagerlöf. But the achievements of two other members of this circle have only recently begun to receive the recognition they deserve. Ernst Josephson and Carl Hill both became mentally unbalanced at an early stage in their careers but continued to paint, and indeed produced their most striking landscapes and figures while in this state; as might be imagined, their art broke right through the bounds of Impressionism into a deeper world.

France was undoubtedly the dominant source of inspiration

[1] See p. 261.

for Swedish painting in the latter half of the century, after a period in its middle years when the German schools of Düsseldorf and Munich had been the most powerful magnets for Scandinavian artists. As during the earlier period of French dominance a hundred years before, a stream of them now again visited Paris, some, like Roslin in the eighteenth century, to spend most of their lives there, some for briefer visits; it was in the French capital that Gustaf Cederström in the 70's—though in a thoroughly Romantic manner—painted the most famous of Swedish historical pictures—that portraying the carrying of the body of Charles XII across the snow-covered mountains to its last resting-place.

There were few hints in Scandinavian architecture of the nineteenth century of the qualities which were to give it such renown in the twentieth. The models here throughout most of the period were German rather than French. The only real exception was during the decades immediately after the Napoleonic Wars, when a kind of modified Neo-classicism or Empire Style named after Charles XIV was introduced; it can be seen in the building at Uppsala known as Carolina Rediviva, now the university's library but originally intended to be its central edifice. But the rebuilding of Paris during the Second Empire of Napoleon III did influence the designs for a new Stockholm drawn up in 1866; the old seventeenth-century plan was no longer adequate for a city whose population rose threefold between 1850 and 1900. The original project—with Kungsgatan forming a great boulevard approaching Karlaplan from the west, as Karlavägen approaches it from the north-west—proved too ambitious; Karlaplan did not become another Place de l'Etoile, and Kungsgatan was made too narrow to be another Champs Elysées.

By 1910, however, the capital had changed its face considerably. No distinct architectural style succeeded that of Charles XIV; Sweden for much of the remainder of the century was, like the rest of Europe, a battleground for the advocates of the revival of various models from the past—Renaissance, Baroque and, above all, Gothic. A leading exponent of the latter was Helgo Zettervall, who, besides restoring and building churches up and down the country, was responsible for the present tower on St. Claire's (Sankt Klara) Church in Stockholm. But a reaction against this antiquarianism set in towards 1900. Already in the 1880's Gustav Clason was calling for the honest use of brick and stone as well as of new materials; his Nordic Museum (built to house the collections of Artur Hazelius, the great enthusiast for a Swedish culture fast disappearing), while still a mixture of styles, does have greater unity than many earlier buildings of the nineteenth century. But the real breakthrough came with the arrival from Germany of the *Jugendstil* (better known in Britain as *Art Nouveau*); Stockholm's General Post Office (one of the first buildings the traveller sees after leaving the main railway station) was built in 1904 to the designs of Ferdinand Boberg, the chief apostle of the movement in Sweden.

Although his output was considerable and varied, the works of Sweden's greatest composer, Franz Berwald (1796–1868), were almost wholly neglected even by his own countrymen during his lifetime, and he never acquired anything like the reputation of the Norwegian, Grieg. It was a performer and not a composer who put her country on the musical map in this period; Jenny Lind first sang in her native Stockholm in 1835, and for the next thirty years entranced audiences throughout the world with her beautiful voice and wide repertoire. At the beginning of the twentieth century, Richard Dybeck's song *Du gamla, du fria* (You old and free), composed as far back as 1844, became generally accepted as Sweden's national anthem.

The cultural revival (for it was no less) which took place in Sweden in the last quarter of the nineteenth century was firmly based on the improved educational facilities which had by this time become available to the mass of her population; the kingdom could boast one of the highest literacy rates in Europe. Under the School Law of 1842, for which the Estate of Peasants had been pressing for some time, every parish was obliged to establish a school to teach reading, writing, arithmetic and the rudiments of religion under the supervision of a lay and elected board, and every province was to provide a training college for teachers, for whom a minimum salary was fixed. Only rather vague standards of attainment were laid down in the Act, and no compulsory period of school attendance was specified; this had to wait until 1882, when seven years between the ages of seven and fourteen was demanded. The Law was still far from being fully implemented when, in 1849, the old 'trivial'[1] and grammar schools were merged into standard six-year secondary schools to prepare brighter children for the matriculation examination necessary for entry to a university. Modern (as distinct from the time-honoured classical) subjects found a place in most of these schools, but it was a very subordinate one and not until 1878 were separate 'modern' sides set up, against fierce opposition from those who believed in the pre-eminent educational value of Latin and Greek. Finally, in 1905, distinct 'modern' schools (*realskolor*) were established, but the grammar school (*gymnasium*) still provided the only channel for university entrance. The two systems had been integrated to a certain extent in 1894, when the curriculum of the last three years of the elementary school was linked to that of the first years of the secondary school, so that it became possible for a child to pass from one to the other. A certain number of private schools continued to exist, but they never acquired the prestige of the English public schools linked so closely to the ancient universities, and were made even less attractive by the low fees charged in the State colleges.

But it was not only while he was a child that the ordinary Swede was given greater opportunities to broaden his outlook during the nineteenth century. Many of the early trade unions grew out of workers' study circles, formed in the 1850's in imitation of German models, and education always played a prominent part in the Swedish labour movement; the first Workers Institute was founded in Stockholm in 1880. Temperance, co-operative and Free Church societies also performed valuable services in this field. An educational establishment of a rather different type, in so far as it was not intended to convey any specific message, was residential and served almost exclusively the older adolescents of rural areas, was the Folk High School, which arrived from Denmark in 1868. This movement never had quite the impact it had in its country of origin, but by 1900 there were thirty such schools in existence in Sweden, running a variety of short courses in the liberal arts with the help of State subsidies.

While in 1905 Sweden still had officially only two universities, higher education had been by no means neglected during

[1] See p. 129.

the previous hundred years. A host of specialist academies for teaching and research sprang up in the capital in the early part of the nineteenth century, led by the Caroline Medical Institute, a State-controlled body with university status founded in 1810, and the Technological Institute of 1825. Almost equally important was the Chalmers Technical Institute in Gothenburg, which dates from 1829. Fresh advances were made after 1870. In 1877, the Technological Institute was raised to the dignity of a 'High School' (*Högskola*) or technological university, and the following year a privately endowed High School for arts subjects was opened in Stockholm. When Gothenburg also obtained one of these in 1891, Sweden could be said to possess for all practical purposes four universities.[1]

After Berzelius, Sweden did not produce any pure scientists of international repute, but in the fields of applied science and technology her record is quite exceptional considering the size of her population. Space permits mention of only a few of the inventions for which Swedes were responsible in the nineteenth century: Laval not only revolutionized dairying with his cream-separator but, in 1887, greatly improved Parson's steam turbine; Sven Wingquist's ball bearings gave rise to Sweden's largest industrial concern—SKF of Gothenburg, founded in 1907; Gustaf Pasch, the inventor of the safety-match in 1844, laid the basis for another very important Swedish industry, which became centred in Jönköping. But over all these towers the figure of Alfred Nobel. The dynamite which he perfected in 1867 and the more powerful gelignite which followed it eight years later proved of immense value to his country's miners as well as, unfortunately, to military men throughout the world. But his fame now rests on the use which he made of the great fortune he earned from his discoveries and business activities. By his will, the income from this when invested was to be devoted to five prizes awarded annually—for physics and chemistry by the Swedish Academy of Sciences; for medicine or physiology by the Caroline Medical Institute; for literature by the Swedish Academy; and for work in the cause of peace by the *Storting*. The first awards were made in 1901, and since then sixteen Swedes have been recipients of them.

[1] Gothenburg High School was granted the title of University in 1954; Stockholm High School followed in 1960.

Swedes have always travelled widely outside their own country; some to seek culture at the great European centres, some to look for good farming land across the Atlantic, and yet others to probe the secrets of hitherto-unvisited parts of the globe. By the nineteenth century there were very few *terrae incognitae*, but Sweden had one on her own door-step. She was rather less active in the Arctic than her Scandinavian neighbours, but a series of expeditions led by Swedish scientists in and after 1858 mapped Spitsbergen for the first time, and, this done, one of the most prominent of the participants in them sought adventure further afield; in July 1878, Adolf Nordenskiöld set off from Tromsö in Norway on the steamship *Vega* to attempt to traverse the North-East Passage to the Pacific, for which men had been searching for over three centuries. After almost exactly a year, during most of which time his ship was frozen in the ice, he emerged in the Bering Strait, and returned home to a tumultuous reception. Four years after this, he succeeded in penetrating the great icebarrier on the east coast of Greenland for the first time. Equally celebrated in their own way were the journeys through central Asia undertaken in the 1880's and 1890's by Sven Hedin (not to be confused with the radical politician of the same name, although the explorer did play an important part in political life later).[1]

The Swedish Lutheran Church had successfully rid itself of the disturbing element of Pietism in the early eighteenth century, and Swedenborg had caused little more than a ripple on the smooth and rather sluggish waters of Swedish theological thought. The State Church managed to retain an official monopoly of public worship until the repeal of the Conventicle Act in 1860. But from the beginning of the nineteenth century a new religious revival brought new problems for the bishops and other orthodox ecclesiastical leaders. Various evangelical movements spread swiftly through the isolated peasant communities of Norrland, and from 1830 they were reinforced by the work of Methodists led by George Scott. This able preacher was a Scotsman who came to Sweden in that year to cater for the spiritual needs of the British workmen imported by Samuel Owen, a naturalized Englishman who had settled in Stockholm

---

[1] See pp. 232–3, 234.

to manufacture steam engines and other machinery. After a riot in 1842 Scott was forced to leave Sweden, but his disciples continued to travel about the countryside addressing large and enthusiastic congregations. They exerted a powerful influence on the evangelicals within the Established Church, who, in 1856, formed the National Evangelical Foundation to serve as their main organ. The independent Methodist Church appeared in 1867 but failed to make as much headway as other dissenting bodies. The most successful of these was the Swedish Missionary Society, the result of a break-away from the Evangelical Foundation in 1878 led by Paul Waldenström; it is now the largest nonconformist group in the land, although many of its members also attend Lutheran churches. For some time its most serious challenger was the Baptist sect, which arrived from the United States as early as 1848 and grew rapidly after the repeal of the Conventicle Act. But the Baptists later suffered heavy losses to the last important body to be formed outside the State Church —the Pentecostals, who attracted many to their banner in the early years of the twentieth century. The Salvation Army, which is a considerable force in Sweden even today, and has of course played a leading part in the temperance movement, appeared in 1882.

But even after the removal of the legal restrictions on dissenters, the vast majority of Swedes remained—and remain today —within the Lutheran fold. In the Established Church, two distinct tendencies clearly emerged about the middle of the century—a 'low' movement, associated with Uppsala and the Evangelical Foundation, and a ritualistic movement, centred on the see of Lund and inspired by Henrik Schartau, a member of the cathedral chapter who died in 1825. The latter group was particularly active in the missionary field in India, China and Africa; a Lund Missionary Association was started in 1845, but not until 1874 was a Missionary Department set up for the whole Church. While the size of congregations dwindled appreciably in the later years of the nineteenth century, especially in urban centres, the official hierarchy was certainly more alive to its responsibilities than it had been earlier.

CHAPTER XX

Democracy and the First World War

The outstanding features of Swedish political life in the decade which followed the break-up of the Union in 1905 were the final triumph of democracy and the laying of a firm foundation for the future 'Welfare State'. The election of 1905 was fought largely on the issue of the extension of the still-narrow franchise. Although the Left had long been demanding at least a reduction in the property qualification required of voters, it was not until the 1890's that the movement for universal suffrage became of political significance. A Universal Franchise Union was formed in 1890, and a petition organized by it in 1898 collected no fewer than 364,000 signatures. Two years later, the liberals in the *Riksdag* became united in one party with a programme calling for equality in the parliamentary franchise for local and national elections, which would give the vote to most urban workers. The cause was also furthered at this time by the growing agitation for a strengthening of the country's defences on a democratic basis; the cry of 'one man, one vote, one gun' was raised, and Heidenstam wrote in one of his verses, 'It is shameful, a blemish on the Swedish flag that the rights of a citizen should depend on wealth.' It was to a considerable extent such appeals to patriotism which led even the Right to come out in favour of universal male suffrage, although conservatives insisted on hedging it round with certain safeguards, such as plural voting to give weight to wealth and education and the raising of the minimum voting age. A proposal on these lines was introduced by the Government in 1904, but a majority of Liberals opposed the proportional representation which formed an integral part of it, and secured its rejection.

The election which followed placed the Right in a minority

in the Lower House, to which thirteen Social Democrats were returned, and a Liberal cabinet was formed by the able lawyer Karl Staaff, the first party leader in a modern sense to emerge in Sweden. His franchise proposals were approved by the Lower House but defeated in the Upper, which was still dominated by the Right. Staaff asked King Oscar for a dissolution of the *Riksdag* so that the issue might once more be put to the electorate, and when this request was refused, he resigned. The minority conservative ministry under Rear-Admiral Arvid Lindman which succeeded him introduced its own project in 1907. Under this, the voting age for elections to the Lower House was to be raised to twenty-four, but the only other significant restriction was the demand that taxes for at least one of the previous three years should have been paid in full; proportional representation reappeared. The 1908 elections, in which the franchise question played only a minor rôle, constituted a further set-back for the Right and a striking success for the Social Democrats, thirty-four of whom were returned. Although the latter were not very happy with the Government's bill, most members of the *Riksdag* were rapidly growing tired of the seemingly endless wrangles, and in 1909 it was passed. The local government franchise was revised at the same time; while one man could continue to cast a number of votes by virtue of his wealth or educational qualifications, the limit was reduced from 5,000 in the countryside and 100 in town to a mere 40.

The first elections held in accordance with the new provisions, which enabled nearly 20 per cent of the population to participate, took place in 1911 and inflicted the heaviest blow on the conservatives they had so far suffered; they lost twenty-nine seats to the Social Democrats. The Liberals, however, remained the largest single party in the Lower House, and Staaff formed his second ministry. The conservatives responded to the challenge by organizing, for the first time, a united party of their own under Lindman; officially called the Farmers and Burghers Party, it was popularly known simply as the Right (*Högern*). Something like a modern party system had at last emerged in Sweden.

The two Staaff cabinets and the intervening Lindman administration all left behind them respectable records of social reform. In 1906, committees were set up to mediate between workers and employers; the right of companies to acquire land in Norrland, where unrestricted private enterprise was threatening to turn the farmers into a landless proletariat, was severely limited; the principles of probation and the conditional sentence were introduced into the penal code; teachers' pay was improved following the Education Act of the previous year; and the spelling of Swedish was reformed to eliminate a number of superfluous consonants. In 1907, the Lindman government acquired half the shares of the company which ran the great iron-ore mines in Lappland, with an option to buy the remainder in either 25 or 35 years' time. A move in the same direction was made in 1909 with the setting up of the Waterfalls Board to watch over the country's vast reserves of hydro-electric power, in which the State was showing a growing interest as a substitute for imported coal; three years earlier it had built its own plant at Trollhättan as the first link in a network which was eventually to serve most of Sweden. The pattern of a 'mixed economy', foreshadowed in railway development in the previous century, was thus further developed, not by socialist but by liberal and conservative administrations. More legislation in 1909 banned night-work for women in industry and limited shop hours; and in 1913, after several years of agitation, a scheme was introduced for the payment of small State pensions to the over sixty-seven's.

Taken as a whole, the epoch between 1896, which saw the end of the 'Great Depression', and the outbreak of the First World War in 1914 was for Sweden, as for the rest of Europe, one of growing prosperity. But progress was interrupted by periodic recessions, and, with both labour and management organized (a Swedish Employers Federation was formed in 1902), these were increasingly marked by large-scale strikes and lock-outs (the latter word was adopted by the Swedes unchanged). Such a recession began in 1907 and reached its peak in 1909, when the industrialists decided to answer the unrest among their employees by declaring a general lock-out, which soon involved 100,000 workers. The trade unions replied with an equally unprecedented move—a general strike. This was weakened from the start by the refusal of the railwaymen to join in and by lack of funds, but it lasted a month before the workers' leaders had to advise their followers to admit defeat.

As during the much briefer general strike in Britain in 1926, there was little disorder, partly because of the strikers' self-imposed ban on spirits. Their failure was softened by a subsequent improvement in economic conditions and the rise in real wages which went with it, but the fact that they had failed could not be concealed, and the organized labour movement suffered accordingly; there was a sharp drop in the membership of both unions and the Social Democratic Party, although this was not reflected at the polls.

The acceptance of Boström's project in 1901[1] pushed the defence question into the background for some time, but interest in it revived with the loss of Norway and the continuing growth in the military potential of all the great European powers. Lindman was particularly concerned. His ministry both increased expenditure on the armed forces and set up a committee, containing service representatives as well as civilians, to co-ordinate the work of reform in this field. Such a policy, however, brought attacks, not only from the Social Democrats, who took a doctrinaire pacifist line, and the Liberals, who objected to the new appropriations involved, but also from some members of the Cabinet itself, who feared that the committee would lead to an increase of military influence in politics. Only by holding a joint session of the two Houses could the subsidy for an improved type of cruiser—the 'F-ship'—be obtained in 1911, and when Staaff took office the same year, he announced that its building would be postponed. The 'defensists', led by the explorer Sven Hedin, immediately launched a campaign to raise the sum needed by private subscription, and the total cost was forthcoming in the space of a few months; the ship, named the *Sverige*, finally sailed in 1915. Just before Lindman's resignation, his Defence Committee had recommended an increase in the length of military service, but Staaff would agree to this only after securing a fresh mandate from the electorate. It was widely known that the new king, Gustav V, who had come to the throne on the death of his father in 1907, was on bad terms with his Prime Minister, both over what he regarded as the Liberals' obstructionist attitude to defence problems and over Staaff's failure to consult the monarch before laying his plans before the *Riksdag*. The defensists decided to exploit this breach by appealing direct to the

[1] See p. 212.

Crown, as the Constitution entitled them to do, and in February 1914 a demonstration organized by them marched on Stockholm under the banner 'With God and Sweden's People for King and Country', to be received by Gustav with a sympathetic speech partly composed by Hedin himself. The king had not informed Staaff of his intentions, and when he refused to promise to give prior notice to the Cabinet of any similar pronouncement in the future, the Premier resigned.

A moderate Conservative government under Hjalmar Hammarskjöld (the father of the future Secretary-General of the United Nations) took office, but had almost immediately to face an election. The campaign was a particularly fierce one, and the poll proved to be the highest on record. The outcome was a severe set-back for the Liberals, who were made to suffer for their equivocal attitude on defence, and lost thirty-two seats. Many workers who had voted for them in the past now swung to the Social Democrats; and the middle class made a sharp right turn. The Government gained more from the Liberals than the Socialists did and emerged with command of the largest single group in the Lower House (the Right had never lost its hold over the Upper). Hammarskjöld took heart. He proposed an increase of military service in the infantry to 340 days (it was always longer in the specialist arms) and the building of five new cruisers and destroyers over the coming five years. The outbreak of war in Europe increased the general sense of urgency, and the Liberals agreed to support the plan in exchange for some minor concessions. In new elections, however, such supineness lost them a further thirteen seats to the Social Democrats, who became, what they have remained ever since, the largest party in the Lower House. All seemed set for a fierce battle between Right and Left, but the parties then agreed to observe a truce as long as the war lasted.

In the preceding decade, Sweden's foreign policy had betrayed distinct pro-German tendencies. These were encouraged by Britain's participation in the separate territorial guarantee given by a number of powers to Norway after her independence, which the Swedes chose to regard as an insult; by the old fear of Russia, especially after a revival of tsarist persecution in Finland; by the close cultural and economic ties established with the German Empire; and by the proclivities of the king, who had married a grand-daughter of the first Kaiser. Lindman appointed a pro-German Foreign Minister in 1909, and the following year talks between the German and Swedish staffs were inaugurated. Although there was a movement in, which Sven Hedin again played a prominent part, in favour of Sweden's adherence to the Triple Alliance of Germany, Austro-Hungary and Italy against Russia, and pan-German ideas were prevalent in certain right-wing circles, these discussions did not lead to the political alliance for which the Germans had hoped, and Staaff adopted a strictly neutral attitude in face of the two power blocs; in 1912 he even arranged a meeting between the King of Sweden and the tsar.

And when war did finally break out in August 1914, very few Swedes wished their country to take any part in it. There was still, however, much sympathy for Germany among members of the upper classes; many of them regarded her as the main bulwark against Slav barbarism, and even her excuses for the attack on Belgium were swallowed, while Britain was accused of having betrayed the cause of civilization by allying herself with Russia. Left-wingers were less blantantly pro-Allied than conservatives were pro-German, but their leanings were nevertheless often made apparent, as when, in 1915, three pro-German Social Democrats were expelled from the party.

Hammarskjöld's foreign policy broadly followed the lines laid down by his predecessor. And in his determination to maintain his country's neutrality he received the full backing of the king, who, at the end of 1914, invited the other Scandinavian monarchs to a meeting in Malmö, where they declared their common determination to stay outside the conflict; this Nordic co-operation continued throughout the war and set a precedent for further joint action after it.[1] But the Premier's position was still a difficult one, especially when he was faced with Britain's demands to help her enforce the blockade of Germany by restricting the re-export of strategic raw materials reaching Sweden from the West; with the placing of Swedish firms trading with Germany on a black list, which meant their boycott by British concerns; and with the seizure of Swedish goods and mail on the high seas. Imports into Sweden from the West dropped sharply, and shortages of oil and wheat, half her require-

[1] See p. 246.

ments of which she had to buy abroad, grew alarmingly. Sugar had to be rationed in the autumn of 1916, and bread and flour followed at the beginning of the following year. A ban on the export of wood-pulp failed to wring concessions from the British government, and relations between the two countries were not improved by the peace moves which emanated from Stockholm at the end of 1917.

In spite of all this, the 'activits', who, led by Sven Lidman and his journal *Swedish Destiny*, pressed for an alliance with Germany, found only a limited response even on the extreme right of the political spectrum. And the opening of unrestricted submarine warfare by Germany at the beginning of 1917 increased sympathy for the Allies; the Swedish representative in Berlin was ordered to make a vigorous protest. At the same time, the U-boat menace led to a further worsening of the economic situation in Sweden, and drove down the bread ration. Under such circumstances, it became more and more difficult to maintain the political truce which had been agreed on in 1914. Finally, Hammarskjöld was defeated in the *Riksdag* and resigned. He was replaced by Carl Swartz, a former Finance Minister, at the head of yet another Conservative administration. This did, however, succeed in reaching an agreement with Britain, by which a number of Allied merchantment trapped in the Baltic were to be escorted through the Sound mine-fields by Swedish warships, and a number of Swedish merchant ships with cargoes of food were to be released from the British and American ports in which they had been held.

This brought only temporary relief to the domestic crisis, and did not save the Right from a decisive defeat in the elections of the same year; it lost twenty-nine seats in the Lower House. Only five of these went to the Liberals, but the Social Democrats were weakened by the defection from their ranks of a small radical group led by Carl Höglund, and it was Nils Edén, the new leader of the Liberals after the death of Staaff, who was asked by the king to take over the reins. He did, however, include Branting in his cabinet as Minister of Finance and three other Social Democrats. The situation which the new Government had to face was still a grave one. The harvest had been poor; the cost of living had risen to more than double what it had been in 1914; speculators were making considerable profits from the shortages, in spite of the regulations to curb their activities; imports were dropping; there were serious shortages of fuel, meat and dairy produce; and many merchant ships were being sunk and many Swedish lives lost as the result of the German submarine campaign. A fresh agreement with the Allies was concluded in May 1918. Under it, exports allowed into Sweden from the West were increased, while the Entente Powers were permitted to use up to 400,000 tons of the Swedish shipping in their harbours, and Swedish exports of iron ore to Germany were considerably reduced, the Allies buying up the surplus. The war ended in November, before this could have much effect, but it did enable the bread ration to be restored to its original level.

Sweden through her membership of the Red Cross did much to ease the worst hardships caused by the war on both sides; the work of Elsa Brandström among the German prisoners-of-war in Russian earned her the title of 'The Angel of Siberia'. Individual Swedes, like the new archbishop, Nathan Söderblom, a passionate advocate of Christian unity, worked hard to bring the slaughter to an end, and Stockholm, one of the few capitals in the world where representatives of both sides could meet informally throughout the whole period of hostilities, was the scene of great diplomatic activity, although not always, it must be admitted, in the cause of peace.

In the middle of 1917, Sweden played a minor rôle in the most important event of the twentieth century, when Lenin passed through on his way from Switzerland to Petrograd to prepare for the Bolshevik *coup* in November. The overthrow of tsardom in February had been welcomed whole-heartedly by the Swedish Left, but the events of November were treated with much greater reserve, except by the small group around Höglund. The most significant result of the Russian Revolution from Sweden's point of view was Finland's declaration of her independence immediately after it. Edén's cabinet did not hesitate to recognize the régime in Helsinki, but then found itself faced with the question of what attitude to adopt to the bitter civil war which broke out in the new republic between Reds and Whites. In spite of calls from the Right for Swedish intervention on behalf of the latter as constituting the legitimate government, Edén would go no further than to permit Swedish volunteers to enlist in the White army, German volunteers to pass through Swedish waters on their way to the front and arms privately purchased by the Whites to be exported. With this help, the Whites were soon able to end the resistance of the Red Guards, but Finland remained in the forefront of Sweden's diplomatic problems for several years owing to a dispute over possession of the Åland Islands.

As early as August 1917, the inhabitants of the islands, all of whom were Swedish-speaking, had called for reunion with Sweden, and, in February 1918, at the height of the civil war, two Swedish warships had been sent to evacuate any of them who wished to leave. When the Russian garrison finally withdrew, a Swedish one took its place until relieved in its turn by German troops, who were aiding the Finnish Whites. These left at the end of the year, and a referendum held in June 1919 furnished further proof that an overwhelming proportion of the islanders wanted to be ruled from Stockholm. The Helsinki government, however, ignored their request and, a year later, had two of the most prominent Ålanders arrested and installed a Finnish garrison. The Swedish government replied by breaking off diplomatic relations with Finland but appealed at the same time to the League of Nations, where Branting was now chief Swedish representative, to mediate. A committee appointed by the League to consider the case reported in 1921 in favour of the Finns, but also recommended the granting of extensive guarantees to the islanders aimed especially at protecting their right to use the Swedish language. Both sides accepted the verdict, with the result that, while the islands remained part of Finland, they gained a considerable degree of self-government.

CHAPTER XXI

Between the Wars

For all European countries, whether or not they had taken any active part in it, the First World War brought with it a great acceleration of social change and, for some, actual revolution; the events which took place in Russia in 1917 and in Germany the year after had profound repercussions throughout the Continent, encouraging the Left to raise its demands, and frightening the Right, either into making concessions, or into out-and-out reaction. In Sweden, both parties in the governing coalition favoured the sweeping away all the remaining limitations on universal male suffrage and the granting of the vote to women, and the Right gave in before the rising tension, which might, it was feared, produce a situation similar to that to the south of the Baltic. The first step in implementing this policy was taken even before the end of the war. Early in 1918, the *Riksdag* was promised the abolition of plural voting in local elections, to which the Right agreed, although it managed to obtain a provision in the final act raising the voting age to twenty-three in urban areas and to twenty-seven in country districts. Three years later came the final triumph of democracy in Sweden with the grant of the vote in national elections to all men and women over twenty-three. At the same time, the life of the Lower House was increased from three to four years and that of the Upper from six to eight; the property qualification demanded of members was retained.

The Government which passed these latter measures was, however, no longer the Liberal-Socialist coalition which had ruled during the last few years of the war. The Liberals, while agreeing to the electoral reforms demanded by the Social Demo-

Between the Wars

porting the action of the Unemployment Board in directing
labour to a strike-bound mine (a good example of the independence always enjoyed by the Civil Service in Sweden), he
resigned. The proposer of the fatal resolution was the Liberal
Carl Ekman. The Liberal Party had split over the prohibition
issue in 1923, when the majority of its members in the *Riksdag* had
formed the anti-prohibition Independent Liberals (*Folksfrisin-
nade*); it was this group which Ekman led. Although he could rely
on only thirty-two votes in the Lower House, he agreed to take
office in 1926 with an avowed programme of seeking support
for any particular measure from either side of the House as the
occasion seemed to demand. This was the so-called 'weigh-
master policy' which he had been advocating since the end of
the war. And for a time it worked well. The backing of the
Social Democrats enabled him to pass the great Education Act
of 1927, which made the six-year primary school the basis of the
public educational system. But the Socialists were far less happy
about the other important product of Ekman's ministry—
arbitration tribunals made up of members of the Government,
employers and labours with the power, not only to try to reconcile
conflicting interest, (which they had had since 1909), but also to
interpret collective wage agreements. The trade unions feared
that this would mean a weakening of their power and independence, and staged a brief token strike, but within a few years,
workers were using the new machinery to a greater extent than
the employers.

The economic situation had continued to improve since 1922,
and the years following had been ones of great prosperity for
the country as a whole. This tended to offset any benefits the
Social Democrats may have obtained from the extension of the
franchise, and in the elections of 1928 they lost fifteen seats. The
Government was eventually defeated as the result of a split in its
own ranks, and Vice-Admiral Lindman thereupon formed a
Conservative cabinet which, in spite of being able to command
over twice as many seats as its predecessor, was, in fact, in a far
weaker position to face the economic crisis which burst on
Sweden, as on all Europe outside the Soviet Union, in 1929.

The farmers, who had not shared the prosperity of the 1920's
to the same extent as workers in industry, were especially hard
hit, and called for greater protection; it was after a defeat

Q   241

of his proposals to raise the tariffs on foreign sugar and wheat that Lindman resigned in the middle of 1930. Ekman consented to return, in spite of the fact that he could now rely on even fewer votes than before. As during his first ministry, however, his balancing tactics had considerable success, although the Socialists vigorously attacked what they regarded as a caricature of minority rule. Grain imports were placed under the control of a semi-State organization of the type which was becoming so common in Sweden's economic and social life, and price-increases were curbed by government action.

The slump, however, continued. The number of unemployed rose, and the reduction of wages brought growing unrest which reached its climax in 1931, when, in Ådalen in the province of Ångermanland, troops, who had been called in by the civil authorities to protect strike-breakers, fired on demonstrators, killing five. Although the Government was in no way to blame for the outrage, and after an enquiry, punished those found responsible, its reputation suffered severely from an event which may be compared to the Peterloo Massacre in England over a century before (from which the British government had emerged with much less credit, and in which the Manchester yeomanry had acted with considerably less provocation). No sooner had this crisis blown over, than the news broke of an even greater scandal—the collapse of the vast international industrial empire which had been built up by Ivar Kreuger on the basis of a monopoly of the manufacture of safety-matches in Sweden, and the suicide of its founder in Paris. While the damage was subsequently found to be less severe than had at first been feared, an investigation revealed that the Prime Minister himself had received financial support for his party from Kreuger in exchange for authorization of extensive credits granted to the Match King by the Bank of Sweden. Ekman was forced to resign, but his cabinet stayed in office until the elections of 1932. These restored the strength of the Social Democrats, now led by Per Albin Hansson; more than wiped out the gains made by the Conservatives in the previous contest; and reduced the Liberals to fourth place behind the Agrarian Party, which had been steadily gathering votes since its formation in 1921.

In fact, the long period of instability in Swedish politics was at

an end, but when the Social Democrats took office for the fourth
time, they were no nearer an absolute majority in the Lower
House than they had been in 1920, 1921 or 1924. That they
managed not only to retain power but to increase their hold, and
eventually to secure complete control of the *Riksdag* was in no
small measure due to the abilities (and, some might claim, to the
weaknesses) of their leader, a man who can be mentioned in the
same breath with Staaff, Branting, De Geer and Boström as one
of the most outstanding parliamentary leaders whom Sweden
has produced. Hansson was extremely popular both with members of the *Riksdag*, of whatever party, and with the general public
(to whom he was always Per Albin) throughout the fourteen
years he controlled his country's destiny, and was a master of
political management. Yet it cannot be denied that his successes
were, up to a point, gained at the expense of his principles. Under
the leadership of this ex-firebrand editor of *Socialdemokraten*, the
Social Democratic Party shed much of its socialism and became
even more like a late nineteenth-century radical party than its
British counterpart. But perhaps this was an inevitable result
of its long period of power, and perhaps the party was enabled
by making this change to bring to the country a greater measure
of social justice than would have been possible had it been more
doctrinaire and less broadly popular in its appeal.

   That great progress was made in all fields in Sweden in the
1930's in undeniable. It was during this decade that—thanks
partly to the publicity given to her by writers such as the
American journalist Marquis Childs, whose book *Sweden: the
Middle Way* was first published in 1936—she came to be regarded
by many outsiders as a near-ideal state, which had achieved
social security, equality and economic prosperity while remaining a liberal democracy. But when Hansson first took office, the
prospect looked far from bright. Unemployment figures continued to rise, until in March 1933 they topped 187,000, and
Swedish agriculture was in a sorry plight. The new government
came to the aid of the farmers by retaining the controls already
imposed by its predecessors and raising the fixed minimum
prices of farm produce; the doctrine of free trade, which had
been part of the Social Democrats' platform, was tacitly
abandoned. Industry was encouraged by devaluing the *krona*
to discourage imports. Opposition from the non-socialist

parties prevented the introduction of unemployment insurance, or the replacement of relief work at minimum wages by the integration of the unemployed into normal industry, but a pact with the Agrarians did enable considerable State aid to be given to those out of work, in the form of grants and subsidies.

Conditions improved rapidly during 1933, with the end of the international crisis. Production and real wages rose, and unemployment sank; a period of prosperity greater even than that of the 1920's got into full swing. The situation was favourable for the introduction of further social legislation, although the Government still had to win support from outside its own party to pass any bills through the *Riksdag*; unemployment insurance came at last in 1935. In 1936 old-age pensions were raised appreciably, but proposals for a further increase in benefits were defeated, and in June of the same year Hansson resigned. An Agrarian ministry was formed, but its life was short. The general election of 1936 produced a record poll, and gave the Social Democrats an overall majority in the Lower House for the first time. In the Upper House, however, they were still outnumbered, and to overcome this disability Hansson opened negotiations with the Agrarians, who agreed to join him in a coalition on condition that further aid would be given to agriculture. The building of the Welfare State continued in 1937 with the introduction of family allowances and the extension of the eight-hour day to land workers, and in 1938 with the enforcement of paid holidays for all. The improved relations which now existed between capital and labour are well illustrated by the so-called Saltsjöbaden Agreements reached between the trade unions and the Employers Federation in the latter year; both sides bound themselves to respect long-term contracts, and the risk of strikes and lock-outs was considerably reduced.

In spite of the prosperity—with exports of wood-pulp and iron ore reaching new peaks, the discovery of rich veins of various minerals at Boliden in Västerbotten, a great expansion of the building industry to reduce the overcrowding prevalent in the larger towns, record yields of cereals and dairy produce (helped by the increasing use of farming co-operatives since the depression at the beginning of the decade)—there were several causes for concern. One was the Swedish birth-rate. In the early 30's, this was amongst the lowest in the world at 13.7 per thousand per annum, and in 1934 Professor Gunnar Myrdal, Sweden's leading economist, attracted public attention to the problem in his book *The Population Crisis*. The following year, the Government set up a commission to look into the question, and it was partly as a result of its report that family allowances were introduced in 1937. In fact, however, Sweden had kept pace with the general rise of population in Europe, and in the later 1930's her birth-rate began to climb rapidly again, until in 1944 it stood at over 20 per thousand.

But the blackest cloud was one which hung over all Europe in the later years of the decade, and it was one not so easily dispersed as that of a low birth-rate. Sweden joined the League of Nations in 1920, but only after a vigorous debate, during which the Right expressed serious doubts about the effectiveness of the organization, and criticized its domination by the victorious powers; when put to the vote in the *Riksdag*, a large minority opposed entry. By the time, however, that Sweden became a member of the Council of the League in 1923, there was general agreement that, while every effort should be made to improve its machinery, the League should be supported as the best instrument available for the maintenance of international peace and the best guarantee of international justice; Branting's firm stand that year against both the French occupation of the Saar and Italy's bombardment of the Greek island of Corfu was approved by all parties. Sweden left the Council in 1926, and, while there was a brief outcry against the Japanese invasion of Manchuria in 1930, interest in foreign affairs and in the work of the League waned until Mussolini's attack on Abyssinia in 1935, when the Government supported the decision to impose sanctions against Italy; fears were expressed in some circles that this might jeopardize Sweden's neutrality, but public opinion united in condemning the bombing of a Swedish Red Cross ambulance by the Duce's planes in 1936. The disappointment was all the more bitter when it became apparent that the League was quite ineffective in face of Fascist aggression, and the movement in favour of withdrawal from it gathered momentum. Sweden did not, however, withdraw, and in 1937 was again given a seat on the Council, but any enthusiasm which her inhabitants still had for the League evaporated rapidly thereafter. By 1938 all parties believed that the country should remain strictly neutral in any future power struggle and should not support any further attempts to impose sanctions.

The growing threat to European peace and the failure of the League drove the Scandinavian powers to seek safety in closer co-operation among themselves. As early as 1932, the Foreign Ministers of Denmark, Norway and Sweden began to hold regular meetings, and in 1936 they issued a joint declaration of neutrality, expressing a very cautious attitude to sanctions. Two years later, discussions were held on the problem of mutual defence, but the only outcome of these was a Swedo-Finnish agreement on protection of the Åland Islands and this soon had to be cancelled under Russian pressure. Swedish re-armament began in 1936, but on a far smaller scale than even the Premier would have wished, and it was not until 1938, when war over Czechoslovakia appeared to be inevitable, that the *Riksdag* would approve a substantial increase in military appropriations.

Small pro-Nazi groups appeared in Sweden after 1933, and there were even three Nazi sympathizers (elected as Conservatives) in the *Riksdag* from 1934 to 1936, but Hitler's régime enjoyed little support from the broad mass of Swedes; a large number of its victims took refuge among them, and in spite of official German protests, the Government refused to take any action against newspapers which criticized the Führer's policies. At the other end of the political spectrum, eleven Communists were elected to the Lower House in 1936, and the party always had a certain following in the larger industrial towns and among the poor farmers of Norrland, but the acts of violence perpetrated by its supporters during the Depression (the Ådalen outbreak was Communist inspired) alienated many who might otherwise have been attracted by their professed aims. Sweden had recognized the Soviet Government in 1924 and concluded a trade agreement with her the same year. In the mid-30's Moscow even asked for a Swedish loan, but when this was agreed to, failed to ratify the contract.

CHAPTER XXII

The Second World War and After

The German attack on Poland which began the Second World War was immediately followed by a Swedish declaration of neutrality, and with a further, if limited, increase in the size of the country's armed forces. The Government's attitude to the new struggle, as to that of twenty-five years before, was undoubtedly shared by the vast majority of Swedes but, while on the previous occasion there had been widespread sympathy for the Central Powers, especially among the upper classes, there was now little support anywhere for the Fascist dictators. Sweden's close economic links with Germany had been maintained throughout the inter-war years, and her iron ore played an important rôle in Hitler's rearmament programme, but her cultural ties with her southern neighbour were far less important in 1939 than in the early years of the century. English had grown in importance as a school subject at German's expense; Anglo-Saxon culture had become more familiar through such media as the Hollywood film; and membership of the League of Nations had drawn Sweden closer to the Western Democracies.

While the 'phoney war' in the West dragged on through the autumn, Sweden was faced with a military conflict on her very door-step, a conflict which roused deep emotions in the breasts of all her inhabitants. By the Hitler-Stalin pact in August, the latter had been given a free hand in the eastern Baltic, and in October, Russia demanded from Finland the cession of certain territory which would protect more adequately the approaches to Leningrad. But the Finns refused to yield, and called on the Scandinavian monarchies to promise help in the event of attack from the east. The three kings met Marshal

Mannerheim, the Finnish president, in Stockholm, but Sweden, in spite of the assurances Hansson had given in September of her military preparedness, still had serious gaps in her defences and felt unable to commit herself. When, however, the Russians did declare war on Finland at the end of November, Sweden declared herself, not a neutral, but a non-belligerent, and allowed 12,000 volunteers and large shipments of arms to cross the Gulf of Bothnia to reinforce the Finns. After the Russian breakthrough in Karelia in the new year, the Finnish government asked to be allowed to engage volunteer units of the regular Swedish army, and the Western Powers applied in Stockholm for permission to send troops through Sweden to the Finnish front. Both requests were rejected, the latter because of fears that Russia's German ally might make the granting of it an excuse to intervene, and that the Allies might seize the opportunity to occupy the Lappland iron mines, which continued to feed the Nazi war machine in exchange for much-needed German coal. Peace between Russia and Finland was concluded in March with Swedish diplomatic aid; the fear of more vigorous Swedish action may have persuaded the Soviet government to moderate its terms. The close relations established in this way between Stockholm and Helsinki opened the way for negotiations between the two countries for a closer union, even for political federation, but they had to be broken off after Russian protests.

Hardly had the 'Winter War' been brought to an end, before a much greater danger to Sweden's security loomed up in the west. In April 1940, German troops marched into Denmark and Norway, and Sweden found herself isolated, with half her merchant shipping outside the Baltic. While Sweden's reaction to the crisis may have been an unheroic one, any overt action by her on behalf of her fellow-Scandinavians would probably have simply subjected her to their fate, for she could have put up little military resistance to an invasion. Vigorous efforts were at last made to mobilize her armed forces, but this took time, and, although Narvik was heroically defended by the Allies for a few weeks, Hitler's attack on Holland and Belgium almost immediately after his Nordic *coup* caused the withdrawal of French and British troops to meet the new onslaught. In June, organized Norwegian resistance came to an end.

While the fighting in Scandinavia had been going on, the

Germans had demanded transit through Sweden for their medical supplies and wounded, and the same right for unarmed troops going home on leave when the campaign was over. The Swedish government felt compelled to agree. In fact much war material to reinforce the German garrison in Norway also passed through the country in this way, and protests against the administration's apparent supineness and its toleration of such a breach of neutrality did not come only from Britain and France; a number of Swedes, led by Torgny Segerstedt, the editor of Gothenburg's *Handelstidningen*, who had always been a bitter opponent of National Socialism, launched a vigorous attack on Hansson and his colleagues. These now included Conservatives and Liberals, for a coalition cabinet had been formed at the end of 1939, and it replied by obtaining from the *Riksdag* powers to muzzle any papers which proved to be too outspoken in their condemnations of Nazi policy; Segerstedt was the first to suffer.

While a restriction on freedom of expression was not the only one which Swedes had to suffer during the Second World War, none can be compared with the real privations which they had had to endure during the First; the tight governmental control of economic and social life, which had still been something of a novelty in 1914, was now well established, and the authorities were much better able to cope with the emergency. A new Department of Economics was set up in 1939 to watch over the country's industry, trade and agriculture, and rationing of petrol was introduced almost as soon as war broke out. By 1941, coffee, tea, sugar, bread and meat had joined it, but there was never any serious shortage of essential supplies because Sweden was far less dependent on imports than she had been twenty years before, owing to the great advances made in her agricultural production in the 1930's. Her trade, however, was for long at the mercy of the belligerents, especially of the Germans, who controlled the exits from the Baltic. On various occasions, the Berlin government imposed a ban on Swedish commerce even with other neutral powers, either to compel the Swedes to grant it further favours, such as the transit through Sweden of troops travelling to the Finnish front after the invasion of Russia in 1941, or later, in revenge for favours granted to the Western Allies. Sweden's trade with Germany itself did not cease until the middle of 1944, but the turning of the tide against the Axis did make Allied threats more effective, and in the autumn of 1943 the transit traffic to Norway was stopped and the supply of iron ore to Germany reduced in exchange for larger supplies of oil from America.

The collapse of Germany, however, brought its own problems. Finland had entered the war on the German side in 1941, and Swedish volunteers had fought against the Russians in Karelia. In 1944 there seemed to be a definite danger that Finland might share the fate of the Baltic Republics and be absorbed into the victorious Russian empire, or at least have a puppet Communist régime foisted on her as the result of a Russian occupation. The threat was fortunately averted by the conclusion of an armistice in which Swedish diplomacy again played an important part; the country remained free at the cost of an enormous indemnity, the cession of territory in the far north and the leasing of a naval base near Helsinki. To the west, there was also a danger that the German occupation troops in Norway might embark on an orgy of destruction before giving up the struggle, and Sweden offered to disarm and intern them. The Allies, however, turned the offer down, and when the time came, the fears were not realized.

A third problem was the stream of refugees flowing into Sweden, which grew to a mighty flood towards the end of the war—Jews from Denmark in 1943, over 34,000 Balts fleeing before the Russian advance the following year, and many others; the peak was not reached until 1947. All were welcomed and cared for as well as was possible. But Sweden was not merely a passive recipient of the displaced of Europe; she also did much to rescue those whom the final holocaust in Germany threatened to swallow up. It was natural that her first concern should be for fellow Scandinavians, and early in 1945 negotiations were opened with the S.S. leader Heinrich Himmler for the evacuation of Danes and Norwegians imprisoned in Germany. He eventually gave his consent to their release as well as that of a number of non-Scandinavians; nineteen thousand souls in all were eventually brought to safety, largely thanks to Count Folke Bernadotte, the king's nephew, who conducted the whole operation through the Swedish Red Cross. Such an action was wholly consistent with Sweden's neutral status, but some activities in which she had indulged before the German collapse were difficult to reconcile with it—the help, for example, she gave to Norwegian resistance groups across the border, and the military training on her soil of refugee Danish and Norwegian police in preparation for the day of their countries' liberation.

By the time Sweden entered the United Nations in 1946, the wartime alliance was rapidly breaking up, leaving her in a particularly vulnerable position during the 'Cold War' which followed. Although the Communists had gained fifteen seats in the Lower House in the elections of 1944, there could be no doubt where the sympathies of the vast majority of Swedes lay in the subsequent quarrels between East and West, and these sympathies were strengthened by several incidents which took place even before the war was officially over, among them the disappearance of a Swedish legation secretary in Budapest after the Russian occupation of the city (in spite of persistent Russian denials at the time, he was later found to have died in a Moscow prison), and the Russians' demand for the repatriation of all Balt and German refugees who had borne arms against them. The Government agreed to participate in the Marshall Plan, the Organization for European Economic Recovery and the Council of Europe, but refused, on the other hand, to commit itself so far as to follow the other Scandinavian kingdoms into NATO in 1949 after the failure of attempts to create a Nordic defence bloc; and most of the refugees whose extradition had been demanded by the Soviet government were eventually returned. Many Swedes, especially the Conservatives, strongly criticized the two latter decisions, but the Russian threat to Finland, who, with her large Communist Party, might yet become part of the Soviet bloc, placed Sweden in a particularly difficult international situation which was not always fully appreciated either at home or abroad.

Her strict neutrality, while it undoubtedly brought a certain isolation, at least enabled her to play a useful, because independent, part in the various crises which faced the United Nations during the post-war years. Swedish troops participated in peace-keeping operations in Egypt after the Anglo-French attack on Suez, in the Congo during the troubles which followed the declaration of its independence and, most recently, in Cyprus; Folke Bernadotte was murdered in Palestine in 1948 while attempting to mediate between Arabs and Jews; nonmilitary aid was sent to Korea in 1953; and three years later, a large number of Hungarian refugees joined all the other foreign nationalities which have found a home in Sweden in recent years. Above all stands the work done by Dag Hammarskjöld as Secretary-General of the United Nations from 1953 until his tragic death in Rhodesia. The impartiality shown by the Swedish member of the Security Council in 1957 and 1958 caused dissatisfaction in both camps—and even among a number of his fellow countrymen.

Her isolation is not the only price which Sweden has had to pay for her post-war foreign policy. Her decision to stand outside all alliance systems has necessitated the spending of large sums on defence, especially on the building up of a highly efficient air force, and this expenditure has still further increased the financial difficulties which have been the main concern of her government since 1945.

The coalition Cabinet did not survive the war. Although Hansson himself appears to have favoured its retention, many within his own party as well as the other party leaders wanted their freedom and the opportunity to tackle post-war problems in their own way. In July 1945, therefore, Sweden returned to being ruled by a purely Socialist administration. Hansson died a little over a year later and was succeeded by the present Premier, Tage Erlander. His position when he first took office was by no means an enviable one. The Social Democrats had suffered heavily in the 1944 elections to the Lower House (for which the voting age was reduced to twenty-one) and had been left with only the same number of seats as the other parties combined; which encouraged these to launch a vigorous assault on all aspects of government policy. The Right especially was critical of the neutralist attitude adopted in the Cold War, and in 1947 the Minister of Commerce was compelled to resign after concluding disappointing trade treaties with Poland and Russia. As in Britain during the same period, the Conservatives, again the party of economic *laisser-faire*, led the attack on the retention of war-time controls, especially rationing, which was not abolished until 1949, and the pegging of rents at their 1942 level, which was blamed for the very serious shortage of houses and flats. They also criticized the increase in taxation. Part of this was devoted to the social services, felt by some to be undermining individual responsibility, but part was used to build up of a strong defence, on the necessity for which all parties except the Communists were agreed. Such assaults made their mark in the elections of 1948, and had the trade slump which had followed the war not taken a turn for the better about this time, the Social Democrats might have fared far worse than to lose only three seats. But the Conservatives themselves suffered a far worse defeat, which reduced them to the smallest party in the Lower House, largely to the benefit of the resurrected Liberals, who gained no fewer than twenty-six seats.

Inflation continued at an alarming rate, to reach its peak in 1951. Erlander, having lost his overall majority, looked round for another parliamentary group with whose support to carry through the measures which he felt to be necessary to weather the storm. Since these took the form largely of more controls, he could expect help neither from the Conservatives nor the Liberals, but the Agrarians were not opposed to controls on principle, especially if they benefited agriculture, which was again hard hit by the crisis owing to over-production and the difficulty of disposing of surplus produce on impoverished foreign markets. Their leader, Gunnar Hedlund, agreed to enter a coalition. Little change of policy resulted, but the elections of 1952 placed the Agrarians in a very favourable position *vis-à-vis* their new allies, for the Social Democrats lost their majority over the other democratic parties. The Coalition suffered further losses four years later, and on this occasion it was the Conservatives who were the chief beneficiaries; since the débâcle of 1948, they had made great efforts to broaden the basis of their appeal and to destroy the popular image of themselves as representing the interests of the old ruling classes, and now returned as strong as they had been at the beginning of the war. By this time, the links binding the Social Democrats and the Agrarians were beginning to wear very thin, and it became extremely doubtful whether they would hold in a serious political crisis. Such a crisis came in 1957 with the announcement of the Socialists' pension policy.

A State-run old age pension scheme had been in existence in Sweden in one form or other for nearly half a century, and there were in addition various private superannuation schemes which could be used to supplement its rather meagre benefits. What was now proposed was the introduction of a fully-integrated system, offering additional grants sufficient to enable every citizen to enjoy a retirement both free from financial worries and with a standard of living not uncomfortably below that of his working years. While all parties agreed in principle—at least in public—on the desirability of such an end, they diverged widely from each other on the means to attain it. The Social Democrats wanted the setting up of a central pensions fund made up of contributions from all workers, the redistribution of which was to be administered by the State. The Conservatives, Agrarians and Liberals objected to the compulsory principle, and many feared the power which the central fund would place in the hands of the Government. They therefore each put forward their own solutions, and demanded that these and the Socialist plan should form the subject of a consultative referendum. The ministers agreed. The referendum had been neglected since its first application in 1922 to the prohibition issue, but it had been revived in 1955 to help decide whether Sweden should continue to be the only country in Europe, except Britain, to drive on the left; the result was a large majority against change but in 1963 the *Riksdag* nevertheless decided that the switch should be made in 1967. Now, on the third occasion it was used, it failed to give much satisfaction to any of the groups concerned; the Social Democrats' plan obtained more votes than either of the others proposed, but less than half the total cast. The Agrarians, having changed the name of their party to the more non-committal one of the Centre, were encouraged to withdraw from the Cabinet, and Erlander was consequently defeated in the House.

The elections which followed seemed to justify the Centre's action, for it gained thirteen seats. The Liberals, however, lost twenty, and the Conservatives became once more the largest Opposition party. The Social Democrats made enough gains to give them a paper majority in the Lower House, but when their pensions scheme (a slightly modified version of the one which had been the subject of the referendum) was introduced there, it was passed only with the help of a dissident Liberal member.

With the pensions question settled for the time being, the general economic situation returned once more to the forefront of political life; unemployment figures were rising, and there seemed to be little hope that the budget could be balanced. In view of the latter, the Opposition parties demanded that economies should be made—cuts in subsidies and even in the social services; and they were supported in the report of a committee which had been appointed to study the problem. But the Government preferred to close the gap by means of a general sales tax of 4 per cent. The measure could be passed through the *Riksdag* only by holding a joint session of the two Houses, in which the Socialists had a majority, but it achieved its objective, and the latter made limited gains in the elections of 1960; these gave them a majority over the combined democratic parties such as they had had before 1952, but they could still be defeated by an adverse Communist vote.[1]

The political battles over pensions and the economic situation must not be allowed to obscure the fact that a host of reforms have been carried out in Sweden since the Second World War with the support of all parties, or at least with opposition only on matters of detail. Three weeks' paid annual holidays for all were introduced in 1953. The basic old age pension (which, unlike the supplementary pension, is not related to income) was raised appreciably in 1959, and linked to the cost of living. Family allowances were made general in 1947, and the strict means test applied to them before the war was at the same time swept away. The only limited effectiveness of the Bratt system of liquor control led to a successful campaign for its abolition, although the State has retained its monopoly of retail selling through the *Systembolag* (whose shops are made as inconspicuous as possible), and restrictions on the sale of drinks in bars and restaurants remain. The immediate result of the end of liquor rationing was a sharp increase in prosecutions for drunkenness, but this development proved short-lived, thanks partly to exemplary punishments meted out to drivers found to have consumed even a very small amount of alcohol. Such drivers often have to serve for short terms in open prisons. These were introduced in 1945, and the whole attitude to crime in Sweden has been increasingly marked by an emphasis on re-

[1] The figures were: Social Democrats, 114; Conservative, Agrarians and Liberals, 113; Communists, 5. The elections to the Lower House in September 1964 resulted in the gain of three seats each by the Social Democrats and the Communists; of the non-socialist parties, the Conservatives lost eleven seats, and the Centre gained two. The Government is thus no longer dependent on the Communists.

habilitation rather than correction, which has always been the hallmark of enlightened penal theory. But the most important piece of social legislation of these years was that which governed the setting up of a national health service. A decision to introduce this by 1950 was taken in 1946 but, owing to the post-war economic crisis, it did not finally come into operation until 1955. Even then, it was in some respects less comprehensive than the British plan put into effect ten years earlier; hospital treatment is free, but only a percentage of the doctor's fees and the cost of medicine is usually remitted, and dental services are not covered.

In 1950, the first steps were taken in a revolution in Swedish public education, a revolution which is still going on and which will take many more years to complete. It is in essence a more thorough-going application of the idea which lay behind the 1927 Act—that every Swedish child should have precisely the same educational opportunities and should be taught in the same type of school throughout the years of compulsory attendance. Every large parish will in the end have a nine-year comprehensive school, to which most of its children will go, but the precise moment for the introduction of such a school will depend on the local authority concerned. It should be noted that, while the basic theory behind them is similar, there are two considerable differences between the English and Swedish comprehensive school: while English children pass from a primary to a quite distinct secondary department at the age of eleven, most Swedish children will eventually spend the *whole* of their school lives at the same institution; and the Swedish child who wishes to go on to university (where, while the tuition is free, the student can support himself only with loans not, as in Britain, with maintenance grants from the State or local authorities) must still do so through the *gymnasium*, entered after leaving the comprehensive school at the age of fifteen or sixteen.

CHAPTER XXIII

The Swedish Image

More than most other countries, the Sweden of today has become a symbol to the world beyond her borders, a symbol singled out by some foreign critics for fulsome praise and by others for equally vigorous condemnation. But symbols are by their very nature simplifications, if not serious distortions, of reality; and it is the purpose of this final chapter to attempt an assessment of the 'Swedish Image' in the middle of the twentieth century.

It is hoped that parts of the preceding narrative will have done something to dispel some common misconceptions about Sweden's development. But as a whole it should also have helped to dispel another. Sweden is often regarded as an ultra-modern state—'a glimpse of the 21st century', as a recent travel advertisement expressed it—and there is certainly much evidence to justify such a view. But it is misleading if taken to imply that she has uprooted herself from her past, has purposely broken away from her moorings. For Swedes, proud as they are of the very great advances they have made during the last fifty years, are deeply conscious of their past. And this has undoubtedly been helped by the continuity of their history. There have been no sharp breaks in it to match the French Revolution, the unification of Germany and of Italy or the re-emergence of Poland after over a century of national extinction. In this respect, as in others, Sweden's experience has not been unlike England's. But even England suffered foreign occupation in the eleventh century; Sweden has never known it, for, whatever her nationalist historians of the nineteenth century may claim, the Union of Kalmar was never this. In her enjoyment of such an advantage she is probably unique among the nations of the Old World, and such things do affect, in ways often difficult to define, a people's character.

Modern Sweden is very much the child of Sweden past, and she has brought much of her past with her into the present. Her political democracy is, for example, very real, the more so for the long tradition of representative government involving large sections of society; but the Crown retains considerable reserve powers under a constitution which does not recognize parliamentary government (only in practice established since the First World War, and even then given a difficult birth by the unstable nature of politics in the 1920's). The Swedish monarch is no longer crowned (Gustav V was the first king to dispense with a coronation), but he is more directly involved in administration than his British counterpart. Gustav VI (born 1882), who succeeded his father (for whom he had already acted as regent on several occasions) in 1950, adopted as his motto 'Duty above all'. And this has proved to be no empty phrase; he has performed the various functions of a constitutional sovereign, as well as pursued his many artistic and cultural interests, with intense application.

Old attitudes and old customs die hard, especially in the countryside, where half the population of Sweden still lives. But this can be extremely frustrating for the young. And this frustration is perhaps made worse by the conformism of an essentially middle-class society, reminiscent of that of contemporary America, though without such extremes of wealth and poverty; one of the worst faults of the Swedes as a whole is a certain bourgeois smugness which has come with riches and success. Not that Swedish society is egalitarian in the strict sense of the word. Inherited rank or rank based on a privileged educational system are certainly less prominent features of the Swedish than of the British scene; neither Uppsala nor Lund has acquired the peculiar aura of Oxford and Cambridge. But rank acquired by ability or character is still very much in evidence; the managing director and the university professor are both very conscious of their dignity, the more so perhaps because of the rarity of other forms of distinction. Again a parallel with the United States suggests itself, but a consideration of the weight of tradition in Sweden—including a tradition of governmental direction of economic and social

The Swedish Image

life which, as has been seen, is by no means a socialist innovation—prevents one carrying the parallel too far.

The Swedes are undoubtedly well clothed, well fed and well educated. The country is perhaps not comparatively as prosperous as in the 1930's, when her rapid recovery from the Depression was held up as an example to the rest of Europe, and when the popular image of Sweden began to be formed. Yet, in spite of the economic difficulties which she has had to face since the last war, she still enjoys one of the highest standards of living in the world, helped by her century and a half of neutrality and an economic life unencumbered with the age-old practices which tend to impede progress in countries who developed their industry earlier than she. In numbers of cars, telephones and radios per head of population Sweden leads the Continent, and the real wages of her industrial workers, thanks largely to the strength of the organized labour movement, rose by 50 per cent in the decade after 1945 (although other sectors of the community did not do so well, a fact which goes far to explain the gains made by the Right in recent elections).

Sweden has a large trade gap, but she has had this at least ever since she became industrialized, and it is largely covered by 'invisible exports'. Nearly half her exports are accounted for by manufactured metal goods and by the ancient staple of iron ore; after reaching a new low at the end of the Second World War, the production of her iron mines now makes up a good 5 per cent of the world's total. The next most important group of exports (about 30 per cent) consists of wood products, headed by pulp for paper-making. In spite of the considerable growth of her engineering industry, however, machinery heads her list of imports, while the development of hydro-electric power has not eliminated the need for foreign oil and coal.

Only a quarter of the population of Sweden now lives by agriculture, and the extent of cultivated land is continually declining. But the use of artificial fertilizers, improved seed and mechanization (although Sweden is not as advanced as Britain in this respect) has enabled the productivity of what remains to rise by leaps and bounds; post-war harvests set up new records.

Agriculture has been considerably aided by the Government, not only with subsidies, but with a highly-organized advisory

259

service, control of the land market and a programme of rationa-
lization aimed at encouraging the amalgamation of small
uneconomic farms. The State indeed plays a large part in many
aspects of the economy, but a vast field is still left open to
private enterprise. Only about 6 per cent of all undertakings
are 'nationalized' (including the iron-ore mines of Lappland,
which were taken over in 1955, in accordance with the agreement concluded by the Lindman administration at the beginning of the century[1]), with a further 3 per cent run by the
powerful Co-operative Union, founded in 1899. As in Britain, a
semi-public body controls broadcasting (sound and television);
and the Government owns half the shares of the Swedish section
of the Scandinavian Airways System (set up immediately after
the war) and plays a large part in the Atomic Energy Company,
founded in 1947. But even a key enterprise like the supplying
of electric power is, unlike in Britain, half in private hands.
As has been shown, this type of mixed economy has a long
history in Sweden, where *laisser-faire* liberalism never enjoyed
the triumphs it enjoyed in nineteenth-century Britain; while
Conservatives and Liberals may now resist further extensions of
public control, opposition in the past has been much less bitter.

The reputation which the Swedes have acquired for good
taste in the material details of living can be traced back to the
great Stockholm Exhibition of 1930, where 'Functionalism'
(originating in Germany) was the dominant feature of the
model flats and houses put on show. And the reputation is
justified. Late industrialization, which enabled advantage to
be taken of the mistakes made by earlier starters; widely distributed wealth, which has allowed all sections of the community
to benefit from the latest advances in the use of materials; the
survival of a tradition of honest, peasant craftsmanship, encouraged by such bodies as the century-old Swedish Society of
Industrial Design and apparent in the glass of Orrefors and
the ceramics of Rörstrand—all are partial explanations of a
phenomenon which, it should be emphasized, is shared by
Sweden's Scandinavian neighbours. The recognition of the
need for planning in the community, which struck root earlier
than in countries more closely wedded to the doctrines of *laisser-
faire*, is most clearly manifested in the new urban centres which

[1] See p. 231.

began to spring up in Sweden during the Second World War. Of these, the most widely publicized has been Vällingby on the outskirts of Stockholm, completed in 1955 and housing 23,000 people (see plate 8). But it is only one among a number of similar experiments to be found both in the neighbourhood of the capital and in other parts of the country.

While perhaps the most striking feature of Swedish culture to-day is the wide circle of the population which shares in it, individual Swedes have continued to make outstanding contributions to the arts in the twentieth century. In architecture, Gunnar Asplund, the principal designer of the 1930 Exhibition, who died in 1940, was the foremost figure in the first half of the century; the most famous (and the last) of his achievements is the severely functionalist Forest Cemetery on the outskirts of Stockholm. But perhaps more familiar in this field, though hardly typical of what is now thought of as 'Swedish Design', is the City Hall of the capital, completed in 1923 to the Romantic Italianate designs of Ragnar Östberg (1866–1945). In sculpture, Carl Milles (1875–1955) was a worthy successor to Sergel. Many of his works can be seen in a beautiful setting overlooking the waters of the Baltic at Millesgården, easily accessible from Stockholm. His *Orpheus Fountain* (see plate 8) is a well-known landmark in the city itself. Sculpture is well patronized by municipalities and private firms in Sweden.

Among a host of composers who have emerged in Sweden in the twentieth century, Hugo Alfvén (1872–1960) is the doyen, best known abroad for his symphonies and his rhapsody *Midsummer Night*. Of still-living composers working in a more modern idiom, Dag Wirén and Lars-Erik Larsson, both born in the first decade of the century, are well established in the concert halls of the world. The voices of Birgit Nilsson, Kerstin Meyer and the late Jussi Björling have impressed on international opera audiences the high standards maintained by the Stockholm Opera, a complement in Scandinavian artistic life to the Danish Ballet.

Three Swedes have been awarded the Nobel Prize for Literature. Of these, Selma Lagerlöf has already been discussed. The others are the poet Erik Karlfeldt (in 1931, the year of his death) and the poet, novelist and dramatist Pär Lagerkvist (in 1951). Karlfeldt really belongs among the regional writers who

The Swedish Image

emerged at the end of the nineteenth century; just as Fröding (whose influence on his early work was considerable) sang of his native Värmland, so Karlfeldt chose the countryside of Dalarna as the subject of most of his lyrics. Lagerkvist has acquired his widest reputation for the historical novels (though they are much more than this) *The Dwarf*, which appeared in 1944 (English translation, 1953), and *Barabbas* of 1950 (English translation, 1952), both of which brought him world renown rather late in life (he was born in 1891). But he is also Sweden's leading modern dramatist and has produced a considerable quantity of verse. The Swedish literary scene in the twentieth century has become so crowded with talented writers that it is difficult to avoid turning this brief account into a mere list of names which would leave the reader little the wiser. Mention may just be made of the novelist Hjalmar Bergman, a restless and bizarre character, whose later works (he died in 1931) are set in his birthplace of Örebro (which appears in them as Wadköping); of the leading 'proletarian writer' Harry Martinson, who embodied his nautical experiences in a collection of short stories called *Cape Farewell* (1933; English translation, 1934); and of the humorist Albert Engström (1869-1940), a true *Stockholmare*, who became almost as famous for his drawings as for his word-sketches of inhabitants of the capital. Many younger men still await recognition outside Sweden.

In the newest major field of art, Sweden has gained an international reputation which many much larger countries might envy. In the early days of the silent screen, actors and directors like Viktor Sjöström and Mauritz Stiller, working on extremely small budgets, were among the first to realize the artistic as distinct from the commercial potentialities of the cinema. The 'golden age', which they dominated, came to an end with the advent of 'talkies', but during and after the Second World War, under the direction of Alf Sjöberg and his younger contemporaries Arne Sucksdorff and Ingmar Bergman, the film again became the medium through which Sweden made perhaps her greatest impact on Western culture. The actresses Greta Garbo and Ingrid Bergman have maintained the high standards of the Swedish theatre, where both of them received their early training, in face of the Hollywood 'star system', and the close link which has always existed in the country between stage and

screen was recently emphasized by the appointment of Ingmar
Bergman to the directorship of the National Theatre in Stockholm.

There are few who would deny the high quality which
Sweden has achieved and maintained in her cultural life,
although some aspects of this life are too little known beyond her
borders. But the Swedish Image has its dark side too. It would
be useless to deny that Swedish society has serious problems to
cope with, problems which prosperity and equality of wealth and
opportunity have not eliminated and may even have intensified;
statistics of drunkenness, juvenile delinquency and suicides and
a serious housing shortage are all blots on the record. But
they are also blots, sometimes far larger, on the records of
other countries with very different backgrounds, and the overall
picture is far less gloomy than some critics, usually without ever
having visited the country, would have us believe. From other
blots—poverty, ignorance, militarism, intolerance of all kinds—
Sweden is singularly free. It is necessary, though admittedly
difficult, to get things in perspective. And not only for the out-
sider. For the Swedes themselves may be partly to blame for the
publicity given to their problems; they themselves may be
victims of the Swedish Image. Their desire to create a rational,
happy society, encouraged by the sometimes over-lavish praise
given by their friends to their real achievements in this direction, has made them perhaps unduly sensitive to the blemishes
which remain; which has helped to create new tensions and new
difficulties. What needs emphasizing is the bold and imaginative way in which major social problems are being tackled, the
rejection of the second-best and the willingness to experiment,
regardless of whether the desired effect is attained or not. But
Sweden must not, on the other hand, be looked upon merely as a
store-house of examples to support a particular case, nor as simply
a field for social experiments, much as these have to teach the
world outside. She is a country with a past, which must always be
taken into account when attempting to apply her solutions to
outwardly similar problems elsewhere.

In the 1930's Sweden suddenly re-emerged from the comparative obscurity into which she had sunk after the collapse of her
Baltic empire at the beginning of the eighteenth century; and to
a greater or lesser extent she has remained in the limelight ever

since. Yet, in spite of her membership of such bodies as OEEC and the Council of Europe, something of the isolation which dogged her when she was accounted among the poorer countries of Europe has remained with her; even the great advances made in international communications during the nineteenth and twentieth centuries have not wholly overcome geographical factors—her position facing east along what is practically an inland sea. And the strictly neutral attitude she chose to adopt during the Second World War and the Cold War which followed divided her even from Denmark and Norway, in spite of the fact that they were dragged into great power conflicts much against their wills. Yet, while nineteenth-century Scandinavianism is dead, the movement has re-emerged in other forms with the accent on cultural and economic co-operation and integration. To co-ordinate efforts in these fields is the purpose of the Nordic Council, a body made up of representatives from the parliaments of Norway, Sweden, Denmark, Iceland and Finland, which was established in 1952 as a development of the Scandinavian Inter-Parliamentary Union, dating from as far back as 1907. Among the many measures which the Council has sponsored have been the introduction of a common labour market, of uniform postal rates between Sweden, Denmark and Norway and, in 1958, the abolition of the need for passports to travel within Scandinavia. Plans also to abolish tariffs were overtaken in 1959 by the formation of the European Free Trade Area, membership of which has strengthened Sweden's ties with Britain, always her best customer. At the same time, over a third of her trade is with the rival Common Market, which gives her a special interest in any project for uniting the two economic systems.

Suggestions for Further Reading

I n drawing up the following very selective list, I have tried to keep in mind the needs of both the general reader who may wish to know more about some of the topics touched on in *The Story of Sweden* through books and articles in English which are easily obtainable in public libraries and of the student who has access to more specialized collections and command of other European languages. Works suitable for the former are marked with an asterisk, and further titles may be found in N. Afzelius, *Books in English on Sweden* (Stockholm, 1951). Swedish history has not yet attracted the attention it deserves from non-Swedish historians, and in order to study any aspect of it in depth it is necessary to turn to publications in Swedish—not a difficult language to learn to read, especially if one has some German. Here the range is enormous, and I have had to confine myself to standard works on important subjects, recent lives of leading personalities and studies of Anglo-Swedish relations. Further guidance may be had from S. E. Bring, *Bibliografisk handbok till Sveriges historia* (Stockholm, 1934), supplemented by the annual lists printed by the Svenska Historiska Förening as supplements to its journal *Historisk Tidskrift* (Stockholm, 1881). The latter and *Scandia* (Stockholm, 1928) are the principal Swedish historical periodicals. The considerable amount of unpublished material relating to Swedish history in British archives has been catalogued in *A Guide to the Materials for Swedish Historical Research in Great Britain* (Stockholm, 1958). All books published in Sweden are in Swedish unless otherwise indicated.

(a) Works Covering All Periods
The best—as well as the most up-to-date—one-volume history of Sweden is undoubtedly Ingvar Andersson's *History of Sweden* (London, 1956).* C. Hallendorff and A. Schück's *A History of Sweden* (London, 1938)* is mainly political, but A. A. Stomberg's *A History of Sweden* (New York, 1931)* devotes consider-

Suggestions for Further Reading

able space to social and cultural movements. In Swedish, two recent multi-volume histories are to be recommended: H. Maiander (ed.), *Sveriges historia genom tiderna* (Stockholm, 1947–48) is richly illustrated, and S. Carlsson and J. Rosén, *Svensk historia* (Stockholm, 1961–62) contains extensive bibliographies with discussions of disputed questions. The development of the Swedish constitution is examined in N. Herlitz, *Grunddragen av det svenska statsskickets historia* (Stockholm, 1952). Birger Steckzén has written a series of essays dealing with various aspects of Swedo-British relations, collected together in *Svenskt och Brittiskt* (Stockholm, 1959). The country's economic development is traced by her greatest economic historian, Eli Heckscher, in *An Economic History of Sweden* (Cambridge, Mass., 1954).* There is no similar survey of her culture in English, but A. Gustafson's *A History of Swedish Literature* (Minneapolis, 1961)* is excellent and contains a very useful list of translations into English. The most up-to-date history of literature in Swedish is E. N. Tigerstedt (ed.), *Ny illustrerad svensk litteraturhistoria* (Stockholm, 1955–58), while in one volume there is E. N. Tigerstedt, *Svensk litteraturhistoria* (Stockholm, 1948). The best survey of Swedish art is H. Cornell, *Den svenska konstens historia* (Stockholm, 1944–46) and of music T. Norlind, *Svensk musikhistoria* (Stockholm, 1918). Brief surveys in English of music and drama are B. Olander, *Swedish Music* (Stockholm, 1956)* and G. Hilleström, *Theatre and Ballet in Sweden* (Stockholm, 1953).* For those interested in the development of the Swedish language, there is G. Bergman, *A Short History of the Swedish Language* (Stockholm, 1947).* The standard history of the Church is H. Holmquist and H. Pleijel (eds.), *Svenska kyrkans historia* (Stockholm, 1941), six of whose nine volumes have so far appeared; the only work in English on this subject is J. Wordsworth, *The National Church in Sweden* (London, 1911),* to which, however, can now be added Leslie Stannard Hunter (ed.), *Scandinavian Churches* (London, 1965), dealing with those of Denmark, Finland, Iceland, Norway and Sweden. The writing of history in Sweden has been examined by R. M. Hatton in an article entitled 'Some notes on Swedish historiography' in *History*, vol. 37 (1952). Fifteen volumes of the *Svenskt biografiskt Lexicon*, edited by B. Boëthius and B. Hildebrand (Stockholm, 1918), have so far appeared, reaching the letter F. It has not been possible in *The Story of*

266

Sweden to say much about the effects of Swedish rule in Finland;
the gap may be filled with the help of E. Jutikkala's *A History of
Finland* (London, 1962).*

(b) Prehistoric and Viking Times
On prehistoric Sweden, M. Steinberger's *Sweden* (London,
n.d.)* is a well-written and lavishly-illustrated volume in the
'Ancient Peoples and Places' series, edited by Glyn Daniel.
There is no book devoted solely to the Swedish Vikings, but the
following contain information on Viking civilization in general
and Swedish expansion in the Viking Age: T. D. Kendrick,
The Vikings (London, 1930);* J. Brønstedt, *The Vikings* (Pen-
guin Books, 1960);* and P. Sawyer, *The Age of the Vikings*
(London, 1962).* Something of the spirit of the epoch has been
recaptured in F. G. Bengtsson's novel, *The Long Ships* (Fontana
Books, 1956).* For Swedish settlements in Russia, see T. J.
Arne, *La Suède et l'Orient* (Uppsala, 1914). There is an article by
W. Roos on 'The Swedish part in the Viking expeditions' in
the *English Historical Review*, vol. 7 (1892). Pre-Christian reli-
gious beliefs can be studied in E. O. G. Turville-Petre's *Myth
and Religion of the North* (London, 1954) and the arrival of
Christianity in S. U. Palme, *Kristendoms genombrott i Sverige*
(Stockholm, 1959). The most recent book on Swedish runes is
The Runes of Sweden by S. B. F. Jansson (London, 1962).

(c) The Middle Ages
The best general survey in a language other than Swedish is
contained in L. Musset, *Les peuples scandinaves au moyen âge*
Paris, 1951). Various problems of Swedish medieval history are
discussed by E. Lönnroth in *Från svensk medeltid* (Stockholm,
1959), which also contains brief essays on the Vikings and
Gustav Vasa. There is an article by J. J. Murray on 'The
peasant revolt of Engelbrekt Engelbrektsson and the birth of
modern Sweden' in the American *Journal of Modern History*, vol.
19 (1947).* S. U. Palme's *Sten Sture den Äldre* (Stockholm, 1950)
is the best biography of a medieval personality. Saint Bridget
forms the subject of a number of rather unsatisfactory studies;
J. Jørgensen's *Saint Bridget of Sweden* (London, 1954)* is the
best available. For early Swedish foreign policy, see the first
volume of the invaluable series *Den svenska utrikespolitikens*

historia; the period up to 1560 is dealt with by N. Ahnlund (Stockholm, 1956). The beginnings of the *Riksdag* may be studied in the first volume of another series: *Sveriges Riksdag*, edited by K. Hildebrand (Stockholm, 1931–38). The medieval development of Stockholm is described exhaustively in N. Ahnlund's *Stockholms historia före Gustav Vasa* (Stockholm, 1953).

(d) The Sixteenth Century

The only works in English on this period are P. B. Watson's *The Swedish Revolution under Gustaf Vasa* (London, 1889)* and C. J. I. Bergendoff, *Olaus Petri and the Ecclesiastical Transformation in Sweden, 1521–1552* (New York, 1928). The most recent life of Gustav Vasa is by I. Svalenius (Stockholm, 1950). This king's foreign policy is examined in the volume by N. Ahnlund quoted in section c. Ingvar Andersson has both written a life of Erik XIV (Stockholm, 1948) and studied his subject's relations with England in *Erik XIV's engelska underhandlingar* (Lund, 1935). The Swedish economy in the sixteenth century is the first subject of Eli Heckscher's monumental *Sveriges ekonomiska historia från Gustav Vasa* (Stockholm, 1947–48). An important aspect of Swedish economic history in this as in earlier periods is the subject of an article by K. G. Hildebrand on 'Salt and Cloth in Swedish economic history' in the *Scandinavian Economic History Review*, vol. 2 (1954), where he is critical of Heckscher's findings. In the same field is an article by I. Hammarström on 'The Price Revolution of the sixteenth century: some Swedish evidence' in the same journal, vol. 5 (1957). The sixteenth century saw the arrival of Scots in Sweden for the first time in large numbers; T. A. Fischer's *The Scots in Sweden* (Edinburgh, 1907)* is still the only study of them.

(e) 1611–1660

M. Roberts's *Gustavus Adolphus* (London, 1953–58)* is not only a masterly study of early seventeenth-century Sweden, but has much on the sixteenth century also. N. Ahnlund's *Gustaf Adolph the Great* (Princeton, 1940)* is the best life by a Swedish historian. The same author has also written a life of Axel Oxenstierna to 1632, *Axel Oxenstierna intill Gustav Adolfs död* (Stockholm, 1940), while Professor Roberts has contributed 'The political objectives of Gustavus Adolphus in Germany, 1630–1632' to *Tran-*

Suggestions for Further Reading

sactions of the Royal Historical Society, 5th series, vol. 7 (1957), 'Queen Christina and the general crisis of the seventeenth century' to *Past and Present*, no. 22 (1962) and 'The abdication of Queen Christina' to *History Today*, vol. 4 (1954).* Swedish relations with England during the period received considerable attention at the end of the last century with: A. Rydfors, *De diplomatiska förbindelserna mellan Sverige och England 1624–1630* (Uppsala, 1890); A. Heimer, *De diplomatiska förbindelserna mellan Sverige och England 1633–54* (Lund, 1893); and G. Jones, *The Diplomatic Relations between Cromwell and Charles X Gustavus of Sweden* (Lincoln, Neb., 1897). Cromwell's envoy to Stockholm, Bulstrode Whitelocke, left behind an excellent account of Sweden under Queen Christina in *A Journal of the Swedish Embassy in the Years 1653 and 1654* (latest edition: London, 1885). French relations after 1648 are surveyed in the introduction by A. Geffroy to *Recueil des instructions données aux ambassadeurs et ministres de France : II Suède* (Paris, 1885). For Swedish foreign policy in general, see vol. I pt. iii of *Svenska utrikespolitikens historia* (1648–1697) by G. Landberg (Stockholm, 1953), and for New Sweden, A. Johnson, *The Swedish Settlements on the Delaware* (New York, 1911). A good general survey of the period is the chapter on 'Scandinavia and the Baltic' by Jerker Rosén in the *New Cambridge Modern History*, vol. V (1648–88) (Cambridge, 1961). For economic developments, see Heckscher, *op. cit.* (section d), and for the *Riksdag* in the period, *Sveriges Riksdag* (section c).

(f) 1660–1718

Besides his novels and essays, F. G. Bengtsson has written a *Life of Charles XII* (London, 1960),* but the best study of this king is O. Haintz, *Karl XII* (Berlin, 2nd edn. 1958). For the regency for Charles XI, consult R. Fåhræus's life of Magnus Gabriel De la Gardie (Stockholm, 1936) and for Charles XI himself, an article by Professor Roberts in *History*, vol. 50 (1965). Diplomatic relations between Britain and Sweden in the later half of the seventeenth century are covered to a limited extent by: the introduction by J. F. Chance to *British Diplomatic Instructions, 1689–1789, I: Sweden 1689–1727* (London, 1922); his 'England and Sweden in the time of William III and Anne' in the *English Historical Review*, vol.

Suggestions for Further Reading

16 (1901) and *George and I the Northern War* (London, 1909); and three articles by J. J. Murray—'Robert Jackson's mission to Sweden (1709–1717)' in the *Journal of Modern History*, vol. 21 (1949); 'The Görtz-Gyllenborg arrests—a problem in diplomatic immunity' in the *Journal of Modern History*, vol. 28 (1956); and 'Sweden and the Jacobites in 1716' in the *Huntington Library Quarterly*, vol. 8 (1945). On Swedish foreign policy during the Great Northern War, see J. Rosén, *Den svenska utrikespolitikens historia*, vol. II pt. i (1697–1721) (Stockholm, 1952), and for its earlier phases, Landberg, *op. cit.* (section e). The forthcoming sixth volume of the *New Cambridge Modern History* will contain a chapter on the Great Northern War by R. M. Hatton, who has kindly allowed me to see the manuscript. Many articles on the Caroline period will be found in the volumes of the *Karolinska Förbundets Årsbok*. Heckscher, *op. cit.* (section d) covers the economy, and *Sveriges Riksdag* (section c) the history of the Estates. On Gothicism, there is an article by E. Ekman entitled 'Gothic patriotism and Olof Rudbeck' in the *Journal of Modern History*, vol. 34 (1962).*

(g) The Era of Liberty
A good summary is given by R. M. Hatton in the chapter on 'Scandinavia and the Baltic' in the *New Cambridge Modern History*, vol. VII (1713–1763) (Cambridge, 1957).* The basic political history is still C. G. Malmström, *Sveriges politiska historia från Karl XII:s död till statshvälfningen 1772* (Stockholm, 1893–1901), although later research has naturally modified many of the conclusions in it. There are lives of Ulrika Eleanora and Frederick I by W. Holst (Stockholm, 1956 and 1953 respectively) and of Louisa Ulrika by O. Jägerskiöld (Stockholm, 1945). The composition and powers of the most important class in Swedish society in the eighteenth century have been described in an essay by M. Roberts in *The European Nobility of the Eighteenth Century*, edited by A. Goodwin (London, 1953).* See also, *Sveriges Riskdag* (section c). Foreign policy as a whole is dealt with by O. Jägerskiöld in *Den svenska utrikespolitikens historia*, vol. II pt. ii (1721–1792) (Stockholm, 1957) and various aspects of it in: J. R. Danielson, *Die Nordische Frage 1746–1751* (Helsingfors, 1888); E. Armburger, *Russland und Schweden 1762–72* (Berlin, 1934); and in an article by R. Lodge on 'The Treaty

Suggestions for Further Reading

of Åbo and the Swedish succession' in the *English Historical Review*, vol. 43 (1928). British relations with Sweden may be followed in the introduction to J. F. Chance (ed.), *British Diplomatic Instructions 1689–1789 V: Sweden 1727–1789* (London, 1928), as well as in the same author's introduction to the first volume of the series, while S. Rydberg in *Svenska studieresor till England under Frihetstiden* (Uppsala and Stockholm, 1951) deals with the visits made by Swedes to England during this period. Economic developments in the eighteenth century are best studied in the appropriate volume of Eli Heckscher's work quoted in section d, but this should be supplemented by the review article by B. Boëthius, 'New light on eighteenth-century Sweden' in the *Scandinavian Economic History Review*, vol. I (1953). In the second volume of the same journal is G. Utterström's 'Some population problems in pre-industrial Sweden'. The theme of B. J. Hovde's *The Scandinavian Countries, 1720–1865* (New York, 1948)* is suggested by its sub-title, 'The Rise of the Middle Classes'; it covers economic, social and cultural as well as—rather briefly—political developments. The best study of Linné is K. Hagberg's *Carl Linnæus* (London, 1952).*

(h) 1772–1818

The fundamental work on the political history of Gustavus III's reign is C. T. Odhner, *Sveriges politiska historia under Gustaf III:s regering* (Stockholm, 1885–1905). The most recent life of the king is Beth Hennings, *Gustav III* (Stockholm, 1957). In English there is only R. N. Bain's *Gustavus III and his Contemporaries* (London, 1894),* but, in spite of its age, this still has considerable value and contains a lively account of Swedish literature, mainly in the eighteenth century. Gustavus's relations with France form the subject of A. Geffroy, *Gustave III et la Cour de France* (Paris, 1867); there is also Geffroy's introduction to the *Recueil des instructions* (see section e). His relations with Britain are dealt with in M. Roberts, 'Great Britain and the Swedish Revolution, 1772–3' in the *Historical Journal*, vol. 7 (1964) and S. Carlsson, *Sverige och Storbritannien 1787–1790* (Lund, 1944). The same author's *Gustaf IV Adolf* (Stockholm, 1946) is the standard life of that king, and Carlsson's contribution to *Den svenska utrikespolitikens historia* (vol. III pt. i: 1792–1810: Stockholm, 1954) surveys the foreign policy of his reign. For that of

271

Suggestions for Further Reading

Gustavus III, see the volume in the same series by Jägerskiöld (section g). Relations with Britain under Gustavus IV are covered fairly fully by: K. V. Key-Åberg, *De diplomatiska forbindelserna mellan Sverige och Storbritannien under Gustav IV Adolfs krig emot Napoleon* (Uppsala, 1890); R. Carr, 'Gustavus IV and the British Government, 1804-9' in the *English Historical Review*, vol. 60 (1945); and L. K. Wahlström, *Sverige och England under revolutionkrigens början* (Stockholm, 1920-4). General works on Bernadotte are mentioned in the following section; his activities as crown prince form the subject of F. D. Scott's *Bernadotte and the Fall of Napoleon* (Cambridge, Mass., 1935). H. Koht has written an article on 'Bernadotte and Swedish-American relations 1810-1814' in the *Journal of Modern History*, vol. 16 (1944) On Sweden's relations with the United States in general, there are K. E. Carlson, *Relations of the United States with Sweden* (Allentown, Penns., 1921), F. D. Scott's *The United States and Scandinavia* (Cambridge, Mass., 1950) and the same author's 'American influences in Norway and Sweden' in the *Journal of Modern History*, vol. 18 (1946). For economic history, see Heckscher, *op. cit.* (section d); for the Estates, *Sveriges Riksdag* (section c); and for social developments, Hovde, *op. cit.* (section g).

(i) The Nineteenth Century

The standard life of Charles John is T. T. Höjer, *Carl XIV Johan* (Stockholm, 1939-60). In English, there is D. P. Barton, *Bernadotte, Prince and King* (London, 1925),* which is the third volume of a trilogy condensed into one book as *The Amazing Career of Bernadotte* (London, 1929).* The Marshal is also the subject of two articles by Harold Kurtz in *History Today*, vol. 14 (1964).* A whole volume of *Den svenska utrikespolitikens historia* (III p. ii) by T. T. Höjer (Stockholm, 1954) is devoted to his foreign policy. There are lives of Oscar I by A. Söderhjelm and C. F. Palmstierna (Stockholm, 1944) and of Charles XV by S. Eriksson (Stockholm, 1954). General surveys of Swedish foreign policy after Charles XIV are A. Jansson, *Den svenska utrikespolitikens historia*, vol. III pt. iii (1844-1872) (Stockholm, 1961) and F. Landberg, *ibid.*, vol. III pt. iv (1872-1914) (Stockholm, 1958). Particular aspects are dealt with in: C. F. Palmstierna, *Sverige, Ryssland och England 1833-1855* (Stock-

272

holm, 1932); A. Cullberg, *La politique du roi Oscar I pendant la guerre de Crimée* (Stockholm, 1912); P. Knaplund, 'Finnmark in British diplomacy, 1836–1855' in the *American Historical Review*, vol. 30 (1925); and B. J. Hovde, *Diplomatic Relations of the United States with Sweden and Norway, 1814–1905* (Iowa City, 1921). For the latter, see also the books by Scott and Carlson noted in section h. For late nineteenth and early twentieth-century politics, there is D. Verney's *Parliamentary Reform in Sweden, 1866–1921* (Oxford, 1957),* and on relations with Norway, R. E. Lindgren, *Norway-Sweden Union, Disunion and Scandinavian Integration* (Princeton, 1959) and an article on the dissolution of the Union entitled 'The Independence of Norway' by Cyril Falls in *History Today*, vol. 5 (1955).* Scandinavianism at its height is dealt with in Å. Holmberg's *Skandinavism i Sverige vid 1800-talets mitt* (Gothenburg, 1946). The second volume of Hovde's work quoted in section g is mainly concerned with the nineteenth century. A. Montgomery's *The Rise of Modern Industry in Sweden* (London, 1939)* is the standard study of the subject, while for the economy as a whole, see Heckscher, *op. cit.* (section d). There is a series of monographs on *Wages, Cost of Living and National Income in Sweden, 1860–1930* (London, 1933–35) in *Stockholm Economic Studies*. The growth of trade unions in Sweden has been studied by J. Westerståhl in *Svenska fackforeningsrörelse* (Stockholm, 1945) and an aspect of the early history of the Social Democratic Party by D. J. Blake in 'Swedish trade unions and the Social Democratic Party' in the *Scandinavian Economic History Review*, vol. 8 (1960). The experiences of Swedish emigrants to America have been pictured in the two classic novels by C. A. V. Moberg, *The Emigrants* (London, 1956)* and *Unto a Good Land* (London, 1957).* For conditions in the homeland which caused them to leave it, see F. E. Janson, *The Background of Swedish Immigration, 1840–1930* (Chicago, 1931). The best life of Strindberg is M. Lamm, *August Strindberg* (Stockholm, 1940–42) and in English, B. M. E. Mortensen and B. W. Downs, *Strindberg, An Introduction to his Life and Work* (Cambridge, 1949).*

(j) After 1905

The life of the king whose reign covers most of the period has been written by K. E. H. Hildebrand under the title of *Gustav V som människa och regent* (Stockholm, 1945–48). Z. Höglund, *Hjalmar Branting och hans livsgärning* (Stockholm, 1929) and I. Anderson, *Arvid Lindman och hans tid* (Stockholm, 1956) survey political life through the lives of two of its leading participants, while in English, O. A. Rustow's *The Politics of Compromise* (Princeton, 1955)* is concerned mainly with the period after 1920. Foreign policy during and after the First World War is covered by the last two volumes in *Den svenska utrikespolitikens historia*, vol. IV (1914–19) by T. Gihl (Stockholm, 1953) and vol. V (1919–1939) by E. Lönnroth (Stockholm, 1959). Its course immediately after the dissolution of the Union has been studied by F. Lindberg in *Scandinavia in Great Power Politics 1905–1908* (Stockholm, 1958); between the wars by H. Tingsten in *The Debate on the Foreign Policy of Sweden, 1918–1939* (London, 1949) and by S. S. Jones in *The Scandinavian States and the League of Nations* (Princeton, 1939); during the Second World War by F. La Ruche in *La neutralité de la Suède* (Paris, 1953); and after the war in H. Friis (ed.), *Scandinavia between East and West* (Ithaca, 1951). The title of O. F. Ander's *The Building of Modern Sweden: The Reign of Gustav V, 1907–1950* (Rock Island, 1958) is rather misleading as it is concerned almost exclusively with the growth of the economy. An important aspect of Swedish cultural life is surveyed in F. Hardy's *The Swedish Film* (London, 1952).* M. W. Child's *Sweden: the Middle Way* has already been mentioned in the body of the present book (p. 243); chapters on developments since the early 1930's have been added in the latest edition (New Haven, 1947).* Kathleen Nott has provided some very personal but intelligent impressions of modern Sweden in *A Clean Well-lighted Place* (London, 1961).*

Index

s*   275

Index

Index

Breitenfeld, Battle of (1631), 94
Bremen and Verden, 98–9, 103, 106, 119, 122
Bremer, Frederika (1801–65), 215
Bridget, Saint (1303–73), 53–6, 102
Bridgittine Order, 55
Britain and Sweden, economic and cultural relations, in prehistory, 15, 16, 19; in the eighteenth century, 169, 170, 174, 178; in the nineteenth century, 159, 165, 166, 207; in the twentieth century, 264
Britain and Sweden, diplomatic relations, in the eighteenth century, 118, 120, 122, 138, 141–2, 153; in the nineteenth century, 159–60, 162, 166, 167, 168, 181, 187, 188, 197–8, 199, 201, 217; in the twentieth century, 233, 234, 235, 236, 248, 249, 250
Broadcasting, see Radio
Brömsebro, Peace of (1645), 98
Bronze Age, 15–17
Bruk, 125, 171, 174, 208
Brukspatroner, see Ironmasters
Brunkeberg, Battle of (1471), 61–2, 69
Burghers, Estate of, in the Middle Ages, 47; in the seventeenth century, 92, 97; in the eighteenth century, 135, 139, 144; in the nineteenth century, 189, 190, 193, 195, 203
Burials, prehistoric, 14, 16, 19

Cabinet, see Council
Cabo Corso, Swedish colony at, 128
Campbell, Colin (1686–1757), 170
Canals, 171, 172, 191
Caps, Old, 137, 139, 140, 141, 142, 144, 145
Caps, Younger, 144–6, 147–8, 155
Caroline Medical Institute, 226
Castles, prehistoric, 18; medieval, 32, 38, 40, 48, 49, 50, 58, 67; sixteenth-century, 72, 74, 87–8
Catherine I, Tsarina (1725–7), 137

Catherine II (the Great), Tsarina (1762–96), 151, 152, 153, 154, 155
Catherine, Saint (1331–81), 55
Cattle-rearing, prehistoric, 14–15, 17, 19; in Viking times, 25; in the Middle Ages, 41; in the sixteenth century, 85; in the eighteenth century, 176; in the nineteenth century, 209
Cederström, Gustaf Olof (1845–1933), 223
Cederström, Olof Rudolf (1764–1833), 187–8
Celsius, Anders (1701–44), 179
Censorship, in the eighteenth century, 145, 150, 157, 159; in the nineteenth century, 164, 167, 184, 186, 189, 190, 193; in the twentieth century, 249
Census, eighteenth-century, 179
Centre Party (former Agrarians), 254
Ceramics, 260
Chalmers Technical Institute, 226
Chancellor, office of, 36, 90, 104, 142
Chancery, 90, 91, 97
Chapman, Frederick Henric af (1721–1808), 148
Charles, see also Karl
Charles IX, King of Sweden (1604–11), 76, 78, 79–82, 84, 85, 86, 87, 92
Charles X Gustavus, King of Sweden (1654–60), 101–4
Charles XI, King of Sweden (1660–97), 105–9, 112, 113, 124, 130
Charles XII, King of Sweden (1697–1718), 111–122, 124, 223
Charles XIII, King of Sweden (1809–18), 157, 163–8, 184
Charles XIV, John (1818–44), 161, 165–8, 184–92, 199
Charles XV (1859–72), 194, 199–203, 215
Childs, Marquis Williams (1903–), 243
Chivalry, 35, 40

Index

Dacke, Nils (*d.* 1543), 74

Dahlberg, Eric (1625–1703), 130–1

Dairying, in the Middle Ages, 41, 42, 65; in the sixteenth century; 85; in the eighteenth century, 176; in the nineteenth century, 209; in the twentieth century, 244

Dalarna, medieval, 28, 61, 63, 64, 68; sixteenth-century, 70, 73; seventeenth-century 130; eighteenth-century, 141, 179, 182; nineteenth-century, 175, 222, 262

Dalin, Olof von (1708–63), 181

Danielsson, Anders (1784–1839), 186

David, Saint, 27

de Bonneuil, *see* Bonneuil

Defence, government policy on, in the eighteenth century, 142, 148, 151; in the nineteenth century, 211, 216; in the twentieth century, 229, 232, 233, 240, 246, 247, 248, 251, 252, 253

De Geer, Louis (1587–1652), 125–6, 128

De Geer, Louis Gerhard (1818–96), 201, 202, 203, 211–12

De Geer, Gerhard Louis (1854–1935), 239

De la Gardie, Magnus Gabriel (1622–86), 105, 106, 107, 131

de Laval, Carl Gustaf Patrik (1845–1913), 209, 229

de la Vallée, Jean (1620–96), 133

de la Vallée, Simon (*d.* 1642), 133

Denmark and Sweden, in the Middle Ages, 32, 45, 46, 47, 48, 60–2, 63; in the sixteenth century, 70–1, 73, 77, 78, 81–2; in the seventeenth century, 89–90, 92–3, 98, 103–4, 105, 106, 109, 112, 124; in the eighteenth century, 114, 117, 119, 120–1, 122, 151, 152–3, 160; in the nineteenth century, 161, 164–5, 166, 167, 186–7, 191, 192, 196–7, 199, 200–1; in the twentieth century, 234, 246, 250, 251, 264

Descartes, René (1596–1650), in Sweden, 102

Diet, medieval, 65, 66, 67; in the nineteenth century, 209

Dissent, *see* Nonconformity

Distilling, government policy on, in the eighteenth century, 148, 149, 153; in the nineteenth century, 214–15

Dominicans, 38

Drama, *see* Theatre

Dress, *see* Costume

Drink, 67, 148, 214

Drottningholm, Palace of, 133, 183, 199

Dutch, *see* Holland

Dybeck, Richard (1811–77), 224–5

East India Company, Swedish, 138, 170

Economic policy, in the sixteenth century, 75; in the seventeenth century, 100–1, 102, 124, 126; in the eighteenth century, 119, 137, 144–5, 148, 150, 153, 169, 170–2, 173–4, 175; in the nineteenth century, 185, 191, 193, 195, 199, 201–2, 205, 210–11; in the twentieth century, 231, 242, 243, 244, 247, 249, 252, 253, 254, 256, 258, 259–60

Edén, Nils (1871–1945), 235, 236–7, 239

Education, medieval, 37–8, 53, 68; sixteenth-century, 86; seventeenth-century, 128–9; nineteenth-century, 190, 224–5; twentieth-century, 247, 256; adult, 225; elementary, 129, 191, 224, 225–6, 231, 241, 256; higher, 38, 68–9, 86, 128, 225, 256; secondary, 37–8, 86, 129, 194, 225, 256; technical, 226. *See also* Schools

Education Act (1842), 191; (1849), 225; (1905), 231; (1927), 241, 256. *See also* School Law

Ehrenstrahl, David Klöcker (1629–98), 133

Index

Index

Index

Holland, Swedish diplomatic relations with, in the seventeenth century, 93, 98, 102, 103, 104, 106, 109, 112; in the eighteenth century, 114, 119–20

Holland, cultural influence in Sweden in the seventeenth century, 133

Holmgård, 21

Holstein-Gottorp, Duke of, 109, 112, 114, 121, 134, 137, 141. *See also* Schleswig-Holstein

Holsteiners (party), 121, 136, 137, 139, 141

Höpken, Anders Johan von (1712–89), 143, 144

Horn, Arvid Bernhard (1664–1742), 118, 136, 137, 138–9, 140

Houses and housing, prehistoric, 17; in Viking times, 25; medieval, 65–6, 67; sixteenth-century, 88; seventeenth-century, 123, 131; eighteenth-century, 176, 182; twentieth-century, 252

Hydro-electric power, 231, 259

Ice Age, 13

Iceland, Swedish settlers in, 20

Indelning system, 108, 212

Indragningsmakt, 167, 184, 186, 189, 190, 193

Inflation, in the eighteenth century, 144, 155, 158, 166; in the nineteenth century, 185; in the twentieth century, 235, 239, 253

Inge, King of Sweden, 27

Ingria, 90, 115, 122

Insurance, social, 213, 231, 239, 243–4

Iron Age, 17–19

Iron, mining and export of, prehistoric, 17; in the Middle Ages, 43, 51–2; in the sixteenth century, 74, 84–5; in the seventeenth century, 124–5, 127; in the eighteenth century, 158, 169, 170, 171–2; in the nineteenth century, 207–8; in the twentieth century,

231, 236, 244, 247, 248, 259, 260

Ironmasters, 125, 171, 195, 208

Iron Office, 171–2

Italy, Gustavus III in, 149; Swedish relations with, 245

Ivan VI (the Terrible), Tsar (1533–84), 76, 77

Jacobites, 120

Jämtland, 14, 98

Japan, 245

Jarl, office of, 31, 33

Jews, 149, 195, 202

Johansson, Johan (1792–1860), 186

John III, King of Sweden (1568–92), 76, 77, 78–80, 84, 86, 87, 88

John, Duke of Östergötland (1589–1618), 81

Jönköping, 43, 226

Jöns Bengtsson, *see* Oxenstierna

Josephina of Leuchtenberg, Queen of Sweden (1807–76), 202

Josephson, Ernst Abraham (1851–1906), 222

Jugendstil, 224

Junker Party, 194

Justice, in Viking times, 24–5; in the Middle Ages, 40–1, 50; in the sixteenth century, 77; in the seventeenth century, 91, 97; in the eighteenth century, 148, 150, 154; in the nineteenth century, 189–90, 194; in the twentieth century, 231, 239, 255–6

Kalmar, 38, 42, 52, 57, 67, 80, 82, 88

Karl, *see also* Charles

Karl August, *see* Christian August

Karl Knutsson, King of Sweden (1448–57, 1464–5, 1467–70), 60–1

Karl Ulfsson, son of St. Bridget, 54

Karlfeldt, Erik Axel (1864–1931), 261

Karlskrona, 108

Karlstad, 163; Convention of (1905), 217

Karolinska, *see* Caroline

Index

Index

Index

Index

Prussia, 119, 122, 143–4, 146, 153. For events before the eighteenth century, *see* Brandenburg

Pyhy, Conrad von (*d.* 1553), 75

Råd, *see* Council

Radio, 259, 260

Railways, 204–5, 208

Rationing, of food, 235, 249, 252; of drink, 240, 255

Red Book, The (1576), 79, 80, 86

Reduktion, under Queen Margaret, 57–8; in the seventeenth century, 100, 101, 104–5, 107, 108, 109, 111, 113, 124

Referendum, consultative (1922), 240; (1955), 254; (1957), 254

Reformation in Sweden, 71, 72, 73, 79–80

Refugees in Sweden in the twentieth century, 246, 250, 251, 252

Regency, for Magnus Birgersson, 44–6; for Erik of Pomerania, 57–8; for Christina, 96–7; for Charles XI, 105–7; for Gustavus IV, 157–8

Religion, pre-Christian, 14, 16, 18, 19, 25–6, 27–8

Religious life, *see* Church, Nonconformity, and Religion

Reuterholm, Gustaf Adolf (1756–1813), 157–8

Reval, 77, 81

Riddarholm Church, 36

Riddarhus (building), 133

Right, *see* Conservative Party

Riksdag, origins of, 47, 91–2

Riksdag, powers and composition of, in the Middle Ages, 64; in the sixteenth century, 81; in the seventeenth century, 89, 92, 97, 107, 118; in the eighteenth century, 135, 139–40, 143, 147, 153; in the nineteenth century, 164, 184, 185–6, 193, 195, 202–3. *See also* Parliamentary reform

Riksdag, meeting of (1359), 47, 91; (1435), 59, 91–2; (1527) 72;

(1543–4), 74; (1562), 77; (1569), 78; (1593), 80; (1595), 80; (1650), 101–2; (1652), 101; (1655), 104; (1680), 107; (1682–3), 108; (1693), 108; (1697), 111; (1710), committee of, 118; (1719), 134, 136; (1720), 134–5, 136–7; (1726–7), 136, 137; (1734), 139; (1738), 139; (1742–3), 140; (1746), 141; (1751–2), 142; (1755–6), 142; (1760–2), 144; (1765–6), 145; (1769–70), 145–6; (1772), 146; (1778), 149; (1786), 150, 152; (1789), 153–4; (1792), 155; (1800), 158–90; (1809–10), 163; (1810), 165; (1812), 166–7; (1815), 185; (1828–30), 185, 186, 193; (1834–5), 189; (1840–1), 190–1; (1847–8), 195, 197; (1850–1), 195; (1853–4), 201; (1862–3), 202; (1865–6), 203; (after 1866), 205, 210, 211–15, 216–17, 229, 232, 233, 235, 238, 239, 241, 242, 244, 249, 255

Rimbert (*d.* 888), 26

Roads, 127, 171, 205–6

Rock-carvings, 14

Rock-drawings, 16

Rogslösa, 39

Roman Empire, trade with, 17

Rörstrand, 260

Rosen, Adolf Eugène von (1797–1886), 204–5

Roskilde, Treaty of (1658), 104

Roslin, Alexander (1718–93), 182, 219

Rudbeck, Olof (1630–1702), 131

Rudbeckius, Johannes Johannis (1581–1646), 97

Runes, 18, 20, 130

Russia, Vikings in, 21–2

Russia and Sweden, in the sixteenth century, 78, 81; in the seventeenth century, 90, 103, 105, 112; in the eighteenth century, 114, 115–17, 119, 120, 121, 122, 123, 137, 138, 139, 140, 141, 143, 144, 146, 151, 152, 154, 155, 160; in the nine-

288

Index

Index

Index

Temperance Movement, 214–15, 225. *See also* Prohibition, and Rationing

Tessin, Carl Gustaf (1695–1770), 142

Tessin, Nicodemus, the Elder (1615–81), 133

Tessin, Nicodemus, the Younger (1654–1728), 182

Teushina, Peace of (1595), 81

Teutonic Knights, Order of, 58, 60

Textile industry, 125, 172, 174, 176, 208

Theatre, 183, 262–3

Things, in prehistory, 19; in Viking times, 24–5; in the Middle Ages, 40, 41, 50

Thirty Years War (1618–48), 92–4, 98–9

Thomas Simonsson, Bishop (*d.* 1443), 69

Thorild, Thomas (1759–1808), 219

Thralls, 24

Thyselius, Carl Johan (1811–91), 211

Tilsit (1807), 161

Timber industry, 172, 207, 214

Toleration, religious, in the nineteenth century, 149, 174, 195, 202

Torgils Knuttson (*d.* 1306), 44–5

Torstensson, Lennart (1603–51), 98

Tott family, 61

Towns, in Viking times, 23; in the Middle Ages, 42–3, 52; in the sixteenth century, 85; in the seventeenth century, 126, 127–8; in the eighteenth century, 135, 171; in the twentieth century, 260–1

Town planning, 128, 223, 260–1

Trade, free, *see* Tariffs

Trade, internal, prehistoric, 15, 16, 19; in the Middle Ages, 42; in the sixteenth century, 75, 85; in the seventeenth century, 126; in the eighteenth century, 170–1; in the nineteenth century, 195

Trade, overseas, prehistoric, 15, 16, 17; in Viking times, 20, 22–3; in the Middle Ages, 32, 35, 42–3, 51, 58, 59, 62–3, 67; in the sixteenth century, 71, 75, 84–5; in the seventeenth century, 101, 102, 109, 126–8; in the eighteenth century, 119, 137–8, 144, 145, 148, 158, 169–70, 171–2; in the nineteenth century, 159–60, 185, 187, 191, 201–2, 207; in the twentieth century, 234–5, 236, 239, 242, 244, 248, 249, 253, 259, 264

Trade unions, 214, 225, 231–2, 241, 244, 259

Trams, 206

Travel by land, in the seventeenth century, 127; in the eighteenth century, 171

Traventhal, Peace of (1700), 114

Treasury, 91

Triple Alliance (1667), 106

'Trivial' schools, 129, 225

Trolle, Gustaf Eriksson (*c.* 1488–1535), 63, 64

Trollhättan, 231; canal at, 171, 172

Trygger, Ernst (1857–1943), 240

Turks, Ottoman, 115, 117, 118–9, 140

Ulrika Eleanora, Queen of Sweden (1688–1741), 121, 134, 141

Unemployment, in the eighteenth century, 145; in the twentieth century, 240, 242, 243, 244, 254

Union and Security, Act of (1789), 153–4

United Nations, 251, 252

United Provinces, *see* Holland

United States of America, 207, 209–10, 215, 228

Universal Franchise Union, 229

Universities, *see* Lund, Uppsala, and Education, higher

Uppland, prehistoric, 18; in Viking times, 24, 27; in the Middle Ages, 41, 45, 51, 61; Code of, 41

Index

Uppsala, medieval, 31, 37, 38; sixteenth-century, 80, 88; nineteenth-century, 206, 219, 228; Old, 19, 25, 27, 31, 37; University of, 68-9, 86-7, 128-9, 131 note, 179, 195, 220, 223

Vadstena, 70; monastery at, 54, 55, 68, 81
Valdemar Atterdag, King of Denmark (1340-75), 46, 47, 48
Valdemar Birgersson, King of Sweden (1250-75), 34-5
Valdemar Magnusson (d. 1319), 44-5
Vällingby, 261
Värälä, Peace of (1790), 154
Varangian Guard, 22
Värmland, 76, 128, 220, 221
Varnhem monastery, 38
Vasa, see names of kings of the dynasty
Västerås, 37, 42, 51-2, 70, 72, 74, 129
Växjö, 37, 220
Viborg, 44, 81
Visby, 38, 42, 47

Wachtmeister, Hans (1641-1714), 108

Waldenström, Paul Peter (1838-1917), 228
Wallenstein, Albrecht Wenzel Eusebius (1583-1634), 93, 94
Warfare, see Army, and Defence
Waterfalls Board, 231
Waterstone, John, 85
West India Company, Swedish, 170
Westphalia, Peace of (1648), 98-9
Wetterstedt, Gustaf af (1776-1837), 187
Wieselgren, Peter Jonasson (1800-77), 214
Wingquist, Sven Gustaf (1876-1953), 226
Wirén, Dag Ivar (1905-), 261
Wismar, 119, 159, 168
Witches, 130
Women's rights, 193, 213, 215, 231, 238
Wood-pulp, 207, 235, 244, 259
Wool, see Textiles
Workers, urban industrial, 172, 176, 259
Wrangel, Karl Gustaf (1613-76), 131

Zettervall, Helgo Niklaus (1831-1907), 223
Zorn, Anders Leonard (1860-1920), 222

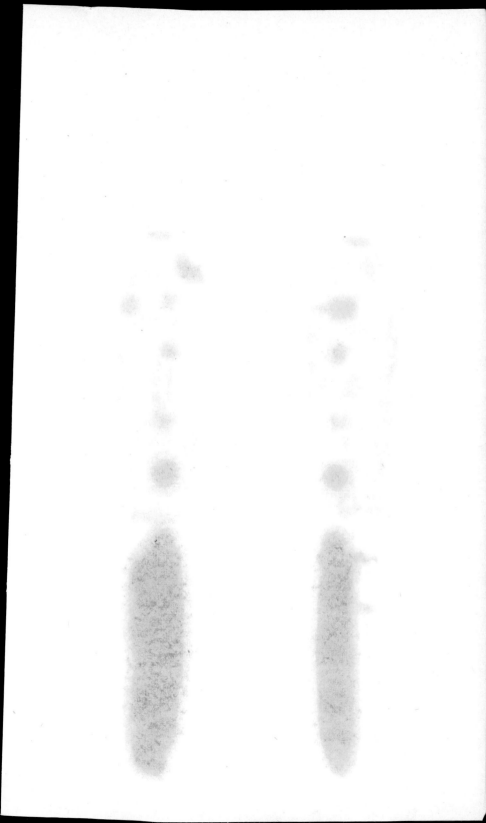

11/22/66

DATE DUE	
NOV 16 1993	
FEB 22 1995	
SEP 29 1998	
MAR 29 1999	
JUL 26 2006	

GAYLORD   PRINTED IN U.S.A.